THE UPPER ROOM

Disciplines

2022

UPPER
ROOM BOOKS®
NASHVILLE

AN OUTLINE FOR SMALL-GROUP USE OF *DISCIPLINES*

Here is a simple plan for a one-hour, weekly group meeting based on reading *The Upper Room Disciplines*. One person may act as convener every week, or the role can rotate among group members. You may want to light a white Christ candle each week to signal the beginning of your time together.

OPENING

Convener: Let us come into the presence of God.

Others: Lord Jesus Christ, thank you for being with us. Help us hear your word to us as we speak to one another.

SCRIPTURE

Convener reads the scripture suggested for that day in *Disciplines*. After a one- or two-minute silence, convener asks: What did you hear God saying to you in this passage? What response does this call for? (Group members respond in turn or as led.)

REFLECTION

- What scripture passage(s) and meditation(s) from this week was (were) particularly meaningful for you? Why? (Group members respond in turn or as led.)
- What actions were you nudged to take in response to the week's meditations? (Group members respond in turn or as led.)
- Where were you challenged in your discipleship this week? How did you respond to the challenge? (Group members respond in turn or as led.)

PRAYING TOGETHER

Convener says: Based on today's discussion, what people and situations do you want us to pray for now and in the coming week? Convener or other volunteer then prays about the concerns named.

DEPARTING

Convener says: Let us go in peace to serve God and our neighbors in all that we do.

Adapted from *The Upper Room* daily devotional guide, January–February 2001. © 2000 The Upper Room. Used by permission.

THE UPPER ROOM DISCIPLINES 2022

The Upper Room Books® website: upperroombooks.com

Cover design: Left Coast Design, Portland, Oregon

Cover photo: moosehenderson/Shutterstock.com

At the time of publication all websites referenced in this book were valid. However, due to the fluid nature of the internet some addresses may have changed, or the content may no longer be relevant.

Revised Common Lectionary copyright © 1992 Consultation on Common Texts. Used by permission.

Scripture quotations not otherwise identified are from the New Revised Standard Version Bible © 1989, Division of Christian Education of the National Council of the Churches of Christ in the United States of America. Used by permission. All rights reserved.

Scripture quotations marked AP are the author's paraphrase.

Scripture quotations marked CEB are from the Common English Bible. Copyright © 2010 Common English Bible. Used by permission.

Scripture quotations marked KJV are from the King James Version of the Bible.

Scripture quotations marked NIV are from the Holy Bible, New International Version®, NIV®. Copyright © 1973, 1978, 1984, 2011 by Biblica, Inc.™ Used by permission of Zondervan. All rights reserved worldwide. www.zondervan.com.

Scripture quotations marked NLT are from the Holy Bible, New Living Translation, copyright © 1996, 2004, 2007. Used by permission of Tyndale House Publishers, Inc., Carol Stream, Illinois 60188. All rights reserved.

Scripture quotations from The Message. Copyright © by Eugene H. Peterson 1993, 1994, 1995, 1996, 2000, 2001, 2002. Used by permission of NavPress Publishing Group.

The week of March 28–April 3 originally appeared in The Upper Room Disciplines 2013. Reprinted and used by permission.

Writers of various books of the Bible may be disputed in certain circles; this volume uses the names of the biblically attributed authors.

ISBN: 978-0-8358-1957-2 (print)

978-0-8358-1958-9 (enlarged-print edition)

978-08358-1959-6 (mobi) | 978-0-8358-1960-2 (epub)

Printed in the United States of America

Contents

Foreword

My formation as a Jesus follower has been profoundly shaped by occasional sojourns among our monastic siblings in retreat settings. Folding myself into the daily rhythms of prayer, work, and rest in their communities for a week or two always reminds me that there is no real separation between the sacred and the secular. God and grace walk among us wherever "the soles of [our] feet shall tread" (Deut. 11:24, KJV). The Lord truly is Immanuel.

As we endeavor to move through this season with the COVID-19 pandemic abated but still snapping at our heels, and with the never-ending cycles of injustice and disparity rerouting our designs to build bridges to God's beloved community, it is imperative that we find ways to internalize the presence of God that transcends the false dichotomy pitting secular against sacred. We hope this annual collection of daily encounters with our Creator will awaken or strengthen your awareness of God's presence everywhere along your life's path.

In *Every Step a Prayer*, Dr. Thomas R. Hawkins reminds us, "Walking as a spiritual practice is more than a pleasant walk through the countryside or a way to stay physically fit. It influences how we interpret and experience God's presence in our lives and our world." Indeed, the metaphor of walking permeates the biblical witness. From the very beginning God walks in a garden among the people of the earth (see Genesis 3:8). We see Abraham and Moses being bidden to sojourn in the land (see Genesis 12:1 and Exodus 3:10). The confessional statement of the people called Israel begins, "A wandering Aramean was my ancestor; he went down into Egypt and lived there as an alien" (Deut. 26:5). Jesus walked everywhere and calls us to do the same: "Stand up, take your mat and walk" (John 5:8);

"follow me" (Matt. 19:21). The apostles encourage us to "walk by faith, not by sight" (2 Cor. 5:7) and "walk just as [Jesus] walked" (1 John 2:6).

I believe the writer of Hebrews gives the best direction for all who want to walk the path of holiness: "Lift your drooping hands and strengthen your weak knees, and make straight paths for your feet, so that what is lame may not be put out of joint, but rather be healed. Pursue peace with everyone, and the holiness without which no one will see the Lord" (12:12-14).

My beloved siblings in Christ, may you be truly strengthened for the journey ahead through *The Upper Room Disciplines.*

KIMBERLY ORR
Publisher of The Upper Room

The Joy of Restoration

JANUARY 1–2, 2022 • MEMORY CHIKOSI

SCRIPTURE OVERVIEW: These scriptures chosen to mark the new year give us a panorama of perspectives, from Ecclesiastes as a poetic musing on how life is measured out in seasons, to the vision in Revelation of what we commonly consider the end of time itself. Psalm 8 asks what the role is for humans in God's magnificent creation, and John speaks of the eternal Word coming into the world. At the core of these scriptures is a strong sense of God's presence and loving steadfastness in which we can rest.

QUESTIONS AND SUGGESTIONS FOR REFLECTION

- Read Ecclesiastes 3:1-13. In what season of life do you find yourself? What are you praying for this season?
- Read Psalm 8. How do you feel when you read the psalmist's words that God has created humans "a little lower than God, and crowned them with glory and honor" (Ps. 8:5)?
- Read Revelation 21:1-6a. How is the vision of a new heaven and a new earth described here good news for you? What do you see God making new in the world around you?
- Read John 1:1-18. What does it mean for you that the true light enlightens everyone?

Elder in The United Methodist Church in the Zimbabwe Episcopal Area; holds a master's degree in theological studies; United Theological College lecturer and chaplain; Amazing Grace circuit associate pastor.

NEW YEAR'S DAY

We are at the beginning—the beginning of a new year and the beginning of the divine mystery. Today's reading poetically describes the pre-existent Christ, the Word, becoming a human being.

John's Gospel explains that the Word was with God, and the Word was God. This Word is the Son of God, Jesus Christ. John shows that this Jesus is equal to God; God is one, yet exists in separate persons. Jesus, the Word, has been there with God before the Creation. So Jesus, the second person of the Trinity, was in the genesis of the world with God. All things in the world were created by God through the Word.

Jesus is alive and is himself God incarnate and expresses all that God wants to say to us about who God is. John the Baptist came to bear testimony to the light so that all who hear John's testimony might have faith.

Today's reading shows us that the same power that the tri-une God used to create the world is the power God is still using to create new life and to bring new life, even in our most hopeless situations. God creates from nothing and can create order where we see nothing but chaos and disorder.

Jesus is the source of all life and the center of our faith and hope. In Jesus, we find life, and his life is light to us—the light that exposes evil and illuminates our lives. Jesus restores our broken relationships and brings life to the dead places of the world. No evil is able to overcome the power of God in Jesus Christ. Jesus is the true life and true light to all who trust in him, and he is the author of our salvation.

God, you create new life and offer new life to us through your Son, Jesus Christ. Help us turn to you when we face situations that seem hopeless, for only in you can we find light and life. Amen.

Since the beginning of time, people have wanted to know a God who is immanent, present with and to them. A God who dwells among the people is a God who is available and accessible. And through Jesus Christ we have this relationship with our Creator. Jesus is both fully God and fully human. In Jesus, we come to know who God is, and we can have a joyful relationship with God.

Jesus is the true light to a better life. When we are guilty of wrongdoing, when our behavior is disgraceful, we know God brings us loving forgiveness. Jesus also reveals the truth and glory of God. Jesus loves and accepts us as we are, but shows us what is true about us, about our lives, and about others.

This light, Jesus Christ, is the focus of our faith and life because, through the fullness of his grace, we receive blessing upon blessing. God gave us the law and its precepts through Moses, but now grace and truth are given to us through the one and only begotten Son, Jesus Christ.

Thus, when we accept Jesus, we are accepting the light of a transformed life of salvation in Christ. The light of Christ has the power to drive away any evil that may threaten us. As we see, hear, and accept the glory of God in Jesus, we enter an intimate relationship with Christ. We bear witness to his message and are thus adopted as children of God. Through Christ, we joyfully dwell in God's everlasting grace.

God, through your Son, Jesus Christ, you dwell among us. Help us to desire nothing more than the relationship with you that you offer us through him. Amen.

I Baptize You

JANUARY 3–9, 2022 • JENNIFER E. COPELAND

SCRIPTURE OVERVIEW: Water is an important theme throughout the Bible. The authors of scripture use water as an image of transition and sometimes challenge, and they tie it back to God's renewing work. Isaiah records the divine promise that God will not abandon Israel, even if they pass through trying waters—a reference to the deliverance of the Israelites from the Egyptians. The psalmist declares that God's voice covers all the waters, so nothing can come against us that is beyond God's reach. In Acts we see the connection between baptism—passing through the water—and the gift of the Holy Spirit. The emphasis is on the inclusion of the Samaritans, a group considered unclean by many but not by God. We see clearly the connection between water baptism and the Spirit in the baptism of Jesus himself.

QUESTIONS AND SUGGESTIONS FOR REFLECTION

- Read Isaiah 43:1-7. Isaiah presents an image of God's favor that is at once particular and universal. How do you experience God's love for you and for all persons as part of the body of Christ?
- Read Psalm 29. God's creation, in its wildness, incorporates destruction. In the face of disaster, how do you find a way to say, "Glory"?
- Read Acts 8:14-17. Our baptism is in the name of Jesus and the name of the Spirit. To what wildness does the Spirit prompt you?
- Read Luke 3:15-17, 21-22. Remember your baptism and listen for God's call out into the wildness of the world.

Executive Director of the North Carolina Council of Churches; United Methodist elder in the South Carolina Annual Conference.

Did you hear that? Did you hear the voice from heaven say, "You are my Son, the Beloved; with you I am well pleased"? Even if you missed the message, you can see the Spirit sitting on his shoulder "like a dove." It is nothing short of a coronation. Much as oil has anointed the heads of rulers and swords have tapped the shoulders of lords, the dove names the royalty of Jesus.

It's not what we expected, but it is, after all, what we were told. The whole of salvation history reveals a God who works upside down and backward. The evidence is clear and consistent.

In spite of the evidence, we remain impressed by might and money, amazed by castles and land (or hotels and golf courses). Perhaps most disappointingly, we revere the rulers who flaunt these things and yearn to have them for ourselves. Selfish power.

We believe it has to be this way. If we show generosity, people will steal from us. If we show mercy, people will harm us. If we show kindness, people will harm us. Fearful power.

To guard against ruin and destruction, we keep more than we need. We amass more wealth than can be spent in four lifetimes. We build walls and fences to prevent others from sharing our fortune. Greedy power.

Contrary evidence kneels before us in prayer, the embodiment of all that the prophets have promised. Beginning with this coronation, the powerful One will demonstrate with the remainder of his life how very misguided we are. Follow him, listen to his stories, watch his actions, know the truth. Power made perfect in love is the only power worth having. Real power.

"Do you renounce the spiritual forces of wickedness, reject the evil powers of this world?" (Baptismal Covenant I, The United Methodist Book of Worship).

Following Jesus always involves a little two-step dance. For United Methodists and many others, baptism is one step—especially baptism for those "unable to answer for themselves," typically babies. And then ten or fifteen years later comes confirmation—those weeks of studying with the pastor (or some other official teacher) about scripture, tradition, experience, and reason—and our part in the journey of faith. This brings us to Confirmation Sunday when we promise to believe and do the things that were promised on our behalf when we were "unable to answer." Being United Methodist is a little like the Samaritan way. We are "baptized in the name of the Lord Jesus," but reception of the Holy Spirit comes later, perhaps at confirmation.

Most of the Christian way is this way. Some days we live as those filled with the Holy Spirit, on fire with a desire to serve God by serving our neighbor. We eagerly mine scripture for inspiration and instruction. We share our convictions with anyone who will sit still long enough to listen. On other days we read the Bible because it's expected of us, but it holds no more joy than reading the dictionary. We have no energy to work for justice, barely enough energy to wash the dishes and walk the dog. And peace—well, that's just so hard to find in the face of so much greed and fear.

The beauty of our faith claims, however, is that we don't have to dance both steps at the same time. Sometimes others live faithfully on our behalf. We are part of a larger community of faith and a greater communion of saints. Any day now, faithful people will join us, pray with us, and lay hands on us until we feel the Holy Spirit welling within us, ready to shine for all the world to see. In the meantime, it is enough to live faithfully.

"Do you confess Jesus Christ as your Savior, put your whole trust in his grace?" (Baptismal Covenant I, The United Methodist Book of Worship).

Chaff, as you know, is the stuff that comes along with a grain of wheat, a sort of outer skin. Think of it like that piece of husk that sometimes shows up in your bowl of oatmeal.

Humans cannot digest chaff; so besides its annoying presence in a loaf of bread or a bowl of oatmeal, it is nutritionally worthless. It's no wonder that John uses this metaphor to describe the in-breaking of God's incarnate One. We don't remove the chaff because it tastes bad—many people find beets to taste bad, but they're packed with nutrients. We remove the chaff because it is worthless; it takes up valuable space needed by those whom Jesus will summon to follow him into the fires of baptism. If the chaff follows, it will be useless. In fact, it will simply burn up.

Disciples are made of stronger stuff, able to withstand the temptation to put self ahead of neighbor, profit ahead of justice, or fear before faith. We don't blow away with the winds of change, but hold steadfast to the call to follow.

We learn something of this unique following when Jesus joins John down by the river. Jesus is dunked beneath the water and rises to hear the eternal words, "You are my Son, the Beloved; with you I am well pleased." Over the next forty days he will face a trio of well-documented temptations. And then he will get on with gathering the wheat, making disciples.

No chaff here; it's blowing in the wind. There is only wheat, solid and nutritious, ready to be made into the bread of life.

"According to the grace given to you, will you . . . serve as Christ's representative in the world?" (Baptismal Covenant I, The United Methodist Book of Worship).

EPIPHANY

Isaiah said they would bring gold and frankincense as gifts to praise the Lord. It would be a joyous occasion, when all the world would see the worth of God's people reflected in the glory of God's light. And so it was when the magi appeared at the home of Mary. Indeed, they were "overwhelmed with joy."

Their joy comes not only in finding Mary and her child at home after a lengthy journey to Bethlehem. Their joy expresses the fulfillment of a prophecy. When Isaiah said that people would come from everywhere and listed all the known nations of his day, those nations clearly listened and continued to tell the story for successive generations. Now they are here as promised; they have come to pay homage to Mary's child.

Isaiah said they would bring gold and frankincense as gifts to praise the Lord. He didn't mention myrrh, an ancient medicine. The magi from the East seem to know something about glory that Isaiah omitted. Glory, especially the kind that produces truth and justice, can be dangerous. Shed too much light into the darkness of deception and the deceivers get nervous. Shed too much light into the darkness of corruption and the corrupters get agitated. Shed too much light into the darkness of exploitation and the exploiters will kill you.

It starts immediately when the magi leave "for their own country by another road," leaving Herod in the dark. It continues to this day as rulers cling to power and the wealthy cling to money, ready to destroy any challenge to their privilege. Myrrh turns out to be the most honest gift of all.

"Do you accept the freedom and power God gives you to resist evil, injustice, and oppression?" (Baptismal Covenant I, The United Methodist Book of Worship).

Another named storm headlines the news. Some years we've run out of letters from the English alphabet and have had to move on to the Greek alphabet. And those are only the storms that make it to the majors. Plenty of other storms create their own level of havoc without names. We, in the path of the storms, know something about cedars breaking, oaks whirling, and floods covering.

At the same time, modern technology gives us another view of storms. We can see them from above. The bigger the storm, the more majestic it appears. My first big storm was Hurricane Hugo (1989). Hugo was a beauty. The satellite images showed a perfectly formed eyewall, with interior solid cloud sheets giving way to spiral bands that stretched across five hundred miles. The heavenly perspective of a hurricane.

The storm's maker loves it. The storm is a thing of beauty, calling Lebanon to "skip like a calf, and Sirion like a young wild ox." The storm from above is a playground. "And in [the] temple all say, 'Glory!'"

Perspective is everything in most of life. If we see the Red Sea from the shore, it looks impassable; from above it needs only a small path of dry land between two water walls. If we see thousands of people (five thousand men plus women and children) waiting for food, it looks hopeless; from above they need only a few loaves and fishes to create abundance. If we see a pool of water, a font, maybe a river, at eye level, it looks ordinary; from above it evokes new life with only three words: "I baptize you."

"The Holy Spirit work within you, that being born through water and the Spirit, you may be a faithful disciple of Jesus Christ" (Baptismal Covenant I, The United Methodist Book of Worship).

Like all my companion authors for *Disciplines* 2022, I am writing during a year fraught with uncertainty. It will be the defining year for this current generation. The names we hear on the news each day will be names written in history and studied by those who come after us in the way I know the names Louis Pasteur and Jonas Salk, people who changed the world for generations before mine. It feels like a year for the ages.

When we read *Disciplines* 2022, we will have some perspective about 2020. Then again, 2022 will present its own level of uncertainty and possibility, as has every year before it. We tend to make each moment about ourselves, as if it were the only moment ever known to creation. But there have been so many fortuitous moments. Consider the people who pondered these questions: *When will the rain stop? How much farther to Canaan? Where are the Babylonians taking us? What are we going to eat? Who will save us?*

Other than the name markers of *Canaan* and *Babylon*, these same questions have been asked by people throughout history, not just in biblical narratives. Exchange *Canaan* for *America* and it becomes a question on the lips of immigrants from Europe, Africa, Latin America, and Asia or any other people who left home in search of a better life. Exchange *Babylon* for *America* and it becomes a question on the lips of indigenous children forced into boarding schools, immigrant children separated from their parents at the border, or Black men arrested on the street corner for being on the street corner.

The answer never changes: Do not fear, for I am with you.

"Sing to the Lord, all the earth. Tell of God's mercy each day" (Baptismal Covenant I, The United Methodist Book of Worship).

BAPTISM OF THE LORD

My first grandchild was born recently. His name is Benjamin, making him the fifth living Benjamin on my side of the family and also the fifth-generation Benjamin on my side of the family. For this child to hear himself called "Benjamin" is to know he is being called by name and that he belongs to something long-lasting and larger than himself.

Naming gains even more significance when family and friends gather at the water. "What name is given this child?" punctuates a litany of promises and assurances that will bracket his life. We promise to live faithfully so that he will know what faithful living looks like. We promise to work toward God's justice so that he will know what justice looks like. We promise to love all our neighbors so he will know what neighbors look like. We promise to teach him that God said, "Do not fear, for I have redeemed you; I have called you by name, you are mine."

This is not normal. Normal is to groom our children for self-sufficiency and independence. Normal is to impress upon them their uniqueness and excellence. Normal is to equip them with survival skills and educational advantages. Normal is to give them control. Baptism upsets all of this normalcy by taking away control and uniting us with a body of believers who are every bit as exceptional and worthy as we are. Not better, not worse, just called by name.

"Will you nurture this child in Christ's holy Church, that by your teaching and example he may be guided to accept God's grace for himself?" (Baptismal Covenant I, The United Methodist Book of Worship).

The Indestructible Light

JANUARY 10–16, 2022 • RAY WADDLE

SCRIPTURE OVERVIEW: Popular conceptions of God sometimes mislead us. Messages coming even from within Christianity sometimes make us think that God is constantly angry, just waiting for us to slip up. This week's readings remind us of the truth. Isaiah teaches us that God delights in God's people just as a groom delights in his bride. This love, the psalmist proclaims, is steadfast and never-ending. The life of Jesus shows us that God even wants us to have a good time in this life. Jesus chooses a wedding as the place to perform his first sign. He multiplies the wine in order to multiply the enjoyment of the guests. Paul in First Corinthians speaks of spiritual gifts. These gifts are all given by God for the good of the entire community.

QUESTIONS AND SUGGESTIONS FOR REFLECTION

- Read Isaiah 62:1-5. Recall a time when you have flourished and a time when your life was far from peace and order. How did you feel God's delight in each situation?
- Read Psalm 36:5-10. When have you felt God's light or taken refuge in the shadow of God's wings?
- Read 1 Corinthians 12:1-11. How can you use your God-given gifts to complement others' and to support the common good?
- Read John 2:1-11. How do Jesus' miracles help you to understand his identity as the Son of God?

Religion columnist and editor; author of three books; published poet; member of Christ Church Cathedral (Episcopal) in Nashville, TN.

The locale of Jesus' first miracle is a party, a wedding, with wine at the center of the action. Scripture dares to place God's abundance in a festive setting here, not a mountaintop vision or a sermon on the plain. The wedding at Cana invites the reader to expect God's activity even in the details of raucous human celebrations that aren't strictly "religious," like a noisy wedding reception.

Momentous news penetrates the scene. Jesus declares a mission focused on a family much larger than his immediate one. He also makes it clear that his hour has not yet come. For the time being, he turns attention to the matter at hand—a lack of wine at a crucial moment in a teeming social occasion. He extravagantly transforms the six massive jugs of water into wine. It's the good stuff, and it's more than anyone needs—the modern equivalent of about nine hundred bottles.

It's usually explained that these verses carry symbolic meaning about Jesus' cosmic nature: The miracle is a symbol of God's power, and the wine foreshadows the Last Supper and Easter drama to come. To me the force of Cana has much to do with the earthy details amid laughter, hospitality, and carousing. This story didn't have to be told. It didn't have to appear in a Gospel in order to make the case for Jesus' unique relationship to God. Yet here he is, at leisure with his friends, the heavenly will of God bisecting the sweet traditions of a wedding.

I know people who feel alienated from religion because they think the Christian message is judgmental or joyless. I hope they'll take another look at the Gospel of John and crash the wedding at Cana.

Gracious God, thank you for the Christ who made his way through earthly celebrations and storms, facing trial, death, and new life, never turning us away. May we find our own discipline and compassion, never turning others away. Amen.

"Providence"—the word has always drawn me in. It has a big inclusive embrace, a protective sweep. I also sense the word is out of favor these days.

Maybe belief in luck rivals it now or trust in fate or fate's cousin, fatalism. Maybe people prefer to believe strictly in their own power of choice, with the motto "I make my own reality."

Psalm 36 is here to reset the coordinates, supply oxygen, a lifeline to Providential confidence—the confidence to believe that God is upholding the world despite the mess we make of it.

God upholds it with patience. Every sunrise is a signature underwriting the renewal of creation once again, as if we're getting yet another chance to make peace, give praise, and get some things right. Nothing is out of reach of God's care or consciousness, the psalm says. God's love is refuge. God's righteousness and generosity are boundless. "They feast on the abundance of your house; and you give them drink from the river of your delights."

How do we harmonize such words with the world's daily cruelties and twisted delusions? This is a tough question. But a deeper question persists: What gets the last word—our violent injustices and politics, or the light of the Creator? A lot rides on the answer we choose. If God is upholding our lives, then I need to hold up my end of things and keep the fires of hope burning.

"In your light we see light," the psalm says. I take that to mean God's truth is always there, accessible, whether we're paying attention or not. We have the freedom to turn in its direction. The capacity to choose it—that too is providential. "O continue your steadfast love to those who know you."

Holy God, you've been constant from the beginning, a presence our whole lives, the Creator who holds us. Make me an instrument of your will in the present moment. Amen.

Gilead, Nineveh, Damascus, Beersheba, Galilee. The place names of the Bible echo back to Sunday-school childhood and thousands of years before that—names forged out of the mysterious encounter of human and divine.

Isaiah features the crowning biblical place name, *Jerusalem,* and its renaming, a sign of God's special devotion to it no matter how traumatic the moment.

I visited Jerusalem years ago. Often it was hard to sense the blessing that is celebrated in Isaiah. What was evident was the menacing tension among the world faiths that compete for it. The jostle of the crowds added to the jitteriness. The Church of the Holy Sepulchre with its dark corridors felt disorienting too.

Then, near sundown on a Friday, a different mood descended. The Jewish Sabbath was arriving. The pinks of dusk reflecting on buildings, the unblinking windless sky, the sudden quiet— everything pointed to an implausible cessation of troubles. The Lord's day was taking center stage once again.

"You shall be a crown of beauty in the hand of the LORD," says Isaiah, and at such moments biblical truth stands right in front of you.

Jerusalem remains at the center of a religious cold war. The political future, as always, is unclear. What doesn't change is the power evoked by these place names on the biblical map and the Power behind them. God stays involved in human affairs— sometimes naming world-historical cities, other times meeting the human heart in small, steady, weekday ways. Bethlehem, Nazareth, Calvary, Emmaus, Jerusalem . . . names that set destinies in motion and are motioning toward us.

Eternal Spirit, thank you for the renewal and astonishment we find in the Bible, in the witnesses who encountered you there, in the towns and cities where your name was first heard and raised up. Keep us open to scripture's power each day. Amen.

I can almost hear Paul sighing as he gazed upon the bickering scene at the Corinthian church and was forced to sort it out. Apparently some churchgoers were lording their gifts of the Spirit over others. In the name of God, their impressive talents were becoming divisive. So Paul took a breath, set them straight, and in doing so made one of the great contributions to Christian thought and practice.

These gifts and services and activities, he says, are to be used for the good of all, for everybody's edification, not personal glorification. Church isn't reality TV, a place for gratuitous drama, performance, and humiliation. Gifts at church are meant to replenish the common good, which is blessed by the one God, the same Spirit, a phrase Paul emphasizes a half-dozen times here.

Then as now, the common good is under siege by other human impulses—egotistical swagger, competitiveness, exploitation, and neglect. Church is where bewilderingly diverse human beings come together and submit to the one Lord. I can't think of anywhere else in society where values of soul and selflessness are upheld decade after decade. In the noise of a cynical age, congregational life dares to claim itself as a zone for these things, honoring the existence of the soul, the cultivation of the needs of others, a wariness of the bottomless ego, the importance of praying together, and hope for the redemption of the whole person, the whole earth—using a dizzying variety of people to do it. This miracle happens every day.

Everybody has personal gifts to discover, celebrate, cultivate, and share. The point, though, is to seek not the limelight but the Light—together.

God in heaven, you've given each of us a path in the adventure of this life. I pray for attentiveness to using my time well and celebrating the gifts of others. Amen.

One time a tearful reader called with a question: "Do you think my Rudy is in heaven?" Rudy had died unexpectedly during routine surgery. Rudy was only eight years old. Rudy was a cocker spaniel.

The reader told me about his church, which was silent about whether pets go to heaven—most churches are. He sounded reassured and relieved when I mentioned that Psalm 36 says, "Your steadfast love, O Lord, extends to the heavens. . . . You save humans and animals alike."

This psalm dares to claim a God big enough to include all creatures great and small in the divine mercy—a Creator powerful enough to carry everything from past to present to future. "All people may take refuge in the shadow of your wings." These are words to fall back on and stake a future on. This psalm's embrace is there when I need it.

Like right now. This era has been a severe test of our health, our politics, our griefs, our planet, our nerves, and our hopes. Yet the world has been in tatters before—think of the economically desperate 1930s, the brutal wartime 40s, the eruptive 60s. Hope is always tested. There's always the risk of seeking the divine truth in the wrong places—in naïve optimism, political utopias, or frightful conspiracies. The Lord's horizon is larger than these, and also closer at hand: in prayer and music, in the faces of others, in actions that heal people and societies, and in the sheer fact that we have been given life. It didn't have to happen. But God has given us time here to share in the all-encompassing divine dream of life abundant—to experience it uniquely, yet as one big family, extending to the heavens.

Eternal Spirit, you are the steady force no matter how uncertain the hour. Help us draw on your indestructible light and cheer one another on. Amen.

Paul lists famous gifts: wisdom, faith, knowledge, healing, miracle-working, prophecy, discernment, tongues, and interpretation of tongues. Apparently some of these gifts were disruptive enough that they needed calling out.

Presumably other gifts and talents are worth honoring too. I think of patience, trustworthiness, serenity, reliability, hospitality. I also think of the quiet competence needed for musicianship, liturgy-planning, and bookkeeping. Churches couldn't function without them. In other words, there's room for all kinds of people, even though it can make for a swarming, combustible mix.

The world these days is obsessed with dividing people. It's always some version of us against them. It drives an addiction to conflict, the temptation to call opponents evil. The real world, God's world, isn't like that.

Paul spells this out. The gifts he lists look irreconcilable. Yet this hodgepodge forces us to acknowledge a truth about the divine creation: Its prodigious diversity is to be grasped and respected, not feared.

Why is there so much diversity and pluralism? Evidently God didn't want a monochrome world, a place of gray sameness. This is God's work, and we're privileged to share in it, for all our differences. I should have the humility and good humor to honor it. We still have individual identity—ultimately in God, not in race, tribe, or party. Those things are too finite—too impermanent, flaky, soon embarrassingly out of date—to bear the weight of eternity.

Paul says to focus on the gifts divinely allotted to each of us and acknowledge that others have been similarly bestowed in turn—all under God.

God of many names, you give us the gift of love and deputize us to do your will. Help us to see your presence in each person we encounter today. Amen.

The world-bending words at the beginning of John's Gospel announce the incarnation of God—Christ on earth walking in neighborhoods and the countryside. The Messiah among us, the Word become flesh—what could this mean? "Come and see," Jesus says. In the Gospel of John, he wastes no time finding followers. A ministry of action is underway. Soon he will scatter the moneychangers, teach, heal, forgive, and turn fatefully toward Jerusalem. But not yet.

First, he shows up at a wedding—the Anointed One enjoying the moment, seemingly at rest before he moves on to the convulsive dramas that await. This episode of turning water into wine comes first, as if to reassure us that the bewildering idea of the Lord incarnate isn't incomprehensible after all but at home among everyday human celebrations.

Wherever Jesus walked he was an awakener, stirring the heart's capacity to recognize Christ and respond to him. And so we incarnate the news ourselves. He moves through the world, gathering witnesses, followers—and also denials. He exposes hardened attitudes, urges self-examination, and confronts our resistance to our own redemption, our own potential.

Believers turn water into wine every day, whenever they regard creation as something more than the play of biological elements or the exercise of ruthless power. Creation is the place where incarnation can unfold and meet each person's suffering. It's the field of the Almighty's acts. When people regard life on earth as living proof of God's care and existence, then grace overflows.

O God, through your incarnation we are shown truth on earth, a way forward with compassion and courage through the shadow of death and into resurrection light. Amen.

A More Excellent Way

JANUARY 17–23, 2022 • MARILYN PAGÁN-BANKS

SCRIPTURE OVERVIEW: How do we feel when we read the word of God? The Israelites rejoice in God's law. At the time of the restoration of Jerusalem after the return from exile, Ezra reads from the Law and explains its meaning to the people. They respond by holding a feast because understanding God's teachings is a source of joy. The psalmist says that God's law revives the soul, causes the heart to rejoice, and helps us to see clearly. Paul continues with his teaching on spiritual gifts, emphasizing that all members of the body of Christ have an important role. No one can claim to be any more important than anyone else. In Luke, Jesus reads from Isaiah and declares that his messianic ministry will focus on justice, mercy, and healing.

QUESTIONS AND SUGGESTIONS FOR REFLECTION

- Read Nehemiah 8:1-3, 5-6, 8-10. When has God's word overwhelmed you? How did you react?
- Read Psalm 19. How do you seek to speak or sing words acceptable to God? How does this shape your life?
- Read 1 Corinthians 12:12-31a. Within the body of Christ, as within our human bodies, parts compensate for one another. How do you take on more to support the body of Christ when others struggle? How do you allow others to take on your roles when you struggle?
- Read Luke 4:14-21. In what ways have you rejected Jesus?

Executive Director of A Just Harvest; queer womanist freedom fighter; senior pastor of San Lucas United Church of Christ, Chicago, IL; adjunct professor at McCormick Theological Seminary.

Today we commemorate the life and legacy of one of the greatest prophets of our time—the Rev. Dr. Martin Luther King Jr. In gratitude for all he sacrificed, we call out his name and we say, *Ashé!*

During his last speech, Dr. King shared with the hundreds gathered in that historic church on a stormy April night in Memphis the urgent need to be in solidarity with the striking sanitation workers. As he taught, Dr. King reminded the crowd how faithful and determined people just like them had succeeded in disempowering Bull Connor, Birmingham's virulently racist Commissioner of Public Safety. As he encouraged his listeners, the preacher and Civil Rights leader moved into a spirit of worship—ending his powerful speech with the well-known declaration, "I've been to the mountaintop . . . Mine eyes have seen the glory of the coming of the Lord."

How surprising that in today's text, in his role as governor, Nehemiah is seen as righteous and just. How ironic that while engaging in this work, he witnesses some injustices and reminds the religious leaders of their responsibility to care for and ensure justice for the poor and the vulnerable among them, using his position to help bring restoration to Jerusalem. The call to let go of fear and to worship is made not only by the religious leaders but also by the governor.

Imagine how different it would have been in Dr. King's time if those in powerful positions had been aligned with God's law. Imagine how different it would have been if religious and political leaders had been concerned for the poor and working class.

Imagine if that were the case for us today. Imagine how much closer we would all be to seeing the Promised Land.

God, we thank you for the leaders and prophets you send to teach us and compel us to live and love in a more excellent way, trusting that we never do this work alone. Amen.

The psalmist beautifully describes creation in a posture of praise and worship. If we close our eyes, we can almost see the sun in all its splendor responding to the call of the Creator with excellence and expectancy. If we read slowly and listen closely, we can hear the wind inviting us to join the celebration.

Here creation reminds us that true worship does not happen in isolation and that there is no worship without accountability to the Creator. Creation reminds us of the laws of God and calls us back to our covenant with God and all of creation.

You do not have to be an environmentalist to believe that creation is fighting for its very existence—our existence. Airborne pandemics, devastating storms, wildfires, earthquakes, mudslides, droughts, melting ice caps, floods—these are just some of the ways that creation is crying out and demanding accountability and care from us humans. Creation is making itself heard. Wisdom is directing us toward restoration and healing.

The psalmist declares that God's law is perfect and that each decree is meant to revive and to reestablish all of creation to its divine purpose. Every precept is intended to cultivate righteous abundance and radical joy.

Creation has no words, but, thank God, we do. Let's use our voices, our keyboards, our social media platforms, and our phones to demand that those who institute and enforce the regulations that protect the environment follow the law of God and put the planet and people before profit. Silence is not an option.

Creator, forgive us for ignoring the groans of creation. May our confession swiftly lead to acts of healing and a commitment to new ways of living that benefit all creation. Amen.

Jesus returned to Galilee, and "a report about him spread through all the surrounding country." Wait, Jesus had been gone forty days and we know he wasn't livestreaming his experience, so what was in the report? That he had survived all that time in isolation with no food? That not even the promise of power and position could tempt Jesus to turn his back on God? Did Jesus start his public ministry by testifying about his battle with the enemy? We don't know. But we do know that the story was spread and passed along because we have it.

There is power in offering testimony. Sharing what we have gone through might just be the encouragement that someone needs to leave an abusive relationship, stand up to an unjust employer, finish a degree, conquer an addiction or fear, seek help, write a book, or give love another chance.

Not only did Jesus' spiritual practice prepare him for the struggles he would face; it also created space that allowed him to be "filled with the power of the Spirit" and to teach and lead with conviction, clarity, compassion, and courage.

From the very beginning of his ministry, Jesus embraced vulnerability. He knew the importance of sharing his experience and the lessons he had learned. He wanted people to get to where he was in their relationship with God and to be clear that he was the example of God's love made flesh and not the exception. Jesus wanted them to know that they too could overcome obstacles and that evil did not have to have the final word.

In a fast-changing world, many of us have the gift of social media as a space to share our wilderness experiences and to realize that we are not the only ones going through such trials. Social media help us celebrate the many ways we have found joy, strength, and hope on our journey. Often we have the pics to prove it!

Holy Spirit, fill us and use us as we offer ourselves this day as a living testimony of your grace, power, and love. Amen.

I don't think it is too far-reaching to describe this familiar pericope as Jesus' "mission statement." The pieces are all there.

When creating a mission statement, it is important to know why you are undertaking a particular project and how you will go about it to be successful. Knowing and naming your target population are also key.

The people in this story were under the rule of the Roman Empire while simultaneously being oppressed by the religious institutions. Jesus knew all this when he stepped up before them, read from the scroll of the prophet Isaiah, and boldly declared his mission. Jesus was clear on his context when he invited listeners to take part in what he was describing and reminded them they were accountable to the God they claimed to serve.

Context matters. I am writing this devotion during a pandemic, a contentious presidential election, and the constant threat of racial and civil unrest. But just as in Jesus' time, no matter what is happening when you reread this text, the message is the same, and God's call is clear: If we declare that we are in relationship with God—right relationship—then we must do all we can to move out in this relationship and into right relationship with all in our community.

As he prepares to begin his public ministry, Jesus reminds his listeners and us that the start of anything new is always a great opportunity to pause, revisit our mission, and reclaim "who we are" and "whose we are." This space of intentional reflection ensures that we show up in the most excellent way, bringing our full and authentic selves and all our gifts in faithful service to God and all God's people.

Jesus, today we join you as we reclaim the persistent presence of the Holy Spirit and God's clear mission for our lives. Amen.

Ubuntu—"I am because we are"—is a South African philosophy that speaks to our interconnectedness, interdependence, and interrelatedness as humans. Our humanity is only fully actualized in relationship with others.

In a letter to the church in Corinth, Paul teaches this concept to a people accustomed to hierarchy, a caste system, exclusion, and separatism. This makes Paul's work twice as challenging. Not only is Paul planting a new church with all the work that entails, but he is also guiding the people to a new way of being in community and leading a more excellent way of life.

It's sad to say, but the church today is still working to figure this out. Oh, sure, most traditions are a lot further along than the early Corinthians were. However, far too many still find ways to exclude people who don't look like them, don't pray like them, worship differently, don't fit the "norm," are too "worldly," too gay, too poor, too Black, not progressive enough, don't have the right accent, live on the wrong side of town, sing too loud . . . are the "other" and don't belong.

The church is to embody God's love in the world. This starts by opening our hearts to build inclusive communities that honor all gifts, welcome all gifts, acknowledge all gifts, and affirm all gifts. This starts by honoring all people, welcoming all people, acknowledging and affirming the humanity of all people.

The world today still needs a church that is ready to show up united and in solidarity for collective liberation. Here I am God; use me. Amen.

My current Facebook cover is an image with the words "Comparing yourself to others is an act of violence against your authentic self."

While the psychological concept "impostor syndrome"—a persistent doubting of one's abilities leading to the fear of being exposed as a fraud—may seem like a modern-day phenomenon, Paul is addressing in today's text the issue of comparison among the community, indicating that perhaps individuals have struggled with this for millennia.

I can personally attest to how feeling unqualified, not trusting my experience, and having unresolved trauma and a deep sense of unworthiness (just to name a few characteristics of impostor syndrome) can and will stunt your personal and professional growth. Too often I get stuck comparing myself to others. Like the people in the early church, I need clear reminders of who I am.

This is what Paul does for the church in inner turmoil. In this section of his letter, Paul clearly affirms for the church, "You are the body of Christ." Paul saw them, knew their gifts, and believed in their potential. He acknowledged their fears and questions. Paul did not want them to get stuck. He wanted them to keep growing. The risk was too great. The world needed the radical message of Jesus, and the church was called to bring it!

The world pushes a fraudulent "bootstraps" and dog-eat-dog mentality. As the church, we are to proclaim grace, unconditional love, and right relationship with God, neighbor, self, and all of creation. Today, let's stand on Paul's affirmation so we can authentically live into our unique role in the body of Christ. Impostor syndrome be damned!

Dear God, help us to see you in our face and in the faces of everyone we encounter today. Only then can we fully be one body. Amen.

I cannot tell you how many preachers I have heard recite these words over the years. All kinds of preachers from an array of traditions, cultures, and backgrounds. Sometimes this is the entire prayer offered right before the sermon. Sometimes it is added at the end of a much longer prayer.

It tells the congregation that words matter. What we say matters. How we say it matters. Why we say what we say matters. What we hold in our heart matters.

These days it would be helpful if political leaders would take a moment to recite this verse before speaking, tweeting, posting, casting a vote. At the minimum we hope that they would take the time to weigh the consequences, count to ten, or get feedback from a trusted and responsible source.

But many of our leaders and many within the Christian community don't believe their words matter at all. They do not understand the power of their words. They do not take any responsibility for the harm they cause and don't seem to care one bit if God is displeased with their hateful, racist, anti-Black, misogynist, homophobic, elitist, white supremacist rhetoric and messaging.

Unfortunately, this distorted and individualized concept of free speech—"I can say whatever I want to say"—is now combined with the ability to hide behind a keyboard, leading to destruction. We claim to follow Jesus, the Word made flesh; yet we often speak, type, or post as if words don't matter, forgetting that "death and life are in the power of the tongue" (Prov. 18:21).

Word who lives among us and within us, "Let the words of my mouth and the meditation of my heart be acceptable to you, O LORD, *my rock and my redeemer" (KJV). Amen.*

God Calls Us

JANUARY 24–30, 2022 • JOHN GOOCH

SCRIPTURE OVERVIEW: The readings from the Hebrew scriptures share a common theme of calling. Jeremiah is called at a young age to be a prophet. God knew and set apart Jeremiah even in the womb. The psalmist also expresses confidence in God's call, because God knew him even before he was born. In the same way, God knows each one of us and has a plan for our lives that is not an afterthought. In this First Corinthians passage (often read at weddings), Paul speaks of love. But this love is not infatuation and is not based on emotion. It is intentional, strong, gritty, and unselfish. In Luke we see that many struggle with the fact that Jesus' calling is also to serve the marginalized. Jesus reveals that God has a missional heart.

QUESTIONS AND SUGGESTIONS FOR REFLECTION

- Read Jeremiah 1:4-10. What is God calling you to do? How does your passion intersect with the world's needs?
- Read Psalm 71:1-6. God promises not to make our lives easy or perfectly safe but to be with us when we face challenges. In a world that seems increasingly violent, how do you find assurance of God's continuous presence?
- Read 1 Corinthians 13. God calls us to a vocation of love. How can you be more loving in your daily work or activities?
- Read Luke 4:21-30. How do you see God's call in those you know best? How can you look to minister to the outsider and the oppressed?

Retired elder in the Missouri Conference of The United Methodist Church; former staffer at Board of Discipleship and the Publishing House of The United Methodist Church; author, historian, teacher.

Jeremiah lived in troubled times. His kingdom of Judah was nearing the end of its political life under the threat of Babylonian expansion. At the same time, there was a movement to reform religious life under the leadership of King Josiah. And God was calling Jeremiah to become a prophet.

Like Moses, Jeremiah had excuses. He thought he was too young ("only a boy" may be an exaggeration, but he was young). He thought he wasn't up to the task of political and international work. He was being called to proclaim the rise and fall of nations! But then the Lord touched Jeremiah on the mouth, signifying that what he says will be the words of the Lord. That's guaranteed.

What do we learn from this? First, that God calls whom God will call. Even though he was young, Jeremiah was chosen, consecrated, and appointed. How do we think about God's calling us? Is there a sense of predestination in these verses that we need to take seriously? Do you believe that God really has a plan for each of us? People talk as if that were the case. Or does God leave us to figure out the best way to fulfill our calling to minister to others? What do you think?

We also hear that our call to ministry is where our passion intersects with the world's needs. What is your passion? Is it writing? Is it working with children? Is it gardening? Should gardening, in fact, be your passion, then contributing to the local food bank could be God's call to you for ministering to the world's hungry people.

To what is God calling you in these days of suffering in the world? What passion do you have that meets the world's needs?

God, I hear your call. Give me the will to explore what that means and how I can make a difference in the world. Amen.

God calls us to be responsible citizens. Jeremiah's call included being overwhelmed by national and international events—to be set over nations, to build up and tear down. He lived in a time of governmental corruption, of wars and the destruction of his homeland. And God called him to pronounce judgment on the corruption.

John Wesley reminds us that we are called to live "acts of mercy." For him, that meant meeting the immediate physical needs of persons—food, housing, medical care, and employment. Each week, the people called Methodists were asked to contribute to a fund for meeting the physical needs of the poor. When there is a crisis today, God's people respond well to efforts to meet the same kinds of need.

Wesley didn't use the language of "acts of justice," but he lived them out. He was always calling for reforms, such as cutting the size of the military to free up funds for the care of the poor. Christians in our day are also called to seek justice for the poor and disenfranchised in our world.

Biblical justice means dealing with the social, political, and economic structures that cause hunger, homelessness, and lack of healthcare. Why is it that children are not getting adequate food in the richest nation on earth? Why are there people who die because they don't have health insurance and can't afford to go to the doctor? What do we do about racial and economic disparities? We feel overwhelmed when we think about all these issues and wonder what our faith calls us to do about them. Jeremiah tells us that God calls us to change our world.

Lord, grant me courage to put my faith to practical applications to help others. Amen.

As I write in the summer of 2020, the COVID-19 pandemic is at its height. People are getting sick. People are dying. People are losing their jobs. The economy is going in the tank. Above all, people are afraid. We all stay in our homes, hunkered down, wearing masks if we go out for groceries, trips to the pharmacy, or to see the doctor. Some people are angry because of closures.

You remember those times. They may have become better after I wrote this. Or they may have become worse. Either way, they left their mark on you.

So you can understand the psalmist when he pleads with God for help. "Deliver me," the psalmist says. "Rescue me. Save me." That's the way we felt, too. "Help me, God! Deliver us from this pandemic. Don't let me lose my job. Keep my family safe."

Life is sometimes not "the best" for either the psalmist or us. But notice one thing: The psalmist never gives up on God. The psalm begins by saying, "In you, O LORD, I take refuge." God is the rock and fortress on whom the psalmist builds his life. God is the source of his hope. Like Job, he cries out to God for help but never doubts God. From the time of his birth, he has learned to lean on God.

These were words of hope as I began writing in the middle of a pandemic. God is faithful. God is the source of our hope. God doesn't always answer our prayers the way we want, but God is always present for us. In times of fear, when hope seems absent, when life is not good to us, God sustains us.

O God, teach me always to trust in you. Amen.

One little-noted event during the bleak time between January 6 and the beginning of Lent is the story of Jesus' baptism. And that reminds us of the act of remembering our own baptism. Many of us can't. We were infants and don't remember. But rituals like the United Methodist Reaffirmation of the Baptismal Covenant help us to remember the grace of God in our lives baptism promises. As a congregation, and as individuals, we are called to remember the "mighty acts of God" and our own commitments to the faith.

Which brings us back to the faith of the psalmist. In other psalms, the writer is asking God to save him from his enemies, protect him from those who would harm him, save him from some troubling time in his life. In this one, the psalmist is remembering God's protection and saving power in the past and is beseeching God to continue to be his Rock and Fortress throughout the remainder of his life. He is reaffirming his faith, allowing him to find courage and strength for living and to find hope for his future.

How often, though, do we affirm such gratitude for God's help in past days and promise to seek God's will in all our days to come—only to panic when the "days to come" turn into nightmares? Do we question God's faithfulness and spend precious time wandering in and out of obedience when we could be living in continued trust that God is working for our good?

Maybe it is good for us to remember our baptism as a way of recalling what God has done in the past and to affirm our desire to trust God for help in the present—recommitting ourselves to the service of God and neighbor.

God, I remember your working in my life in the past. I remember your call to rely on you, to serve others in your name. Lead me, I pray, to joyful service of your children. Amen.

God calls us to love one another. That's what Paul is saying to the Corinthians and to us! We think, *That's really hard. How can I love her? I don't even like her! He's such a jerk. I did all the work on that project and he took the credit. Love him? Forget it.* That's life, right? Those same feelings carry over into public relationships as well. How do we love people who are different from us?

Read today's scripture again and think of all the things Paul was saying as simple steps to loving our neighbors: Patience. Kindness. Civility. Hope. Not tooting one's own horn or looking down on others. Not being jealous of what another person gets credit for. This description still doesn't sound like love. Love is, somehow, bigger than that, more mystical.

No one of those attributes by itself is love. But taken together they make a good plan for loving our neighbors. How do we learn these attributes? By practicing them. Someone once said, "You make a path by walking in it." We learn patience and civility and all those other traits by living them.

Begin with civility, for example. Be polite. Treat other people with respect. Or start with patience. Practice being patient, even if you don't feel patient. If you practice, one day you'll discover how patient you've become.

When we make loving our neighbor an abstract ideal, we make loving them difficult. Paul tells us these simple attitudes and practices taken together make up the practice of love. Living them out is one way we answer God's call to love one another.

God, show me how to live out your love in the daily tasks of life. Amen.

Today this scripture has been fulfilled in your hearing." That must have sounded like great news. The scripture was coming true. Surely that meant the Messiah was coming. The people would be free again!

Jesus had just read the words from Isaiah about the deep needs in people's lives being fulfilled. We react the same way today when we hear about new progress on coronavirus vaccines or about businesses being reopened and people going back to work. It's exciting, but we are also skeptical.

But what about today? How could those scriptures be fulfilled in today's crises? Because of unemployment, food banks are being overwhelmed by hungry people. Cars line up for miles to get food. And we're told that the majority of the people who come have never been to a food bank before. I look at scenes of food banks on television and think that ordinary people are fulfilling the scripture about feeding the hungry. It's not some big miraculous event, like Jesus feeding the five thousand. It's about volunteers and members of the National Guard passing out food so children can eat. It's about people like you and me donating food so the food banks can feed people. Scripture can be fulfilled in ordinary ways in our lives.

Of course there are others who don't see the need to help. So fulfillment of the scripture means we have to work for justice and public concern for peoples who are poor, hungry, and oppressed. Jesus mentioned freeing the oppressed as well as feeding the hungry. We need to do both. We need to meet immediate personal needs and, at the same time, work to change the structures in our society that create those needs. Then the oppressed can truly go free.

Lord, grant me the eyes of faith to see ways I can fulfill the scriptures today—and the energy to do what is needed for that fulfillment. Amen.

Who would have thought that Joseph's boy would grow up to be a prophet? That's what they were asking in Nazareth that day. Who would have thought?

But there are some issues under the surface. The congregation wants Jesus to heal someone in Nazareth, just as they heard he had done in Capernaum. Maybe they want to see proof for themselves. Maybe they want the benefits of Jesus' healing for the people of their town. Or maybe the people of Nazareth just want bragging rights over their neighboring towns. What's going on here?

Then Jesus talks about a prophet not being accepted in his hometown. Where did this come from? Why is it important? He reminds them that Elijah was sent to the widow in a pagan community during the drought, even though there were many widows in Israel. And he says that Elisha healed a pagan (and enemy) from leprosy when there were plenty of people with leprosy in Israel he could have healed. Why outsiders? Why not heal among the chosen people?

The old issue of "us" and "them" rears its ugly head. Who is included? Who is excluded? Who decides? How do you know? The morning paper tells me a lot about *who is* and *who is not*, but not much about *why*. Jesus is saying here that God has a different understanding about who is included. God's grace, he says, is not just for a select few but for all people. That's why Elijah and Elisha went outside the chosen people. Faithful ministry always looks for the outsider, the neglected, the oppressed.

It's easy to be angry at people who are exclusive, who think their way is the only way. We too often feel superior to those people; after all, we're Christians. But what if we are as exclusive as those we look down on? Would we be among those who would try to kill Jesus because he said God's grace is for all?

God, I want to be open to your call, even when it makes me uncomfortable. Amen.

Invitation to New Beginnings

JANUARY 31–FEBRUARY 6, 2022 • GENNIFER B. BROOKS

SCRIPTURE OVERVIEW: The theme of calling is continued in this week's readings. Isaiah has a vision of God on the throne and is terrified because he knows that he is unworthy; yet he is being called by God. The psalmist, traditionally David, praises God for having a purpose for his life and bringing it to completion. Paul echoes Isaiah's sentiments of his own unworthiness to the Corinthians. While assuring his readers of the reality of Christ's bodily resurrection, Paul recognizes that he preaches only by the grace God. When Jesus is calling his disciples, Simon Peter recognizes him as the Lord and cowers because he feels unworthy—much like the prophet Isaiah had done. These readings teach us that God's call is based not on our worthiness but on our willingness.

QUESTIONS AND SUGGESTIONS FOR REFLECTION

- Read Isaiah 6:1-13. When have you heard a difficult call from God? How did you come to finally say, "Here I am; send me"?
- Read Psalm 138. How have you seen God uplift the lowly and the humble? How have these experiences changed the way you live out your faith?
- Read 1 Corinthians 15:1-11. How does your life witness to Christ's resurrection?
- Read Luke 5:1-11. How has Christ called you? Whether or not you feel worthy to the call, Christ wants you to follow.

Styberg Professor of Preaching and director of the DMin program and the Styberg Preaching Institute at Garrett-Evangelical Theological Seminary, Evanston, IL; elder in the New York Conference of The United Methodist Church; author of *Good News Preaching, Unexpected Grace,* and the devotional book *Bible Sisters.*

The first flush of excitement that comes with the opening of a new year is fading fast and may even have dissipated completely for you. And yet there is still the glow of the leftover sparkles from New Year celebrations, and, in some cases, the Christmas lights still hang from the eaves of frozen rooftops. All are reminders of the new that has come with the start of the year, and these reminders stir our hearts and invite us to offer songs of praise and thanksgiving to God. Perhaps the journey to this place has been fraught with pain and sorrow, but here we are, in the realization that it is God who has brought us to this time and place.

This song of thanksgiving—offered by one who has been delivered from distress—calls us to make our individual offerings of praise to the One who makes all things new each moment, each day, each year. The new is inviting because it speaks of possibilities. When that newness follows on the heels of deliverance, it speaks of limitlessness that begins with the blossoming of new hopes and dreams that have been set free to flourish through the expansive grace of God.

The experience of God's enlivening presence calls forth praise. The new has come and brought increase for those who have been blessed by it. That is the promise that resonates through the words of this psalm in these early days of the year. Who knows what awaits? Yet the present moment of new beginnings is worthy of thanksgiving to God, who not only makes all things new but comes with the promise of new opportunities, new growth, and great flourishing.

God of new beginnings, accept the praise of our hearts for what has been, what is, and what is yet to be. Amen.

What an invitation this is, overwhelming in its majesty and awesome in its presentation. It is a call to consecration, dedication, newness, growth, unimagined purpose, possibilities, and even power. It's a set-up. It draws the would-be prophet into the web of God's invitation, and the reader expects the recipient of this extravagant revelation to balk at the whole situation. But that's not what happens. Isaiah immediately volunteers. Why? What has he heard and seen in this highly sensuous experience? What does he perceive and where does his imagination of what is to come take him? Why is he so quick to offer himself?

How in this new season can we hear the new possibilities awaiting us? As I write this, with new national leadership in the United States, many of us are waiting with cautious hope for the new that needs to come—for the uniting of people separated by political differences, for an end to oppressive policies and systems, for a world that epitomizes justice for all people, and for civility and compassion and care that honor the entirety of God's human creation. So where do I fit? How much am I being called to give for the cause of justice?

The call here is to the prophetic, and, despite the individuality of the response, it is important to recognize the universality of the call. It is not simply to the one. This questioning reaches into the community that strives in its ever-new iteration to respond in word and deed in acceptance of the divine invitation. It is the call to grow in love for the sake of the reign of God in the world.

God of new possibilities, we hear your call, and we want to respond in faith. Forgive our hesitations and fill us with strength to do your will in all things. Amen.

It does not make sense, or at least it seems contradictory to the possibilities presented by divine invitation and the human acceptance. Isaiah seems to have been given a message that will work against accomplishing his divine task. Why take a message if it will not be heard? But is that really what this report from the prophet portrays? Or is it that the text, written after the fact, is in actuality a reflection of events that have already happened? Perhaps the most we can say is that the final line—"The holy seed is its stump"—hints at growth and rebirth.

This text speaks to the reality of many preachers. So many who come with great excitement in response to their call to the ministry of proclamation are disheartened by the response of those to whom they have been sent. One of my homiletics colleagues has written a book titled *I Refuse to Preach a Boring Sermon*. But this message from Isaiah—if taken at face value—is calling the preacher to preach a message that will not find an audience, a boring sermon. It may well be an invitation to those who are called to the ministry of proclamation to recognize that even the best developed and delivered message may not take root—immediately or later.

To those who are called to other areas of ministry it seems a similarly depressing prospect: to offer oneself as a witness of Christ's light, only to see oppression and injustice prevail in society and the world. But if "the holy seed is its stump," if the core of the message is divine grace, then, by God's grace, growth is always possible.

God of all life, move us beyond our failures, and give us courage to live out the message of love and life. Amen.

"Preaching is the proclamation of good news." This statement represents the core message of my teaching and preaching. Many preachers—perhaps even most—will concur with my statement, but few of them interpret the meaning of that good news in the same way. In fact, Paul's description of the substance of the good news—namely the life, death, and resurrection of Jesus—is the same as that presented by many of today's preachers. And those events taken together are indeed good news. But is the memorial of the past enough? Is that repetition sufficient for these days or for any day?

For me the good news that bears proclamation at every event of preaching is God's active transformative presence in human life. Paul's declaration to the Corinthians exemplifies the truth of that definition. In his summary of the good news, he names Jesus' active presence in several lives, including his own. In each case the life Jesus touched was transformed in some way. Paul sums up his argument by recounting the transformative impact of Christ's call on his own life. He wants to make clear to his audience his belief in the incarnate power of the gospel to transform the lives of those who accept Christ's call to believe in the good news.

Jesus' appearance to the apostles and to those who followed his teachings had consequences for their lives. His coming fulfilled the divine promise, and his presence changed the state of things for those who accepted his invitation to receive the good news. The message for today's church is the same as it was for the Corinthian church: Believe in the good news of Jesus Christ and watch the change happen.

Life-sustaining God, inspire us to receive your good news. May it change our hearts and lives to be more closely in accord with your will. Amen.

What does it take to be accepted by those to whom God sends us? In an earlier reading this week, the prophet Isaiah volunteers to join the new thing that God presents and is confronted by a task that seems destined to be unsuccessful. The apostle Paul is confronted with a church community that has internal struggles, theological questions, and leadership challenges. He tries to legitimize his position by focusing on the message that is the foundation of any Christian community, namely the good news of their salvation through Jesus Christ.

Paul then asserts that he has been called as an apostle in spite of himself. He is an apostle because Christ made him an apostle. Paul knows that trying to justify oneself as worthy of being a proclaimer of the message of Christ is futile. One is better advised to take the path of the prophet Isaiah and admit one's unworthiness. Success comes not because one is worthy or even because of diligence in doing the task of ministry. Regardless of the form of one's proclamation—by word or deed—faithfulness to the task is the only requirement. It is only the grace of God that brings growth through the acceptance of the good news.

The COVID-19 pandemic forced preachers to find new ways to deliver the gospel message. Many who adapted quickly to the technological requirements were able to deliver the message with greater facility, and some even garnered an expansive online following. However, with a plethora of preachers and sermons to choose from, it was the substance of the good news— the grace of God—that sustained the increase and claimed new believers of the gospel proclamation.

Gracious God, direct our thoughts, actions, and words so the good news of your amazing grace will reach those who need it most. Amen.

It's a pattern: God calls; the one who is called demurs, claiming unsuitability for the task; and then, in a startling turnaround, the one who is called accepts the task. Isaiah did it, and now Peter does it. How many of us—the called of God—have followed this pattern. I know I have, and perhaps that is your story as well.

Prior to calling Peter, Jesus models a way of being with people that is instructive for us as proclaimers of the gospel. He touches people by speaking directly into their lives. Those upon whom his attention is centered experience his presence in tangible ways. The crowd demands his attention, and they get it wholeheartedly. We are called to touch the people to whom God sends us with the good news that transforms lives.

Jesus invites Peter into a relationship with him in a field of endeavor that is totally new. It is one that promises growth of an unexpected nature. Peter was not necessarily listening to Jesus, and Jesus' request starts Peter on a course that alters his entire life. How has your life changed and perhaps grown since you responded to Christ's call? Consider where that affirmative response has led and what growth has resulted from that turn-around decision to be a proclaimer of the good news, whether in word or deed. Consider also if your present location is still where Christ's call would have you. Is there another field to which you are being called? The call of Christ may come again and again throughout our lives.

Open our ears, our minds, and our hearts, O God, to hear and heed your call on our lives. May our journey now and in the future be a response of faithfulness. Amen.

Christ began to call me to ordained ministry eleven years before I answered. Even when I did, it was not a straight or certain path. As I prepared to preach my trial sermon that was to be submitted to the Board of Ministry, I had a conversation with God. Well, it was me yelling at God in denial of that call, with no response. However, later that day, God's response was so clear and definitive that I could not deny it. My acceptance of that divine invitation changed the trajectory of my life forever, and the subsequent growth changed me in ways I could never have imagined.

Kudos to those who, like Isaiah, hear and accept God's call immediately. But for most of the people with whom I have had a conversation on the subject there was definite reluctance to make the seemingly all-or-nothing commitment required by Christ's call.

Peter models the way we use our lives to avoid making the changes that the divine invitation (or demand) requires. It is interesting that both Peter and Isaiah protest their worth to be recipients of the grace that accompanied the call. Both say they are sinful. But then, is that not everyone's situation? Clearly, sinlessness cannot be a requirement for doing the work of God, or else no one would be worthy of being a proclaimer of the good news of Christ. The acceptance of the divine call brings grace that enables and empowers faithful proclamation of the good news.

Christ, our Savior, you alone make us worthy to proclaim your gospel. Grant us strength, hope, and power to serve you faith-fully and with joy. Amen.

Trust the Paradox

FEBRUARY 7–13, 2022 • BRANDAN ROBERTSON

SCRIPTURE OVERVIEW: God wants us to be rooted firmly in our faith. Jeremiah contrasts those who put their trust in themselves with those who trust in God. The latter are like healthy trees with deep roots and a constant water supply, never in danger of drying up or dying. The psalmist uses the same image to describe those who meditate on God's teachings. Thus, as you do these daily readings and reflect on them, you are sinking deep roots into fertile soil. Agricultural imagery is continued in Paul's letter. Paul describes Jesus Christ risen in the flesh as the first fruit, meaning that he is the first of many who will be resurrected. In Luke's version of the Beatitudes, worldly success is not necessarily an indication of God's blessing.

QUESTIONS AND SUGGESTIONS FOR REFLECTION

- Read Jeremiah 17:5-10. Examine your heart. Do you place your trust in "mere mortals" or in the Lord?
- Read Psalm 1. How do you seek to meditate on God's Word day and night?
- Read 1 Corinthians 15:12-20. How has your understanding of the resurrection of the dead changed your living?
- Read Luke 6:17-26. How do you understand the paradoxes of Jesus' blessings and woes?

Activist and public theologian working at the intersections of spirituality and social renewal; author of eight books on spirituality, justice, and theology; founder of Metanoia, a digital faith community for progressive Christians; has a bachelor of arts in pastoral ministry and theology from Moody Bible Institute and a master of theological studies from Iliff School of Theology.

Faith often requires us to trust in a perspective other than our own, which is an incredibly hard thing to do. It often asks us to suspend our rational judgment for a moment and trust that our Infinite Creator has a much better grasp of our situation than our finite minds do. In today's passage, the prophet Jeremiah tells the people of Israel something they've been reminded of again and again—when they rely on the human way of doing things, rather than the way of God, they will find themselves dried up, parched, and dying. They will, the prophet says, miss out on the prosperity that God has promised to bring when they trust in the divine will.

Too many of us have been conditioned to feel as if God's commands (or the commands of anyone) are to keep us from doing what we want to do. The truth is, however, that the principles and lessons of scripture are intended to guide us on the path of abundant life. They seek to provide a corrective to the finite and flawed human belief that working hard enough, earning enough money, or experiencing the most pleasure will lead to a fulfilling life.

Not only does this path not lead to fulfillment; it actually drains the life out of us. Jeremiah's message is clear: Don't trust in the limited perspective of humans, or you will be greatly disappointed.

As we go about living day by day, it is important to ask if we are looking at our circumstances from a self-centered, limited, human lens, or if we are seeking to align with God's perspective, even if it doesn't make immediate sense to us. Our answer to that question will determine the quality of the life we will live.

God, help me not to rely on my own perspective but to have the faith and courage to trust that your ways are higher than mine. Amen.

The grass in my backyard remains constantly brown unless we water it every day. But we live in southern California where droughts are common, so water conservation is more important than the condition of our grass. We just let it be brown and dry most of the time. In the same way that our grass withers without regular attention and watering, our spiritual life withers when we do not set aside regular time for its nourishment.

In today's passage, the prophet Jeremiah tells us that a regular practice of seeking and then trusting in God's presence will connect our lives to a continual source of nourishment and growth. This may sound simple and obvious, but few of us treat our lives with this sort of care. In the busyness and stress of life, it's easy to allow our "natural" mind to take over. We see our to-do list growing longer, the bills piling up, and our family concerns growing more intense. When this happens, we usually resort to thinking like a superhero: "I've got to press on, power through. I can carry this load." We begin to believe it is irresponsible or selfish to take time for ourselves to connect with God and center our souls. Yet it is this very connection that we need the most if we are to have the strength to carry on with our responsibilities.

The God revealed in Jesus wants to support us and renew our strength. In order to tap in to this gift, we have to spend time with God, whether by reading scripture, walking in nature, or simply being still. When we spend time with God, learning to trust God's direction, we will find the grass of our soul nourished and growing greener each day.

Holy Spirit, nudge me throughout the day to take time to be with you. Renew my strength and guide my path according to your will. Amen.

The people we surround ourselves with shape our perspective and lifestyle the most. We've all had the experience of being around someone who is always negative, always expecting the worst thing to happen, always saying a critical word. Such people draw out negativity from within us, and we find ourselves becoming just as negative as they are. The same is true with people in our lives who are genuine and kind—they ignite the flame of authenticity and charity within us.

In today's scripture, the psalmist reminds us of this very point: The people we keep "counsel" with will determine whether we have a life of blessing or a life of judgment. This wisdom may seem to be common sense, but how often do we allow people to pull us into the "way of the wicked"? How often do we allow ourselves to be influenced in a way that makes us doubt God's faithfulness or our sense of purpose in life?

If we seek to be healthy, spiritually rooted people, then we must seek relationships that draw us toward our higher selves and create boundaries that can keep us from those who pull us in the opposite direction. This will not always be easy; but if we are to experience life that flourishes, that bears good fruit, we must be willing to trust the wisdom of God revealed through the words of the psalmist.

Take some time today to reflect on your relationships. Where should you invest more? Where could you create better boundaries? Take steps to align yourself with the ways of God's blessing.

Creator, help me to walk with those who draw me closer to your path for my life. Amen.

The Resurrection is one of the most challenging claims that the Christian faith makes. It takes a lot of faith to believe that Jesus died on the cross for the sins of the world, rose from the dead three days later, and has continued to remain alive, active, and at work in the world. Yet billions of people throughout the world believe just that and experience a palpable hopefulness about the direction of their lives and of our world.

In today's passage, the apostle Paul claims that the faith of Christians would be useless if Jesus had not risen from the dead. What does it mean for us in 2022 to say that Jesus Christ is risen from the grave?

I believe that the hope of the Resurrection for us in the modern world is twofold. First, if Christ is risen then we have hope that we too will rise from the dead. If Jesus is alive, then we have a strong reason to believe that our lives will extend beyond this reality when we die. Such a belief not only helps quell our fear of death but gives us an imperative for living well. Resurrection means that what we do in this life matters. Second, if Christ is risen, then we are not alone in this world. The Spirit of Christ is at work, even in moments of darkness and tragedy.

As Paul says, "Christ has indeed been raised from the dead." We then should be a people of hope—hope for our lives, hope for our world. Thanks be to God for that hope!

Risen Christ, breathe new life in me today. Open my eyes to see you at work around me, and stoke the flame of hope within me that I may live faithfully in the light of eternity. Amen.

Today's Gospel reading makes a curious claim about Jesus. Luke says that "power came out from [Jesus] and healed all of them." This is one of the most compelling claims about how Jesus showed up in the world—that tangible energy radiating from Jesus that brought healing to all who needed it simply by being in his presence.

Jesus embodies healing in his time and in ours. He so sought to conform his life to the values of his Father that he became a channel through which the Spirit of God could bring healing and redemption to the world.

All followers of Jesus are challenged to imitate Jesus' behavior here. We're called to be healers and ministers of reconciliation. (See 2 Corinthians 5:18.) We're called to live our lives with eyes wide open to the pain and brokenness in our world, and we should work to extend healing and grace in every moment.

This is a high calling, but it's also precisely what our world needs to see from disciples of Jesus. We are to step into the divisions and establish justice. We are to be willing to sacrifice our self-interest to ensure the well-being of others. We're called to bear witness to the powerful love that Jesus embodied and to help the world see that these are the ways to abundant and joyful living. This is the high calling we choose when we decide to follow Jesus: to be a people whose very energy and presence bring healing and grace to broken places.

Through us, the Spirit of God can bring healing to our world—often to one person at a time. When we allow God to use our life of sacrificial love, we will be surprised at how God can use a surrendered heart.

God, make me a channel for healing and grace in the world today. Flow to me and through me to embody your love for those who need it the most. Amen.

God's way of seeing the world is fundamentally different from the way we see it. This is never more clearly illustrated than in the Beatitudes that we read today. Every statement that Jesus makes in this teaching says exactly the opposite of what the standards of our world would expect it to say. Jesus says that the poor in spirit, the hungry, those who weep, and those who are hated, are blessed by God.

When we hear these words, there is still a sense of scandal within them. Realistically, even most Christians do not treat the poor, the hungry, and the broken as if they are God's treasured people. And our social institutions certainly don't always act out of this perspective.

But at some fundamental level, we know that Jesus' words are actually statements of what is already true. They expose the fake world that most of humanity lives in, a world that believes that we are what we produce.

The way God sees and has organized the world gives blessing to the humble, those who serve others, those who walk with others through dark valleys. As subversive as it sounds, those are the only ways to experience the life we were created for. May we learn to trust and live in accordance to this simple, sacrificial way of Jesus.

God, help me conform my mind to the wisdom of Jesus, seeking fulfillment in loving you and loving others as myself. Amen.

One of the biggest misconceptions about Jesus is that he expected and wanted his disciples to suffer. As the Rev. Naomi Washington-Leaphart said, "Suffering is not redemptive."

These words fly in the face of what many Christians have been taught; but the statement, I believe, is true. When we read passages like the one we're meditating on today, it is easy to believe that God is opposed to those who are rich, well-off, and highly regarded. But it is not that simple. Throughout scripture, God uses and delights in people of great wealth and influence as well as those with no wealth or influence.

The "woes" that Jesus warns about in this passage are focused on those who believe that these good things are ends in themselves. Jesus is warning that trusting external blessings to be the foundation for our lives sets us up for great suffering and pain. When the rich store up money in palaces of gold, using all their wealth for their own pleasure, they are cutting themselves off from the only path that can bring lasting satisfaction—that of sacrifice and service. Those who laugh and are joyful when others around them are suffering and facing oppression have joy that is shallow and cruel, disconnected from the heart of God.

Christ calls us to use our gifts to spread love and justice in the world around us. These gifts become gateways to a joy that is much deeper and richer than material wealth.

God, help me to use the blessings you have given us to make the world look a bit more like your kingdom each day. Amen.

Becoming the Body of Christ
FEBRUARY 14–20, 2022 • KATHY KHANG

SCRIPTURE OVERVIEW: Joseph had experienced betrayal by his brothers and then had been sold into slavery. At the time, he no doubt felt abandoned by God. However, after God raises up Joseph in Egypt, Joseph is able to provide for his family in a time of drought. Although others have acted with evil intentions, God uses those actions for good. The psalmist offers a similar encouragement. We struggle in the real challenges that face us, but we believe in a God who can carry us through them. In First Corinthians, Paul explains that God carries us even through death to resurrection glory on the other side. Jesus teaches us to respond to evil with mercy. Because we believe in a God who will ultimately bring justice, we do not need to serve as judge and executioner.

QUESTIONS AND SUGGESTIONS FOR REFLECTION

- Read Genesis 45:3-11, 15. How would considering your children's children to seven generations change the way you make decisions?
- Read Psalm 37:1-11, 39-40. What is your relationship to the land where you live now and the land where you lived as you grew up?
- Read 1 Corinthians 15:35-38, 42-50. How do you live out the characteristics of God's imperishable realm?
- Read Luke 6:27-38. How do you respond to Jesus' call to love your enemies? How does your community of faith follow this gospel requirement?

Writer, speaker, and yoga teacher in the north suburbs of Chicago; author of *Raise Your Voice: Why We Stay Silent and How to Speak Up*; currently looking for a church home.

It is not unusual to see "TW" (trigger warning) on a syllabus or on social media to alert readers that the content may include references to issues, ideas, or stories that could trigger trauma.

Joseph's family got no such warning when they found themselves standing in front of the brother whom they had sold into slavery. Joseph got no such warning when his family arrived in Egypt, convinced that there was no possibility that he would be alive. He even tested them in their stated purpose to find relief from the famine.

Eventually the trigger of being reunited with his family and his oppressors sets off the trauma physically. Joseph weeps so loudly people cannot help but notice, and his brothers are silent in their terror. Trauma changes us not only spiritually but physically, affecting our thoughts, feelings, and bodies. Living out our faith, even in times of deep distress, must include space and grace for a physical response.

But what happens next is not quite what we have come to expect from the TWs of today. Instead of silence, resistance, or separating into opposite "sides," there is love, forgiveness, understanding, reconciliation, healing, and restoration. There is space for the pain of trauma to be acknowledged in a visceral way, and there is space for Joseph to name the trauma and to name his process of healing in front of his family.

While Western methods of therapy and counseling are most often focused on individual healing, this example pushes us to consider how God can bring about the healing of communities.

Help me heal from the deep wounds of trauma, O God, so that I respond not from a place of pain but from a place of love and hope. Heal our communities from the deep wounds of trauma so that we can be an example of a healed and healing body. Amen.

The fact that Joseph's story—the story of being sold into slavery by his own family, finding healing, and coming into power to ultimately save his people—became a hit Broadway musical is perhaps the happiest ending to a story with an already improbable happy ending. But not everything in life ends in a neat, tidy bow.

Joseph used the power he gained in Egypt to save his family, but in the process he also consolidated power for Pharaoh. This man who was himself once enslaved contributes to a system that enslaves uses enslaved labor to enrich the powerful.

The story makes me consider how my sense of justice sometimes becomes too narrow, too limited to the people and places I hold nearest and dearest.

Joseph believes his suffering was not in vain, and there is something for us to wrestle with in that proclamation. What if it is *not* true that everything happens for a reason? What if there is *not* a silver lining to every act of injustice and harm? Does everything happen for a reason? Or at the very least, does everything happen for a reason that we can intentionally act on?

Joseph's open arms and warmth to his family should inspire us all. The forgiveness and healing that happened come from a place my time in therapy and spiritual direction still cannot access. But I cannot help but wonder how different things could have turned out had that love and care extended to the Israelites and Canaanites.

How can our love and influence be forces for good in our immediate family and in our communities?

Poetry was my first introduction to creative writing. A staple assignment of the first few days of most years of elementary school included writing an acrostic poem using our first names—each letter of the name starts the first word of each line, and each line is a self-description. Acrostic poems became a way I wrote about my children when their elementary school teachers asked me to describe them. *Brave for Bethany. Caring for Corban. Energetic for Elias.* Each letter revealed a little more of what I saw in each child and what I hoped their teachers would discover.

The psalmists used Hebrew acrostics to draw listeners and readers into a pattern and rhythm as each pair of lines invites us to consider what faithfulness and faith look like. The acrostic nature of the poem gets lost in translation, so imagine that the lines build on each other, taking us deeper into our own heart and into God's impact on our lives.

This poem of Psalm 37 starts with a reality check: We aren't bothered by evil itself. Rather, we are actually jealous of what people manage to get away with. The psalmist reveals more and more the contrast between how we actually exist in the world and God's alternative ways of being. We are being invited line by line into a deeper understanding of God.

Choose a word you might use to meditate on God's character. Use that word to build an acrostic poem of your own. Reflect first on where you are spiritually, and then move toward naming God's character and how you could live your life differently.

Christian life is a matter of focusing our motives and actions not on short-sighted pleasure or success but on understanding God's true nature.

What motivates you to live the way you do? For example, I find such great satisfaction in physically checking a task off my list that I sometimes write down things I've already done so I can check them off. I am motivated by the pleasure of seeing the checked-off list, even though I have not done anything extra by adding a finished item. Further, the payoff is quite temporary and doesn't change a bad habit or even reflect how God has changed me.

But here we are invited to examine our true motives. How many times have we looked at the good fortune of someone we considered less than godly and wondered why good things happen to bad people? Faithfulness can mistakenly look like a list of dos and don'ts, when actually a life of faithfulness happens by allowing our lives, daily actions, and motivations to be shaped by God's character.

Trust. Commit. Be still. Do not get upset. Let go of anger and leave rage behind. None of this makes sense in a world that offers temporary success, temporary riches, temporary delight. But the psalmist knows these are the characteristics of the very God we claim to believe and follow.

O God, help me be honest with myself and name the jealousy and envy in my life. Help me seek you so that I may live a life that reflects your refuge and rescue. Amen.

My friends are my friends because we like each other. We are kind to each other. We celebrate one another. Friendships take time, energy, and patience, but, in the end, the relationship is based on agreed mutuality.

I am a good friend, but I have one friend who is a great friend. She remembers birthdays and sends a card and gift at least one week before. She remembers what is going on with my children and asks how they are doing. She sends me links to articles she thinks I would find interesting, and she has been known to send me a gift because she noticed on my social media that I was having a rough go of it.

I am probably a better enemy than a friend. I am excellent at carrying a grudge for slights that happened months if not years ago. People who mistreated my children when they were young are still on my list. I don't seek revenge, but I've mastered cold politeness. We call it "Midwest nice."

But I am also a Christian, and this is when Jesus pushes me to the edge. Honestly, I read this passage and I want to scream. I want Jesus to know why my enemies are my enemies. How can Jesus want me to love the very people who have been the cause of pain for my family and friends?

"What about the racists, Jesus? Do I love them?"

"Yes."

"What about the people telling me to go back to where I came from? Do I love them?"

"Yes, love them."

"Why?"

"Because I love you."

How have I been someone's enemy? What have I done or become that would make it impossible for another person to love me? Jesus, help me not only to love my enemies but to become less of an enemy. I love because you first loved me. Amen.

At the start of fall, my mom and I would harvest seeds. A summer of marigolds, lettuce, peppers, tomatoes, and perilla leaves would give way to fall. Those seeds looked so unlike and unrelated to the plants from which they came. Bright orange compact blooms would dry into narrow, black and brown seeds, some with a hint of orange at the end. Stalks of perilla, green spade-shaped leaves sometimes as big as my hand, would grow a small shoot of flowers from which we get the tiny black seeds.

When my own children were young, we planted watermelon, broccoli, and brussels sprouts from seed. Sometimes the payoff would take too long for them to remain interested in the necessary daily watering and weeding. But when harvest time came, there was always a moment of awe.

The image of seeds dying into new life requires faith and imagination. Who could have imagined a resurrected Christ? What does that imagination dare us to dream? What if it's not just seeds and bodies but also the church? We know what it looks like for seeds to die and return in full bloom to provide beauty and food. But what does it look like for our lives as they once were to die and return as intended on earth as reflections of God the Creator, as creators bringing flourishing and peace? What would it look like for the church in its buildings and programs to die and return in full bloom to live out God's kingdom on earth as it is in heaven?

God, creator of all living things, grant us the imagination to bring forth your kingdom on earth as it is in heaven. Amen.

A few years ago my parents wanted to talk with me and my sister about their eventual death. I had anticipated a sad conversation, but my dad brought a great deal of levity and some perspective as he and my mom had been discussing cremation. I was rather surprised to realize that somewhere along the way I had believed cremation was a sin. My dad shared with us an article laying out options for the ashes, including having one's ashes made into pencils, buried with a tree seedling, or used to make diamonds.

As Christians we must never forget resurrection. It is not merely symbolic. Nor is it simply about individuals guaranteeing their way into heaven. Paul is not saying the physical body doesn't matter or that an individual's "arrival" in heaven is the only goal. Paul is writing to the church in Corinth, a body of believers, embodied souls whose work in the flesh mattered and matters. Embodiment reminds us to consider not only a spiritual resurrection but also how that transformation affects the body of Christ, the church.

My dad joked that his ashes should be split between me and my sister so that we could each have a part of him remain in our lives. My mom joked about having two diamonds made so that we could wear her near our hearts. My husband learned his ashes could be pressed into a vinyl record; I opted either to become pencils or to be buried with a tree. Regardless of what actually happens, we have peace knowing that what matters is not what happens to our physical bodies at death but how we have lived to reflect the transformative power of the Spirit of God. That is what it means to become the body of Christ.

O God, grant us wisdom and joy to live out our spiritual realities in our physical lives. Amen.

The Call to Love and Serve

FEBRUARY 21–27, 2022 • MARY C. EARLE

SCRIPTURE OVERVIEW: God's glory is always revealed, even if never completely. When Moses encounters God on the mountain, his face undergoes a physical transformation as a reflection of God's greater glory. The psalmist reminds us of how great God is and how even Moses and Aaron bow before God's throne. Paul refers to the story of Moses, but because of Christ, God's glory is now more openly revealed. There is no need to wear a covering as Moses did, for Christ reflects openly the divine radiance. Luke recounts the Transfiguration, when the face of Jesus, like that of Moses, begins to shine. God's voice reinforces the revelation of the Transfiguration, declaring Jesus to be God's Son and the revelation of God's glory.

QUESTIONS AND SUGGESTIONS FOR REFLECTION

- Read Exodus 34:29-35. Consider the ways you provide evidence of your faith. Do you display it for your glory or for God's?
- Read Psalm 99. How do you seek a healthy balance of awe and intimacy in your relationship with God?
- Read 2 Corinthians 3:12–4:2. What "veil" separates you from God—a sense of unworthiness, a hardened heart, a lack of understanding?
- Read Luke 9:28-43a. Jesus shines with God's glory, but then he gets back to his work of healing. Consider how God might transform you to do better the work you are already doing for God.

Author, poet, retreat leader, spiritual director, and Episcopal priest; faculty member of The Academy for Spiritual Formation; lives in San Antonio with her husband, Doug, along with a border collie, Fiona, and a cat, Leftovers.

Moses has been on the mountain. He has conversed with God and received the Commandments. He has been enclosed in the uncreated light of the Holy One, encircled by the radiance of this God who has brought the Israelites out of bondage in Egypt and into the desolations of the desert. While his people have fallen prey to all kinds of longings and temptations, Moses has gone apart for this intimate time with God. Moses is spending time alone with the One who has led them by pillars of cloud and of fire. He has been immersed in the light of God. He comes down from the mountain a changed man with a changed face.

The human face is a mystery. We can never see ourselves. Of course, we can see our reflection in a mirror. But that is a mirror image; the reality of our face is reversed. We need one another to have a sense of the beauty of our faces. We need one another to discover what our faces may be showing. Those who know us best let us know that our faces reveal more than we can ask or imagine.

Moses' face was shining. He was changed from glory into glory. Yet this stunning appearance was disconcerting for others. He knew that his face was different—radically changed—because of the reactions of others. Moses was changed in every respect. Even his physicality reflected the encounter with divine glory. His face was radiant and full of light.

In pastoral work as an Episcopal priest, I have on occasion had the privilege of seeing a truly physical shift in a person's face. Not a momentary change, but a transformation from the inside out.

Living, loving God, change our faces to infuse our being with the light and love of Sinai so that we may bring light into the world. Amen.

Revelation is a strange phenomenon. It both shows and conceals. This truth is right in the etymology of the word, which means "to veil again." We tend to imagine revelation as a process of something being made clear. Yet in scripture, a revelation is also a veiling. Such is the case with Moses.

His time on Mount Sinai has been singularly transfiguring. He is still Moses, but he is more Moses than he ever has been. He is shot through with glory, so much so that he must veil his face to spare his community the full radiance. His practice of veiling when he is with them and then unveiling when he is with the Lord becomes a kind of vesting and unvesting.

Though he cannot see his altered face, Moses does behold the response of those around him. Out of kindness and respect, he veils. He chooses a way of humility (which, it might be noted, has not characterized his leadership). In his ongoing encounters with God, he removes the veil because the One in whom he lives and moves and has his being is the author of this glory, the creator of this light.

In the life of prayer, the charism of humility allows for breathing room in the gathered community. Leaders who know when to "veil themselves" so that others may speak create space for transformation. This chosen self-limitation is fruitfully cultivated in silence, solitude, and stillness. When we cherish our times of deep prayer, opening ourselves to the working of the Holy Spirit, we are led to listen to our neighbors. In choosing to be veiled, we join in a tradition going back to Moses, a tradition of quiet confidence and trust.

In quiet confidence, may we be open to the glory that is at work within us, bestowing justice and beauty beyond our imagining.

Most of us, truth be told, do not think of the Lord as king. At least, we don't think of the Lord in images of the royalty of countries here on earth. If we do, we are missing the point of the good news.

The psalms were Jesus' prayer book, which is why he quotes them in times of distress. As we make our way toward the Transfiguration, we are walking with Jesus, who prayed the psalms. His reign of love leads to justice and abundance of life.

I am led to remember John Lewis, whose skull was fractured at the Edmund Pettus Bridge in Selma, Alabama, as he marched for voting rights. I am led to remember all who have marched chanting, "Black Lives Matter!" I am led to remember my friend Olga Samples Davis, an African American poet here in San Antonio, who said to me, "Marching is fine. Now Jesus is telling us to make justice the king."

When we, both as persons and as communities, begin to notice inequity, a transformation is taking place. When we listen to the stories of immigrants, people of color, women and children who have been abused, we cannot un-hear them. The mercy and compassion of Jesus spring forth when we seek the justice and equity established in the beginning by God.

Imagine that. Imagine if this country, this community of nations, and this planet were places where all were given the respect due their sacred humanity. Imagine a planet transfigured by equity and compassion. Let that holy possibility take hold of your whole being, body and soul.

And then, today and throughout the coming season of Lent, ask God to show you what offering for the sake of justice you might make—not out of inflated heroics but out of that deep desire to embody the life-giving Spirit.

Grant me, gracious Friend, to act on your invitation to be your life here and now and to bring equity to all. Amen.

In my ministry as a spiritual director, I often hear directees, especially those new to the walk of faith, become over-wrought by what they perceive to be an unanswered prayer. God may seem distant or not present at all. This hiddenness is disconcerting, troubling, and challenging to them.

And yet, throughout the tradition of Christian spirituality, we are reminded that progressing in the way of love, step by tiny step, will sometimes lead us to a time of unknowing. We begin to find that our prayer dries up, or our long-loved images of divine presence fall apart. As hard as it may be, the tradition tells us that these moments are of God. We are being led deeper into the mystery of God, and anything that was becoming a bit idolatrous goes by the wayside.

To use the words of Psalm 99, we are encountering that pillar of cloud. Often this occurs in the midst of personal difficulty or tragedy. Sometimes it just happens for no discernible reason. Many of the saints tell us that this passage, while disorienting, happens when God is drawing us closer to God's own self. John of the Cross goes so far as to say God is weaning us off mother's milk and getting us to stand up. Any of you who have nursed a baby know that there's a tenderness in weaning for both mother and child. That said, failure to wean at the right time is truly problematic.

As your own walk in love unfolds, may you trust God, your companion on the way. May you know that the voice in the pillar of cloud is a voice of love.

As I walk through this day, dear Friend, may I heed your voice, and may I trust that you are ever with me, even when I am feeling bereft of your presence. Amen.

At our baptisms, we are baptized into the glory of God. One of our Episcopal prayers for the season of Epiphany asks that we might "shine with the radiance of Christ's glory." To what end? Clearly, as we move toward the Feast of Transfiguration on Sunday, we are being led to see that this glory, this splendor, this eternal uncreated Light leads us to the hallowing of our wills. Our God-given capacity to live in the joy of loving service becomes stronger as we practice that capacity in small ways.

I think of my neighbor who has been homeschooling her middle-school–aged children during the COVID-19 pandemic, while also making sure that they get outside, play, and come to help out with chores from time to time. Glory in the household.

I think of all of the volunteers at the San Antonio Food Bank, tirelessly offering food to families in need—with smiles and kindness. Nothing smacks of condescension.

I think of the medical personnel who are laying down their lives in the hospitals to bring healing to those who can't breathe.

I think of all who have worked for racial equality and those who continue to put themselves at risk in the hope of bringing a renewed society into being.

All around us, every day, we are witnesses to that Spirit-led freedom to love and to serve. It is an honor to behold. When we see this love in action, it truly is glorious. We see the whole human family radiant with the freedom to choose love. Christ lifts the veil from our faces so that we can be transformed by seeing and accepting the new freedom to choose to love the whole human family. And God is glorified.

Gracious God, grant me the wisdom to know the freedom you have given me to choose loving service. And grant me the courage to live and act from that freedom. Amen.

Peter, John, and James have accompanied their friend and teacher up the mountain for time apart. Jesus wants to pray—to be with the One who has sent him. He also senses the need to bring these companions. No doubt we have this story of what happens on that mountain because of those three. At some point, they told of the wonder they had beheld.

In the depths of prayer, the uncreated light of life shines forth from Jesus. That light has been there all along. But now, in this moment on the mountain, the three disciples receive the stunning gift of seeing the truth of their friend's being. They see his glory. Their eyes are filled with divine radiance. Their skin is warmed by this phenomenal light.

They are invited to receive this gift of revelation, and they are transfigured by wonder. The events on the mountain shift their perceptions. Yes, this is Jesus their teacher. Yes, this is Jesus their friend. Yes, this is the companion who has told them stories over dinner. And Jesus is also the Anointed One. He is also the One for whom the whole world longs, for whom we are created.

The change in Jesus' face, a face that is loving and compassionate, will remain in the disciples' memory. As they remember and feed on the memory, they will also be changed. Each one, in his own way, will be led to serve in love. Each one, in his own way, will shine with the radiance of Christ's glory. And so will we.

Beloved, we give thanks for the splendor of your light, the abundant generosity of your life, the stunning strength of your love. May we mirror your glory as we walk in your way. Amen.

TRANSFIGURATION

Affter the events on the mountain, Jesus, Peter, John, and James return to their lives. Immediately they are met by a great crowd. A father in agony over his son's malady approaches and begs for his son to be healed from the seizures that have convulsed him. His heart and soul long for his son's wellness.

Jesus, fresh from being enveloped by the light of God, heals the son by rebuking a demon. The true identity of Jesus continues to shine through. When he heard, "This is my Son, my Chosen; listen to him!" he returned to the people who walked in darkness. That led to his immersion in the great crowds of those who were hungry, thirsty, sick, lonely, and frightened.

Luke doesn't mention Peter, John, and James in the story of healing, but I can imagine their watching what happens. I imagine their realizing that, despite their desire to stay on the mountain and build three dwellings, they are learning anew and at a deeper level that deep prayer always opens us to loving action. Deep prayer—prayer in which we listen with our whole being and receive the light of Christ—will inevitably lead us, step by step, to the places where we can offer compassion and hope.

Just as Jesus is transfigured, so are we—through our baptism, our Communion, our prayer. We are led by the Friend who goes before us, preparing good works for us to accomplish.

Gracious Friend, may I walk in your ways and continue to praise you not only with my lips but in my life, as I give myself to your service. Amen.

Call Upon the Lord

FEBRUARY 28–MARCH 6, 2022 • WILL WILLIMON

SCRIPTURE OVERVIEW: As we begin the season of Lent, the readings provide several images of how we might prepare our hearts. Deuteronomy focuses on gratitude with a recitation of the history of God's faithfulness. The people are instructed to offer their gifts to God as a response to God's generosity. The psalmist focuses on faithfulness. If we put our confidence in God, God will protect and sustain us. In Romans, Paul emphasizes faith. Our confession of faith from the mouth should come from the heart, and this heart confession saves us. The story of the temptation of Jesus admonishes us to know biblical truth. The devil tempts Jesus with half-truths—even scriptural quotes—but Jesus counters with correct understanding of God's Word and God's character.

QUESTIONS AND SUGGESTIONS FOR REFLECTION

- Read Deuteronomy 26:1-11. We no longer offer physical sacrifices to God. How do you give the "first fruits" of your labor to God in thanksgiving?
- Read Psalm 91:2, 9-16. Recall a time you have felt abandoned or insecure. How did God respond to your call?
- Read Romans 10:8b-13. Paul learned to see those he once despised as his equals in Christ. Whom does God call you to learn to love?
- Read Luke 4:1-13. How do you follow Jesus' example to use scripture to resist temptation?

Professor of Christian ministry, Duke Divinity School, Durham, NC; retired bishop of The United Methodist Church.

R emember where you came from.
 Good advice, Deuteronomy. It's all too easy to claim that we're here because we worked hard or because we deserve to be here. It's easy to forget the helping hands that others offered. Self-advancement, self-creation, self-help, and self-care are lies.

At the end of Deuteronomy, entering the land of promise, the Israelites are urged to remember how they got there: We were starving, enslaved, immigrants without land or hope. We "cried out for help," and the Lord with "outstretched hand" brought us out and gave us land. Remember you would not be here, you would not have the life you are living, if not for God. Your life—everything that you call your own and all that makes your life joyful and worthwhile—has come to you as gift, as grace.

Remember: You wouldn't be Christian—reading these scriptures, thinking these thoughts, walking this way—if not for the gifts of others. No one is born Christian. If you have faith, if you believe that the story Deuteronomy tells is truthful about what God is up to and who you are, then that is gift. Someone had to love Christ and love you enough to tell you the story to show you the way.

"When I discovered Christ . . ." "When I gave my life to Christ . . ." *No!* We must remember how we got here and where we came from. Our relationship to God is a gift from God.

We wouldn't have life if it were not for the God we have—the giver of gifts, the protector of immigrants, the Savior of the enslaved—and if that God had not relentlessly, constantly reached out to us and put us where we are, without much assistance from us. That's the God that Deuteronomy names, the same God who comes to us in Christ, giving us the life we didn't earn or deserve.

Remember the people who gifted and guided you to where you are today.

Many's the time I've had someone show up at church after a long absence, explaining their return like this: "I've been going through a tough time in my life. Big problems. I thought I needed to get back with God."

"I tried drugs. Only made things worse. Then I got addicted to alcohol. Hit bottom. Now, I think it's time for me to try Jesus," said another.

As a pastor I've chafed at their no-atheists-in-foxholes religion. They ignored God until the bullets were sailing past, until they had tried everything. And then, in utter desperation, they decide to "try Jesus."

People should love God at all times of our lives. God ought to be on our minds in good days as well as bad. What does it say that some people only pray when they are going down for the third time, having exhausted all other alternatives, and are at the end of their rope?

It says that they are at last ready to meet the God who reaches out to us in scripture.

"Then you will call, and the LORD will answer; you will cry for help, and God will say, 'I'm here'" (CEB).

So many times in scripture, God says, in effect, "Though you forgot me, I haven't forgotten you." When we call out to God in times of deepest distress, we are calling out to the God who in every moment of our lives—through good times and bad—constantly calls to us.

What should I say when people who were absent from God or forgetful of God show up at church or seek spiritual help in their times of desperation? "Wonderful! God's been waiting for you to call."

Lord, our help in time of need, help me to call on you even when I don't feel that I need you. Amen.

Ash Wednesday

On Ash Wednesday the church makes us admit our mortality, finitude, and sin. Not too many will be in church on this day. Few of us are willing to hear—in spite of any of our alleged accomplishments—that we are dust and to dust we shall return.

How can deceitful people (like us!) be that honest? We're able to confess our sin because we've heard a gracious word from God, "You will cry for help, and God will say, 'I'm here'" (CEB). Only people who are confident that God is here for us can risk honesty about our need for God's help.

I know someone whose testimony illustrates this truth: "I worked hard in college and did well. Got into the medical school of my choice. A year after finishing medical school I was pulling down $200,000 a year. My practice was booming. Then late one night, returning home at my usual hour, I saw a note on the kitchen table. The note said, 'We don't know you anymore. We're leaving.' My wife and the kids were gone. For the first time in my life, I fell down. For the first time, my life was out of control, and there was nothing I could do to get it back. I fell down, ten thousand fathoms down into this dark pit. Just before I hit the bottom, I reached out for the first time. And it was like this hand was there waiting for mine. Maybe that hand had been waiting for mine my whole life. I don't know. All I know is that hand grasped mine. I was pulled up. I was saved."

Once you know the truth of God's identity—once you understand that God is the one who says, "I'm here"—you can risk the honesty required by Ash Wednesday.

Thanks, Lord, for being here for us, even in those times when we are not there for you. Amen.

There. That wasn't so hard, was it? Yesterday, Ash Wednesday, we committed an unusual act: We confessed our sin. Feel sorry for those who brag, "I will never apologize for anything." Confession is a gift.

An unverifiable but still useful story says that somebody asked C. S. Lewis, "Why are atheists some of the best people I know?" Lewis responded, "They must be good, mustn't they? They have to get it right; they don't know a God who forgives."

Christ, when told that no respectable Messiah would hang out with disreputable people, responded, "I have come to seek and to save the lost. I've come for sinners, only sinners" (see Luke 15). If you don't know a God who saves sinners, then you are forced to keep up the pretense that you are a nice person who can get along just fine on your own.

"Whenever you cry out to me, I'll answer" (CEB). Sometimes we overlook the gift of knowing a God who, even in our sin, welcomes our cry for help, reassuring us, "I'll be with you."

When a child wakes up in the middle of the night and calls for a parent, the child trusts that the parent will respond. The parent may not be able to explain why the child had a frightening dream, but that's okay. It's enough for the parent to answer, "I'm here. No need for fear."

We can be honest because we know a God who responds to our cries for help. We sinners need not fear entering the season of Lent, these forty days of forthright honesty about our sin and our need for salvation.

Whenever we cry out—whether it be a time when life is difficult or a time when we have once again messed up, stumbled, and fallen—that's when we're glad to have a God who says, "Whenever you cry out to me, I'll answer."

For the gift of your loving forgiveness, O God, we sinners give thanks. Amen.

How reassuring to hear Paul proclaim, "All who call on the Lord's name will be saved." Christians are those who, at least on a weekly basis in our worship, "call on the Lord's name." The rituals, teaching, and proclamation of the church are training in the art of calling upon the Lord's name.

The trouble is, Paul doesn't say "those who have their names on the membership roll of the church" or "believers who are as morally upright as you" or "people who resemble you and your friends" will be saved.

Paul says "all." *All?*

John Wesley, the founder of Methodism, got into big trouble for consistently preaching Paul's message of "salvation for all." Against those who said that Christ died for many but not all, or who said that God's love was conditioned on our ability to love God in certain ways, Wesley exuberantly proclaimed that Christ's work is without boundaries. *All?*

How wonderfully reassuring to know that Christ has stepped over all the barriers and obstacles that kept us distant from his love! And yet, to tell the truth, it's disconcerting to hear that Christ has done for all what Christ has done for me. *All?*

Surely that doesn't include horrible people who have committed terrible crimes. "All" must not mean those who are steadfastly cruel and unjust to their neighbors. How about the guy who cheated me on a business deal? And the person who said that my sermons are boring? *All?*

The first Bible verse I learned by heart was John 3:16: "For God so loved me, and people in my church who look and act a lot like me, that God gave God's only begotten Son . . ."

Isn't that how that verse goes?

God so loved the world? *All?*

Lord Jesus, help us to give thanks that your love extends beyond us. Amen.

Jesus begins his ministry not by joining with family and friends to celebrate his ordination but rather by being cast into the wilderness where he is tempted by Satan.

When I think of temptation, I think of sin—lust, pride, greed, the seven deadlies, and other self-evident wrongs. Sin is complicity with evil, doing wrong, succumbing to bad desires.

The temptations put before Jesus by Satan are different. "Jesus, I know you want to help people. Think of the good you could do for hungry people by turning these stones into bread."

"No? I can see your point. Feed somebody today, and they'll be hungry tomorrow. You should do sustainable good by the only means we have of doing systemic, effective good—politics. Take over the kingdoms of the world."

"No? That's true, you are a spiritual leader. Throw yourself down from the pinnacle of the Temple. Give solid, miraculous proof to struggling believers!"

Jesus refuses.

Satan's temptations are not sexual, abusive, or immoral. Bread for the hungry, power used responsibly, and miraculous evidence—these are good things. And yet Jesus says, "No."

Note that Satan begins by saying, "Since you are God's Son" (CEB). "If you are who the voice at your baptism said you were, God's Son, act like it! Be the Messiah we thought we deserved, not the Messiah you are. Prove you are the God we wanted" (AP).

Jesus says, "No."

Why did Jesus refuse such tempting offers? What kind of savior would refuse to align with our expectations for God? We must wait and watch Jesus in action for the next forty days of Lent. Satan departs and Jesus goes his way not as the God we thought we had to have but rather as the Savior he is.

Lord, help us to follow where you lead, rather than walking where we think you should go. Amen.

First Sunday in Lent

Upon entering a church, I noticed that the children were picking up small bags and taking them to their seats. "What are those?" I asked.

"Those are activity bags with crayons, Bible picture books, and other activities to occupy the children during the service," explained the pastor.

Imprinted on each child's bag was "Worshiper in Training."

Satan tempts Jesus by offering power over "all the kingdoms of the world," saying, "It's been entrusted to me and I can give it to anyone I want. . . . Worship me, it will all be yours" (CEB).

Satan connects worship with politics. Politicians dominate our news. The nation has become our source of security, our protector from the cradle to the grave, our only means of doing good, the functional equivalent of God.

Jesus responds, "It's written, You will worship the Lord your God and serve only him" (CEB).

Both Satan and Jesus understand that the chief issue is not the politics of the left or the right. The question is, "Whom do you worship?" Our persistent, chief temptation is idolatry. God's people belong to the God who delivered and loves them; but we're still tempted to bow before other altars.

False gods come in many guises; detecting them requires honest self-examination and discernment. The story of Jesus' temptation prompts us to ask, "To whom do I give my allegiance? Where have I placed my hope? On what altar am I laying my life?"

So at church this first Sunday of Lent, as we attend to the reading and preaching of scripture, as we pray and praise and journey with Jesus toward his cross, this is our main business, the task of a lifetime—Worshiper in Training.

God, we call on you to save us from the temptation to worship anyone but you. Amen.

God's Love Is Always Greater

MARCH 7–13, 2022 • MOLLY VETTER

SCRIPTURE OVERVIEW: This week's readings give witness to God's ways and provide confidence and hope in our faith. In Genesis we read of God's promise to Abram, a promise that seems very unlikely to a man with no children. But God seals the covenant, and the story later shows that God never breaks God's promises. The psalmist, even while mired in conflict, praises God for being his light, his salvation, his stronghold. The psalmist longs to be in God's presence forever, a desire that can inspire all of us as believers. Paul says that in the future reality, we will no longer experience resistance from those who oppose God. One day Christ will fully transform us to our citizenship in heaven. Jesus himself experienced resistance even in Jerusalem, yet he ultimately triumphed, as will all those who trust in God.

QUESTIONS AND SUGGESTIONS FOR REFLECTION

- Read Genesis 15:1-12, 17-18. How can you take a step forward in the dark toward God's seemingly impossible promises for the future?
- Read Psalm 27. Recall a time when you waited in the shadows of your life. What did you learn about God's provision during this time?
- Read Philippians 3:17–4:1. How do you live in the paradox of standing firm in faith by being vulnerable?
- Read Luke 13:31-35. When have you been unwilling to accept love? How can you comprehend the depth and yearning of God's love for you?

Senior Pastor at Westwood United Methodist Church in Los Angeles, CA; elder in the California-Pacific Annual Conference.

When I read ancient texts like this one from Genesis, with details about the preparation of animal sacrifices offered to God, the distance between Abram's time and mine seems immense. I confess that I prefer the verses about looking at the stars!

In the time since Abram's life, we've come to understand more about our universe. We now know that the closest stars to our sun are between four and five light-years away—that is, when we see their light, we are perceiving light that emitted from those stars more than four years ago. And that's just the nearest stars; some of the dots of light we see in the night sky are not individual stars but whole galaxies at such a distance that they appear to shine with a single light from millions of light-years away.

When the Lord tells Abram to "look toward heaven and count the stars," I hear an invitation to broaden our view. And, knowing now what we do about this starlight, we understand that this view requires us to see a bigger picture in both space and time.

The promise Abram received from the Lord required him to see a vision that he would not get to experience in his life—to trust in a promise of descendants that would only become visible beyond the limits of Abram's lifespan. Likewise, in faith we are invited to trust that our faithfulness to God—our persistent work for justice—shines like starlight with beauty we may not yet be able to perceive.

God of all time and space, I rest in trust that your promises for our world are bigger and more beautiful that I can imagine. Give me faith to persist in your work of love and justice, even though I will not get to see it all come together. Amen.

I find the image of living "in the house of the Lord" quite evocative. I think of my living space and how it's the place where I do so many different things. At home I sometimes feel comfortable and at peace, as when I cover myself with a blanket on the couch to read a good book. Yet at times I hide in my room alone when I'm angry or devastated. I cook dinner and clean up the dishes; I start projects and sometimes finish them. In the evening my home can be a sanctuary as I finish my day. In the morning it is where I get myself ready for the day ahead.

In a world where so many people are homeless, I am aware that my home is a great gift. It is a safe place to sleep and has bathrooms, heat, and air conditioning. There's always water to drink and a place to cook and store food. I get to live with my spouse and child, and we can welcome others into our home when we choose to do so. In all this, though, the primary value of my house isn't the house itself but what the house makes possible—how it provides space for life and helps me prepare to venture out.

Similarly, if dwelling "in the house of the Lord" is a goal of our faith, we ought to remember that it's not the metaphorical house we strive for but the life it enables. Living in God's house provides me "shelter in the day of trouble." God's house is "the stronghold of my life," where I need not be afraid. But then, God's house also provides me a jumping-off point when my faith becomes less static and more of an active, engaging life of living out God's love for all to see.

May I live in your house, O Lord, all my days. Amen.

Imitating Christ requires significant humility and sacrifice. I'm always tempted to skip to the parts at the end about the "body of his glory." Glory in Christ, however, is attainable only by way of a cross.

A common misconception is that Christ's saving death on the cross means that we will be saved from all suffering. Instead, it is an invitation to use our lives in imitation of Christlike love for the world. We are called to use our lives, privilege, and hands in self-offering service to others.

I think of a pastor in San Diego who literally opened his church to new immigrants detained at the US-Mexico border awaiting hearing as they sought asylum. Someone took a photo of him during the foot-washing portion of the Holy Thursday worship service. The man whose feet he was washing had a digital tracking device on his ankle. He had to wear it until his hearing.

I think of a family in my church who have just welcomed newborn twins into their home temporarily, expanding their household and hearts again as foster parents. Their expansive love keeps growing more spacious, with room for everyone.

I think of the persistence of a woman at my former church who crocheted shawls for all one hundred participants in a retreat for adults with HIV/AIDS, ensuring that each person would receive a handmade gift that they could wrap around themselves like love.

There are countless ways we can offer ourselves, pouring out love into a world of so much brokenness. The call of the cross is to choose this way of living that gives of ourselves for others.

Christ of the cross, give me courage to imitate your deep love for the world. Amen.

We got chickens for our backyard this year. I've learned that hens can be stubborn, fierce, and protective. We don't have a rooster, though, so I haven't gotten to experience our hens with a brood gathered under their wings.

The chicken coop in our parsonage's backyard is in the shadow of our elegant and imposing church building. The neo-Gothic sanctuary was built in the heady years after World War II, when world peace seemed possible because so many had experienced the destruction of war. There was new enthusiasm for interfaith and ecumenical cooperation, and hopeful optimism about new technologies. It was in those years that my congregation constructed this worship space to welcome all who are willing to gather under Jesus' protection.

Behind the altar is a beautiful window in an unusual style of stained glass: The jewel tones of the glass in daylight transform into a gilded reredos when night falls, persistently depicting the glorious stories of Jesus' life through the rhythms of each day. There are no chickens in the sanctuary decorations even though Jesus depicted himself as a hen. Perhaps the image is just too unsophisticated, or perhaps it is because the brood was not willing to gather.

In a church where we are more comfortable with elegant depictions of the glory of God, I find it refreshing that Jesus compares himself to a hen. It is a reminder that God is present not only in the carefully wrought and beautifully curated sacred spaces but also in life that sometimes squawks and scratches at the ground. Whichever feels more accessible to you, I pray that you will always find God's fierce, glorious love present there.

Holy Jesus, may we accept the offer of your love for us and the world. Amen.

It's possible to trust God and really struggle at the same time. Courage is most visible when it's held in the face of real danger. This psalm reminds us that we are not alone when we experience deep pain in life: in the devastation of abandonment by family, in the harm of violence and lies, in human anger, and at times when we cannot perceive God's presence.

I am frequently tempted by the lie that says having faith means always having it together. I think I should always feel strong. Or, worse, I think that if I'm struggling or experiencing tragedy, it must be because I didn't love God well enough. This way of thinking is destructive and dangerous.

As a counterbalance to this way of looking at myself, I find it helpful to look out at God's world. I love the affirmations near the end of this psalm: "I believe that I shall see the goodness of the LORD in the land of the living." When spoken in the midst of real struggle, destruction, and pain, this is a bold faith claim that insists on a hope found in perceiving beautiful and good things.

There is real struggle, destruction, and evil in the world, not only in our personal relationships but spanning the whole of our earth. Our climate crisis threatens entire communities as changing weather patterns bring devastation.

It's been my experience that even in my most hopeless moments, signs of hope are all around me—even if I don't perceive them until later. Part of the discipline of faith is daring to look for God's presence at all times. This divine presence gives us the emotional boost we need to keep going, and it allows us to muster the courage that goes to our hearts. This courage in the face of danger makes all things possible.

Even when it's all falling apart, God, help me see your beauty here in the land of the living. Amen.

What do you think heaven will be like? Have you thought about who else is there?

"Citizenship" implies we are not alone—we are citizens together, with shared rights, privileges, allegiances, and obligations. We live in and belong to a community—a shared place.

For the people of Philippi, citizenship also brought with it a much more valuable citizenship in Rome because Philippi was a Roman colony. But it is likely that many Philippian Christians were enslaved and therefore without worldly status of any kind. Therefore, when Paul affirms that "our citizenship is in heaven," he is doubling down on its being a collective reality, insisting on "our" belonging there. He is asserting that it is good news that all Christians belong with and to one another.

I regularly struggle with this good news of an eternal community because—I confess—there are people I prefer not to spend any time with, much less all time. (I won't say that some of them are in my church, but I won't say they aren't either.) But I am comforted by Paul's promise that Jesus "will transform the body of our humiliation that it may be conformed to the body of his glory." Scripture reminds us that—beginning with our families and congregations and extending across denominational and national boundaries—our lives as Christ followers give us access to incredible grace and life-changing responsibility.

Our citizenship in heaven asserts that we belong in God's grace together with all those throughout the world who seek it. Above our other allegiances and identities, we claim this holy life together.

Christ, help me desire—more than any other treasure—citizenship in your heaven together with all your children. Amen.

SECOND SUNDAY IN LENT

I sometimes wonder what the Pharisees in this passage were thinking. Did they take delight in telling Jesus that Herod was after him? Were they looking after his safety out of concern for him, or did they just want to avoid further conflict?

Jesus' response is clear and determined. He calls Herod a predatory fox, and then he recommits to his work. Faced with threats and danger, Jesus persists in pursuing the best interests of the people of Jerusalem.

Sometimes, especially when things get intense and threaten institutions or communities we value, we are tempted to ignore the needs of actual people; we may even expect them to ignore their own wounds. Or worse, we inflict new injuries on others—frequently, those with the least power—as we attempt to save or protect something we deem more important. In contrast, Jesus delays his exit from Jerusalem so he can heal more people and cast out more demons.

I find Jesus' actions to be a convicting and sobering call to pay attention to one another. I want to remind you (and myself) that Christ's church existed long before most of the traditions we treasure now. I know that you and I know, in some deep way, that church is bigger than anything we can decide or control. As we grieve the loss of structures and traditions we treasure, as we prepare for shifts beyond what we can fully imagine, I pray that we will have the same sort of compassion and commitment that Jesus had: to tend the hurting and resist what is evil. We should be striving to offer God's grace and compassion to those who have already been pushed to the edges of our community.

Compassionate Christ, help me be a channel for your healing, tending, life-giving work. Amen.

The Power of Vulnerability

MARCH 14–20, 2022 • TOMMIE L. WATKINS JR.

SCRIPTURE OVERVIEW: In the midst of Lent, when many might be giving up a certain food that they love, we read about feasting. The focus is not on physical feasting, but on feasting as a metaphor for communing with God. Isaiah describes food and drink that one cannot buy with money, for it comes freely from the Lord. The psalmist describes the state of his soul as being hungry and thirsty. Only meditating on God's faithfulness nourishes his soul at the deepest level. Physical food is momentary, but spiritual nourishment endures. In First Corinthians, Paul appeals to this imagery. Although the ancients experience this spiritual nourishment, some pursue physical pleasure and stray into idolatry and immorality. Partaking in this nourishment should cause us in turn to produce spiritual fruit, as Jesus admonishes his listeners.

QUESTIONS AND SUGGESTIONS FOR REFLECTION

* Read Isaiah 55:1-9. When has God's grace inverted your expectations?
* Read Psalm 63:1-8. As you mature in faith, what new questions about God do you ask?
* Read 1 Corinthians 10:1-13. Think of a time you have faced great temptation. How did God help you endure it?
* Read Luke 13:1-9. For what do you need to repent?

Rector of Saint Andrew's Episcopal Church, Birmingham, AL; a pilot, social worker, and public health professor.

Who would actually go shopping with no resources and no money? Who would risk the embarrassment, disdain, and humiliation associated with being found lacking? Yet this passage asks us to be vulnerable in trusting our well-founded relationship with God.

Who among us likes to ask for help? The core of this passage pushes us to do exactly this: become uniquely vulnerable, open, and transparent. Imagine the angst and fear that must have surrounded those who trusted in this new manner of living relationally with God. I often wonder if they were angry at God or resentful that—after all they had been through—they would have to trust God's word and covenant again.

That is what God asks of us. Just like the people in the scriptures, we must forsake material things to trust Almighty God. Then and only then can we refocus on God and God's power and ask for God's unwavering help. This trust in God, this repentance, this new birth requires beginning again.

In fact, that is what the Lenten season is all about: desiring God so much that we are willing to let go of all things comfortable and familiar to turn our very souls and bodies to God's will.

In beginning again, we trust God to will and act in our favor. This is the vulnerability that makes the core Christian principles of unconditional love and exceptional forgiveness possible. It is a willingness to turn away from a past that is often riddled with thoughts of *If only* and *I should have* to refocus on *right now*. Lent teaches us to live in the now with God.

Eternal God, make us vulnerable and willing to begin again, trusting you to love and forgive unconditionally. Amen.

In this passage the writer petitions for restoration and guidance from God. It is a cry to God for understanding, compassion, tolerance, and supervision. The writer seeks liberation from shame and fear.

Praying for God's forgiveness and guidance involves being open and honest with God and ourselves in a way that leads to our emancipation. Being totally exposed and unafraid of the intimacy that characterizes our relationship with an all-knowing and all-loving Creator God is the attitude that pervades Isaiah's soul and spirit.

Admitting our faults and the places we have erred requires humility and vulnerability. We can "seek the LORD while he may be found." Yet as the writer says, it is only when we are willing to be mindful of God's mercy, justice, and steadfast love that we can we be emboldened to seek God again and again. This type of praxis is what a new and vibrant relationship with God is all about.

This Lenten season reminds us that by refocusing on prayer and fasting we can reexamine the things within us that bind us and prevent us from seeking God. As we acknowledge those forces in our lives that block God out, we will experience a revitalization of our lives. This is the new relationship of higher thoughts and higher ways.

Let us be animated by God's Holy Spirit. Let us vulnerably seek God as we are then liberated from the expectations of our "enemies" and ourselves.

Forgiving God, make us willing to seek you in truth and be emancipated by your all-encompassing love. Amen.

For many people, Lent is a time of fasting in which we are encouraged to focus on eating and drinking. More specifically, we are asked to examine our relationship with water and food. What do we put our trust in and spend our time doing?

Fasting can be a spiritual practice that helps us to become vulnerable. We abstain from something—indulgent food or some other comfort—that hinders our reliance on God. But the psalmist presents us with a new type of fast that is derived from God's ubiquitous love for all humankind and is exemplified by the Christian values of equality and equity. God makes clear that material things are not so much the focus of fasting but the innate, internal manifestations of "isms" that block God out of our lives and prevent us from living justly.

The fast articulated by God in this passage produces intimacy. God is particularly interested in becoming our sanctuary, sustenance, and security. This is a type of fasting I never contemplated, one that puts us unreservedly in God's presence.

What about our relationships with those perceived as "other"? What might happen if we cease practicing racism, classism, sexism, and exclusionism? What if we refrain from pointing fingers, blaming, and pursing our self-centered wills and instead pursue the will of God? Perhaps that is what repentance is all about. Turning our will and eyes from judgment of one another to love and acceptance. This is exactly what Lent is all about.

Eternal God, make us vulnerable and willing to begin again to love and forgive unconditionally. Amen.

Suffering as a punishment for our wrongdoing is bad enough, but at least it is understandable. However, the scripture tells us that we are assured of the blessings and favor of God when we suffer for doing what is right and just.

What can that mean? It could mean that we will have our reward in heaven, but it might be more subtle than that. Maybe suffering for what is right and just changes us in powerful ways. Maybe those blessings are a growth in empathy and compassion—spiritual tools that can undo the most visible injustice in our world. These are the weapons that animate and empower human rights and social justice movements all over the world.

In our baptism, we vow to respect the "dignity and worth of every human being"; thus we are charged and compelled to "suffer" by becoming uncomfortable, giving up complacency, and working for equality and justice for everyone. This is the spirit of Lent. The season of Lent compels us to give up our privilege and become discontented, abstain from the systematic subjugation and vilification of others, and work toward justice for the marginalized and stigmatized. We then acquire empathy and compassion for others that change us and them.

To obtain this vulnerability, which can manifest a change in ourselves and our communities, we must begin to trust God in ways we have never imagined. We must die to self-sufficiency and self-security and turn our hearts and minds over to the loving will of God. This is the Lenten discipline.

Compassionate God, as you sent your Son, Jesus Christ, to suffer with us and for us, help us to be willing to suffer for our friends and enemies alike as we are animated by your eternal and unconditional love. Amen.

Imagine coming up from your baptism and being driven by the Holy Spirit into the wilderness to be alone in silence for forty days to be tested by God. What? Must we wander around in a desert wilderness to be closer to God?

Perhaps we must. When we are conscious of our barrenness—what is lacking within us—we are free to rely on God. As God compels us either through circumstances, actions, or the words and actions of others to give up our self-sufficient ideals, we become able to see and hear God in a new way. I believe this is what Paul describes in today's passage as the outcome of baptism.

The Lenten season invites us to become vulnerable. On every Friday in Lent, we recall Christ's ultimate sacrifice on a tree. It is in willfully letting go of expectations and his self-determined will that Jesus submits unequivocally to the will of God.

Barrenness, lack, and void are the vital tools that can complete in us a humble state of being that compels us to be "all in" for God. This desert state of being is necessary if we are to acquire a new life in Jesus Christ. This is the new consciousness espoused in our baptism and with which Jesus initiated his ministry.

This is also the conversion Jesus preached and the new life he promised. For us to focus on the now, which is where God abides, and give up focusing on our past or dreaming about our future, requires this "all-in" dependence on God. Let us make haste to get to our "desert living" state in this Lenten season so we will be prepared to hear and see God and God's word anew.

Ever-present God, give us a willingness to become totally barren of earthly things, including our past and future, so we depend on nothing but you. Amen.

The theology of place is shown in Jesus' leaving his hometown of Nazareth in Galilee and journeying through Samaria down into the region where John is baptizing followers. Jesus hears a new message that compels him to forsake the familiar for the unfamiliar and security for insecurity. He willfully submits to a novel idea of ceremonial washing, preparing persons to be used by God rather than washing objects to be used for God. Jesus totally gives up his expectations of himself, others, and even God.

Jesus, perceived as a "lowly Galilean" and an outsider, presents himself to be baptized by John—a process and procedure Jesus no doubt neither needed nor was required to achieve. Nevertheless, Jesus consents to being made common and even one with those individuals who "needed" saving in order to be of maximum use to God. In these actions the floor of heaven opens, and God confirms that true power exists in meekness, humility, and vulnerability. God confirms for us all that we must not exercise power as the secular society does, but we must be powerful as Christ was by being visibly vulnerable.

In baptism, sin is removed from us and we are made one with God forever. In every act of baptism, Jesus claims us as his own. It is as if God is saying to us, "You are my child, the beloved; with you I am well pleased."

This is indeed good news. Surely the gospel proclaims this message: God empowers us not because we are powerful but because we are not. The weak are made secure. Truly this is a new kingdom into which we are brought through Jesus Christ in baptism.

Eternal God, make us willing to begin again and love and forgive unconditionally ourselves and others. Amen.

THIRD SUNDAY IN LENT

Wow! God being angry? I often struggle when contemplating a loving Creator who is capable of such an emotion. Anger is incredibly powerful and tempting to hold on to. But many of us neglect to consider how our own emotions can make us stuck or can make us lash out and crave vengeance.

Who of us can admit we are mad at God, perhaps as our ancestors were when they accused God of leading them out of Egypt to die of thirst in the wilderness? (See Exodus 17:1-7.) What do we do with the anger and resentment we have when we must begin again, or when failing to achieve a goal is entirely our own fault? How do we handle self-directed anger?

The answer can be found in grace: God gives us what we do not deserve. Too often during Lent we fall short of fully understanding God's gift to us of immeasurable grace—grace that we must offer to others. Grace overwhelms anger and vengeance. Grace makes us vulnerable.

Only when we consider God's amazing grace can we refocus on God and God's power. This superb trust in God, this repentance, this new birth comes with the promise that we will never be tempted beyond what we can endure.

This Lenten season, let us accept God's grace as a gift that will turn what we think are failures into successes. And let us thank God for the gift!

God of grace, how grateful we are for your forgiving love! May we so live in your grace that we move among your people with courageous vulnerability, helping you bring hope out of despair and joy out of sorrow. Amen.

Equipped by Grace

MARCH 21–27, 2022 • JULIA SEYMOUR

SCRIPTURE OVERVIEW: Lent is a time for focusing on our need for God and for remembering God's abundant resources for filling that need. When the Israelites finally pass into Canaan, they observe the Passover as a reminder of God's deliverance of them from Egypt. The psalmist, traditionally David, rejoices in the fact that God does not count his sins against him. Paul declares that through Christ, God has made everything new. God no longer holds our sins against us, and we in turn appeal to others to accept this free gift. Jesus eats with sinners and tells the story of the prodigal son to demonstrate that no matter how far we stray, God will always welcome us home with open arms. God never stops pursuing us, even if we feel unloved or unworthy.

QUESTIONS AND SUGGESTIONS FOR REFLECTION

- Read Joshua 5:9-12. What stories do you tell about your faith? What do these stories help you remember?
- Read Psalm 32. When have you hidden from God? When has God been your hiding place?
- Read 2 Corinthians 5:16-21. We are ambassadors for Christ. How does your life display for others that life in Christ eliminates worldly identity labels?
- Read Luke 15:1-3, 11b-32. Do you identify with the prodigal son, the elder son, or the father in the parable? Are you ready to rejoin God's household on God's terms? Are you ready to welcome everyone home?

Pastor to Big Timber Lutheran Church (ELCA) in Big Timber, MT; author of *Nice Is Not a Fruit of the Spirit* from Pilgrim Press; married with two children and assorted pets.

Surely the "disgrace of Egypt" belongs to Egypt. The shame of having enslaved other persons and having them escape, the embarrassment to Egypt's gods—this should be ascribed to the Pharaoh and his associates. Why would the people of Israel, the enslaved people, have disgrace ascribed to them?

We are not only marked by the history of our actions; we are also shaped and scarred by how others have acted toward us. Our ancestors experienced stresses and pains that continue to affect us through family stories. Even more deeply, things like enslavement, pogroms, and wars shape our epigenetics, stirring deep responses within us that are beyond our understanding.

The disgrace of Egypt lingered with the people of Israel in their fear, their questions about their ancestors, and their understanding of the nature of God. If divine intervention could bring them into freedom, why were they permitted to be enslaved at all? They are able to embrace fully the joy and possibility of Canaan only when the reproach and shame of the past is lifted.

This kind of burden does not fall away instantly. God's provision for the people through their wilderness wandering removed the burden slowly. Through each bite of manna, God rebuilt trust with the people of Israel. Through each sip of clean water, the people of Israel perceived the power and mercy of the One in whom their hope was anchored.

The disgrace of Egypt defined them by pain and by the actions of others. The promise of Canaan redefined them as a people who had been led and fed by God. Thus equipped by grace, they ate the produce of the land and feasted on the promise of tomorrow.

Providing God, strengthen my trust that I am not defined by the worst things I have done or that have happened to me. My identity is as your beloved child, equipped by grace to share your hope in the world. Amen.

There are beatitudes found throughout the Bible. Any sentence beginning "blessed are" offers guidance into a life of joy and possibility. Such blessings come from living in alignment with God's will and way. The psalmist offers a road map for reaching one's own beatific destination, but the on-ramp is steep.

Entrance into this blessed way of life comes through speaking honestly to God about one's sins, transgressions, and iniquities. We are compelled to do a thorough housecleaning of our soul, which is only possible with the Holy Spirit's help.

Our sins are the ways we have missed the mark, when we have fallen short or have had things go sideways. Transgressions are more egregious; they are times when we have deliberately chosen not to do better. Transgressions often bring regret and broken trust. Iniquities are the ways, acknowledged and unacknowledged, we have participated in systems of oppression, exploitation, and destruction.

All this brokenness gets in the way of a life of blessing. Such a life is experienced through God's provisions and being part of how Divine Love provides for others. How do we clear the hurdles of sin, transgression, and iniquity so that we can freely run the race of blessing?

The psalmist warns that silence about missteps brings grief and pain to the body. Unburdening ourselves through confession to God brings the wholeness and peace we seek. Whether we engage in a formal rite of contrition or pray alone, God's grace equips us with the assurance of forgiveness. Let us never fail to avail ourselves of this blessing.

Forgiving God, hear my confession of all that causes me to feel separated from your love and from others. Amen.

Some stories are so familiar that it is easy to miss the details right in front of us. Cultural studies of the Prodigal Son narrative from Luke 15 have shown that different people notice different details of the story. In places that are well acquainted with hunger, the note about the famine in the far country stands out clearly. For societies oriented around fatherly leadership, the honor or dishonor of the patriarch is a major detail of the story.

Many small moments are tucked away in this story: the description of what the pigs are fed, the younger son rehearsing what to say to his father, the father spotting the son while he is still a long way off, the enslaved person's report to the elder brother, and the elder brother's mention of a goat for a party with his friends.

Together, they become more than the sum of their parts. We even have details about ourselves that we put on the story. We can reflect on when we have waited for someone's return, felt someone else was unjustly celebrated, or struck out on our own with an adventure in mind. The broad strokes and the small details of this familiar Bible story mean that everyone can relate to these characters.

The phrase "God is in the details" is used to emphasize the importance of attention and precision. Today's story shows us God's presence in details on a grand scale. The God who receives all prodigals with love knows all the little notes and nuances of our lives. Nothing is beyond God's notice—not the pigs, the prodigal, or the patriarch. Remembering God's presence in and awareness of the details of our lives consoles our spirits. This comfort is how we are equipped by grace to live each day.

God of all details, strengthen my awareness of your presence in all things. May that presence bring consolation and courage for all my days. Amen.

The once ubiquitous "All Are Welcome" sign has become disdained in many church circles. It is not that churches do not wish to welcome all people. The tension is between the desire and the execution. Churches often welcome all who are able to fit in. In the light of "the way we've always done it," clearly not all are welcome.

What if the new vogue in church signs were "We See with Christ's Eyes"? This assertion indicates that the church takes Paul's words to the Corinthians seriously. Because of everything that has happened before—Creation, covenant keeping, Incarnation, Resurrection, and the sustaining power of the Holy Spirit—this church sees all people through Christ-tinted glasses.

A church living up to this sign would hold its traditions and habits lightly. It would create new ways when the old ones cause harm or limit the church's ability to share love and power. The people of the congregation would see themselves as a new generation of apostles sent out into the world to see Christ in others and returning every week for prayer, renewal, and to share stories of the new creation.

In this beloved community, no one is considered from a human perspective but in the light of divine love. People are accepted for who they say they are. Good boundaries are established and kept. Honesty is valued, encouraged, and praised. No one grieves alone. Forgiveness abounds and reparations are respected as necessary.

All things are possible with God. Further, the foundation for this new creation has already been laid. If we want to mean "All Are Welcome," then we have to demonstrate how we see all people through Christ's eyes.

God of unity in diversity, help me to see others through Christ's eyes. Enable me to love and welcome all people as you have loved and welcomed me in Christ. Amen.

In 12-step groups, the community rejoices over each sign of progress, no matter how small. One day of sobriety is better than no days. One week of acknowledging powerlessness is better than one day. The testimony of one who has tried and failed is as valuable as that of one who carries a twenty-five-year chip. Community solidarity is part of the program's success and the hope it offers. One who asks for help will never walk alone.

Outside the program, though, consequences and mistrust often remain. Those who have not struggled with addiction and have not been in a relationship with someone who does, usually misunderstand the steps, the process, and the language.

People who grapple with addiction have a story to tell about the relief of sobriety. They also often need to confess their pain, their mistakes, their failures, and their history. In their grief, they talk more than most people are willing to listen.

Confession, though, is a communal activity. It takes strength and hope to tell someone else the truth about the past. If it is safe for us physically, spiritually, and psychologically to hear another person's unburdening, we should consider it a privilege to do so. Equipped by grace, we can listen with love and assure the other person of God's love and power for them and in them.

If we are capable of hearing another's confession but refuse to do so, we become like the stubborn horses and mules of the psalm. We have rejected the opportunity to share another's burdens. We have left them to carry on alone. Friends, there is great peace in confession and the assurance of God's pardon. Let us share that peace with one another.

God of love, I am willing to be an instrument of your consolation and mercy. Open my heart to opportunities to listen to others and assure them of your forgiveness. Amen.

An ambassador is never off duty. Whether inconvenienced, flustered, or frustrated, ambassadors must remember that they represent more than themselves. Their words and actions reflect on the one for whom they work. Belligerent, unkind, or entitled ambassadors show whatever they represent to be unpleasant at best and maybe even dangerous.

Ambassadors must not abuse their position. Being trusted to act on behalf of another means respecting the limits and shape of that relationship. It is not to be used for one's own gain through manipulation of others, resources, or circumstances. Ambassadors must seek the good of the one they represent.

In return, ambassadors are treated with the respect of their office. Such a person is honored, not only as an individual but in accordance with the larger relationship they represent. Ambassadors are responsible for maintaining these relationships—seeking reconciliation in the face of brokenness as well as peace and justice for people and nature.

Through Christ, we have been made ambassadors in service to God's love. We represent God every day of our lives. This is an awesome responsibility we are only able to fulfill by being equipped by God every day. From the most mundane of errands to a once-in-a-lifetime opportunity, we are always ambassadors for Christ.

Let me live a life of service to you, Jesus, that my light may shine and others may come to trust your presence and love and honor your name. Amen.

Fourth Sunday in Lent

The only stories we can tell truthfully are our own. Our stories look different to others than they do to us. Perspectives, experiences, and hopes shape the way we tell our own story. One of the most important things we can do for others is to listen to their stories and to let our truths live next to one another.

The characters in the story of the prodigal are not fully aware of each other's truths. Even as readers of the story, we are not fully aware of each character's truth. The younger son must have his reasons for asking for his inheritance before his father's death. Then, when things don't work out, he tells himself a story about what will happen when he returns to his father's house.

We do not have as much insight into the story the father tells himself. He chooses to grant his younger son's request. We do not know how easy or difficult that was to do. Reading into the father's joy at the younger son's return, we can guess at the grief or loss he experienced in his child's absence.

The elder brother tells some of his own story. He has been diligent in his work and in his dedication to his father. He had never asked for anything, but he is resentful of what is lavished on his brother. Without putting too many words in his mouth, we can safely assume that anyone who has worked diligently and consistently without recognition can understand the elder brother's resentment.

All these stories contain truth, the truth that each man told himself. Every person has a truth, rooted in their perceptions, experiences, and hopes. It is only when, equipped by grace, we listen to one another that our truths can be reconciled in love and become a new story of hope and restoration.

O Holy Spirit, source of all wisdom and truth, guide me in telling and hearing stories to be open to where you are at work in others and in the world. Amen.

Looking Back, Going Forward

MARCH 28–APRIL 3, 2022 • K. CHERIE JONES

SCRIPTURE OVERVIEW: The Isaiah text portrays the redemptive activity of God that is about to be introduced into Israel's life. All paradigms lie shattered before the immensity of God's grace! The joy of Psalm 126 is occasioned by the memory of God's act of redemption in the past and also by the anticipation that a similar intervention is imminent. Paul's autobiographical sketch directed to the Philippians confesses the change that has come into his life as a result of "knowing Christ Jesus my Lord." The story of Mary's anointing of Jesus' feet must be read in the context of Jesus' looming passion. Jesus sets Mary's actions in their proper perspective by linking them to his own death, even as he deflects Judas's counterfeit compassion.

QUESTIONS AND SUGGESTIONS FOR REFLECTION

- Read Isaiah 43:16-21. How do you respond to this God who insists on doing new things for the sake of the people?

- Read Psalm 126. Pray this psalm three times: (1) pray all the verbs in the past tense in thanksgiving; (2) pray all the verbs in the future tense as a prayer for help; (3) pray verses 1-3 in the past tense, verses 5-6 in the future tense. Which was hardest to pray?

- Read Philippians 3:4b-14. What props or credentials do you need to let go of?

- Read John 12:1-8. What motivations does your discipleship reflect?

Retired United Methodist pastor; member of the California-Pacific Annual Conference.

Memory of God's works takes different roles in our faith. Sometimes we recall the past to remind ourselves that God remains with us. I sat with a friend who was suffering greatly from the complications of a rare form of cancer. We talked about hope in the midst of a bleak outlook. She recalled times when she experienced God's provision and faithfulness. It did not change her circumstances, but it encouraged her and renewed her awareness of God's presence and faithfulness.

In this reading, memory plays another role. The people are *not* to recall the past so that they will be ready for God's new work. The opening verses evoke the memory of the Exodus, specifically when God brought the people safely through the sea and into the wilderness—a place of struggle as well as a place of revelation. There they dealt with scarce resources and murmured against God. Now God promises to do a new thing by making a way in the wilderness where rivers will run and praise will resound.

Forgoing that Exodus memory is not a critique of the memory; rather, the focus shifts to awaiting the new thing that God will do for the people. As is true for every generation, our task is to remember the past but even more to ready ourselves for what God seeks to do *now*.

This readiness does not come easily—especially to those who "remember the former things." The church has wrestled with many issues, such as slavery, style of worship, war, and the role of women. It has taken much prayer, conversation, and discernment. Needed change can take a long time, if ever. Still, God promises to do new things and calls us to follow on that new way.

O God, you continue to do new things for your creation. Help us to see and respond to your action. Amen.

Thirty years ago, my spiritual director taught me to pray the psalms. The psalms teach us to pray and bring the truth of our lives to God, including the emotions and habits we would prefer to ignore. Praying the psalms gives us words when we cannot find them on our own. The psalms also teach us about the One to whom we pray and who expects us to need to pray these words at different times in our lives.

Today's psalm is one of the Songs of Ascent the pilgrims prayed as they traveled to Jerusalem for the high holy days. In the Christian tradition, we pray this psalm during Advent and Lent and often at Thanksgiving.

The Bible translation you use when you pray this psalm will shape your prayer. The challenge comes in determining the verb tense of the psalm. Some translate all the verses in the past tense, making the psalm a prayer of thanksgiving. Others translate all the verses in the future tense, making the psalm a prayer for help. Still others split the difference by translating verses 1-3 in the past tense and verses 4-6 in the future tense; this results in remembering God's past acts of salvation and requesting help from God now.

Perhaps this very ambiguity or flexibility among the translations is God's gift, as it encourages us to pray this psalm in different ways depending on the situation. During Advent and Lent, it is a psalm of praise as we ponder anew the humble birth, violent death, and resurrection of Jesus. Other times, it is more appropriately a prayer of praise and a plea for help.

As we continue our approach to Holy Week, perhaps praying this psalm will give voice to the cries of our hearts.

O God, thank you for the gift of the psalms. I take comfort in praying the words that your people have found so helpful. Amen.

In this dinner at the home of the family Jesus loved, we witness discipleship in several forms. First we see Mary anointing Jesus' feet with an expensive perfume, then wiping it away with her hair. Here we see part of the dynamic of discipleship: Jesus loves and cares for her, and Mary responds with an act of devotion. She has listened to and learned from Jesus, has seen him raise her brother from the dead, and has put some of the pieces of discipleship together. She intuitively knows how to respond extravagantly to Jesus—even before he washes his disciples' feet and commands them to love others. Mary chooses the right action for the right reasons and models faithful discipleship.

We see another example of discipleship in Judas's response. Perturbed by Mary's actions, he offers a critique that seems rational when he asks, "Why was this perfume not sold . . . and the money given to the poor?" The question of how to respond to God's persistent commandments to care for the poor is appropriate, one that every generation of faithful people wrestles with. But the Fourth Evangelist essentially asserts that Judas's motivation for asking the question involves greed rather than compassion for the poor. Judas knows scripture and talks piously but does not follow through on his words; thus, he models unfaithful discipleship.

This story calls us to check our motivations as well as our actions to be sure that we are taking the right actions for the right reasons. It also gives us permission to offer extravagant gifts of devotion to Jesus, even a donation to the poor.

Lord Jesus, you know the contours of my heart. I may know the right answers, but I don't always do the right things for the right reasons. Continue to teach me how to be your disciple. Amen.

I serve on a committee of clergy and laity that meets several times a year to certify candidates for ordained ministry in our denomination. There are criteria for the candidates: seminary education, psychological assessments, recommendations from church leaders, etc. During the meetings, we pray, listen carefully to the candidates and to God, and discern if we confirm a call to ministry and if the candidates seem ready to move on in the process. We expect them to meet the criteria and show fluency in theology, leadership skills, and pastoral care. We also want them to be mature Christian disciples who wholeheartedly trust in God.

In this reading, Paul lists the ways he met the criteria for being a faithful Jew: by birth, zeal, and keeping the Law. He knows that while these credentials are good, even God-given, knowing Jesus puts him in a right relationship with God. So he gives up putting his trust in his credentials and instead puts his total trust in Jesus. This does not mean that Paul stopped using the skills of debate or knowledge of the Law that he had honed as a Pharisee or stopped being energetic in living out his faith. When Paul chose to rely first on Jesus, he placed his credentials in the right place, the right order. They then became tools with which he could serve God in remarkable ways.

Whether clergy or lay, we easily slip into relying on our credentials—how long we have attended church or how many mission projects we have gone on—as a way to be right with God. Paul reminds us that we are to trust in Jesus not in our credentials—no matter how good they are.

Lord Jesus, it is easy to rely on accomplishments and credentials rather than on you. Please help me to keep all this in the right order. Amen.

In this short, autobiographical snippet, Paul recaps his little life and places it within the big story of God's activity. He recounts his credentials and religious heritage, then mentions his need for reevaluation of all in light of "knowing Christ." He goes on to state his present intention. Paul's "knowing Christ" has reoriented his entire perspective on life, creating new priorities for his life's direction: how he chooses to expend his energy and for Whom he will "press on toward the goal."

Rachel Beckwith had a goal that reoriented her perspective. At church she learned about the desperate need for clean water in other countries. Shocked that children her age did not drink clean water, Rachel decided to raise three hundred dollars for water wells in Africa. She canceled her ninth birthday party and urged her family and friends to contribute nine dollars each to the project. She set up a web page to make it easier to contribute. It disappointed her to raise only two hundred and twenty dollars by her birthday, but she decided to keep trying.

Six weeks later, a traffic accident left Rachel critically injured. Friends began to contribute to the fund to signal their support. On July 23, 2011, three days after the accident, Rachel was taken off life support and died. But Rachel's dream lived on. As the media picked up the news about her dream of clean water, the contributions poured in. The account was closed on September 30, 2011, with total contributions of over 1.2 million dollars that would help more than sixty-three thousand people.

By God's grace, Rachel's death was not the end of the story. What are your dreams for reaching out to others with Christ's love? How are you helping others press on "toward the goal for the prize of the heavenly call of God in Christ Jesus"?

Holy God, thank you for giving me dreams of how to share your love with others. Give me the courage to see these dreams through. Amen.

On September 11, 2001, my friend Michael Hingson and his guide dog, Roselle, went to work in his office on the 78th floor of the North Tower of the World Trade Center. What started off as a normal day turned extraordinary when the hijacked American Airlines Flight 11 was flown into their building. Not knowing what was going on, Michael and Roselle walked down 1,463 steps and exited the North Tower.

Minutes later, the South Tower collapsed some one hundred yards from them. As the pair turned to flee from the debris, Michael, who had prayed throughout the morning, cried out to God, "Why did you get us out of the building only to let another fall on us?" In the chaos, he heard God's voice inside his heart, *Don't worry about the things you cannot control. Focus on running with Roselle and the rest will take care of itself.* In what was now an urban wilderness, God's words comforted and calmed his heart.

Michael and Roselle ran, dodging debris and then being enveloped by the toxic three-hundred-foot dust cloud. In the utter chaos of those moments, Michael felt God's presence and experienced the "peace of God, which surpasses all understanding" (Phil. 4:7). The deep peace allowed him to totally focus on running with Roselle, who was now temporarily blind from the dust. Michael, who learned echolocation at the age of four, and Roselle simultaneously heard an opening into a subway station and ducked out of the wilderness into a refuge.

It was a few years before Michael talked about his mystical experience publicly, but now he alludes to God's guidance in the wilderness whenever he tells his story. God made a way for Michael on that terrible day. How has God made a way for you in the wilderness?

Thank you, faithful God, for meeting and guiding me in the wild places. Amen.

FIFTH SUNDAY IN LENT

Twenty-five years ago, on the Fifth Sunday of Lent, our organization underwent upheaval. I worked for the General Board of Discipleship (now Discipleship Ministries) of The United Methodist Church. That morning our coworker, Donna, went missing. It soon became clear that she had been murdered. Eight days later, on Monday of Holy Week, a beloved retired staff person named Bobby died of natural causes. On Wednesday, a coworker named Verlia died, also of natural causes.

The deaths of three trusted colleagues and friends rocked the organization. The first response of the staff was to meet daily in worship. We affirmed God's faithfulness and lamented our loss. We prayed for Donna, her family, and those who had been searching for her. During Holy Week, we added the families of Bobby and Verlia to our prayers. We looked for ways to support their families, especially their children. The staff somberly tried to concentrate on work, and conversations were muted. Walking into the building felt like walking into a tomb.

The words of the psalmist resonated: "Restore our fortunes, O LORD." Corporately we had experienced God's faithfulness many times in the past but we desperately needed God's help and faithfulness again—help with our grief and with how to continue in ministry.

Easter brought a new depth of hope in the Resurrection. God met us as we gathered weekly in worship and felt the prayers of so many people outside the organization. Slowly and surely, God gave us the help we needed, and we experienced divine faithfulness anew. I remember the day when, walking through the halls, I heard laughter once more. I knew we had turned a corner, and I offered a prayer of gratitude to the Faithful One.

Eternal God, thank you for your faithfulness in times of need. Be with those who need your help today. Amen.

The Shape of Discipleship

APRIL 4–10, 2022 • MARK W. STAMM

SCRIPTURE OVERVIEW: Blessed is the one who comes in the name of the Lord! Psalm 118 is a song of rejoicing, yet it also includes the prophecy that the cornerstone must experience rejection. Isaiah speaks of physical suffering, of being beaten, disgraced, and spat on. We see elements of this in the Gospel reading, where Luke describes the final moments of Jesus' life. Bloodied and beaten, Jesus hangs on the cross and breathes his last. In Philippians, Paul places this drama within the eternal narrative of God's redeeming work. Jesus leaves his rightful place and becomes flesh. He experiences pain and suffering, even the most humiliating form of death, crucifixion. Jesus can empathize with our suffering because he has suffered. Blessed is the one who comes in the name of the Lord!

QUESTIONS AND SUGGESTIONS FOR REFLECTION

- Read Isaiah 50:4-9a. How does the Suffering Servant speak to your life today?
- Read Psalm 118:1-2, 19-29. How do you hear differently the familiar verses of this psalm when you read them together?
- Read Philippians 2:5-11. Do you find it paradoxical to live as a beloved child of God and as a servant? If so, how do you live in this paradox?
- Read Luke 22:14–23:56. How do you experience the extreme emotional highs and lows of Palm Sunday and Holy Week, even knowing how it will all turn out?

Professor of Christian worship and Chapel Elder at Perkins School of Theology, Southern Methodist University, Dallas, TX.

Today we begin our turn toward Holy Week and toward the complex liturgy with which it begins, Passion/Palm Sunday. Which is it? It's both, Palms and Passion juxtaposed, and there begins the complexity. But it is problematic only if you insist that liturgies sound only one central theme. Realize, however, that the scriptures don't offer us such thematic coherence; they are as complex as our lives.

Consider these narratives not simply as historical accounts. Experience them instead as a contemporary disciple. You could enter today's passage at one of several points—perhaps as the disciple sent to retrieve the colt. Jesus calls us to do such strange things. Or you could enter it as one called to give your very best, even today, offering the colt simply "because the Lord needs it." Each of those pathways leads to both joy and sacrifice. Or you could enter the narrative along with the "multitude of the disciples" who greet Jesus as their king. That is what's going on here; the colt (see Zechariah 9:9) and the variation on Psalm 118:26 ("blessed is the king") make that unmistakable point, and naming Jesus as king changes everything.

In a realm with emperors, naming anyone other than Caesar as king could bring lethal consequences, as it did for Jesus. But what about us today? It's such problematic language. Those who call Jesus *king* may be tempted to see themselves as his royal courtiers, but the Gospel and the other texts that we read this week will have none of that. Yes, we're to follow, as subjects must do, but we are to follow in his way of self-giving love and service. What will that mean for you for the rest of this year?

Help us, O God, to name you as King and follow where you lead, even in the way of sacrifice and self-giving. Amen.

God is addressing you through the scriptures, calling you to participate in what God is doing. That's never truer than in the psalm appointed for the Liturgy of the Palms. Note its dynamism and allow it to carry you forward.

We praise the God who saves and delivers us. We join the procession with the multitude and shout, "Open to me the gates of righteousness." Presume that God answers this prayer, for we thank this One who has become "[our] salvation." Entering the Temple, we might think that we've reached our goal, but we are not there yet. Notice the next prayer, "Save us, we beseech thee, O Lord," and even then the psalm continues to carry us forward toward the altar.

What's going on here, and for what are we praying? Those words *save* and *salvation* are a major part of our faith language, but perhaps we're only beginning to understand what they mean. Sometimes we speak of salvation as if it were a credential; in its worst use it is something like a ticket to heaven that some of us receive and other unfortunate souls do not. What if salvation means far more? I encourage you to hear it as God's ongoing intention to bless the world, using us as willing instruments of that blessing.

In the days ahead, some churches will follow ancient precedent and hold palm processions outside, but I invite you to do your own walk through your community with or without a palm branch. As you walk, notice your neighborhood and those who live there. Imagine their lives and hold them before God's altar. Pray for them and for yourself.

God, thank you for my neighbors and my neighborhood. Help us to see that, in you, the whole world is one neighborhood. Amen.

We turn toward the readings from the Liturgy of the Passion, first to Isaiah's witness to the Suffering Servant. Along with the psalm and epistle to follow, this reading works to shape our perception of the Passion narrative, and so we read with the suffering Christ in mind. Jesus fulfills the dynamic of today's text. He is the faithful teacher who heard and proclaimed God's word, and he suffered for it while believing in the One who would vindicate him. We're grateful that Jesus walked this road before us, but the procession that he began doesn't end. We're called to join him.

What will that mean for you? Notice that our reading doesn't say suffering is good. It is the tragic consequence of truth-telling. Therefore, let there be no exalting of suffering, especially that experienced by others. We admire the martyrs of the faith, but for today let us access the discussion at a lower intensity. We live amid chronic indignation. The church and culture are significantly divided, always ready to engage the latest controversy. We justify ourselves because we're not one of the offensive others.

What if we decided to live as generously and hospitably as possible? It sounds simple, but remember that Jesus was continually criticized for the meal fellowship that stands in the midst of the Passion narrative and as the final word of the Lord's Day liturgy. Generosity that eats with sinners will draw opposition. At the least it will cause us the discomfort of dealing with companions whom we did not choose. But God calls us to this pathway and blesses those who walk it.

Bless all our neighbors, O God, and help us live so that all may be one. Amen.

Having empathy is a first step in the disciple's way of generosity. Today's reading begins, "Be gracious to me . . . for I am in distress, my eye wastes away from grief, my soul and body also." Here is prayer offered in a time of loss and spoken by one who is exhausted. That description may or may not describe you right now, but continue listening to the psalmist's prayer. He feels like he has been forgotten and "plotted against." His sense of dread is all-encompassing, even if his fears and feelings don't entirely make sense.

Perhaps it seems strange to offer this prayer as your own, although there may be times when it's exactly what you would pray. Either way, I invite you to imagine it as someone's prayer today. Here is a key understanding held by those who advocate for use of the full Psalter, even its difficult parts. Ask yourself, "Who might be praying this prayer today?" Then imagine praying it with them, perhaps with someone mourning the loss of a spouse or child, or with a victim of abuse, or with someone struggling to pay medical bills or to find the next meal.

Invite the Spirit into the process, both to enlighten your imagination and to help you bear difficult things, even your own wordless groans (see Romans 8:26). Here is work the Holy One inspires in us as we prepare for the Holy Week journey, and we are able to do it because Jesus walked the journey before us. With him we can complete this prayer with confidence: "But I trust in you, O LORD. . . . My times are in your hand . . . deliver me."

Pray with and for those who are weary and grief-stricken.

Today's reading provides another lens through which we are invited to see the Passion narrative. Paul wrote, "Let the same mind be in you that was in Christ Jesus" as a conclusion to a passage in which he called the community to "compassion and sympathy," telling them to regard "others as better" and to look "to the interests of others" (see Philippians 2:1-4). This call is rooted not in some commonsense morality or in any particular political commitment, but in the nature and mission of Christ.

According to this ancient hymn, Christ was "in the form of God" and equal with God. This affirmation is consistent with the ancient creedal witness of the church that insists that Jesus Christ is "of one being with the Father" and fully human (see the Nicene Creed). Note what God does: "emptying himself" and "taking the form of a servant" even unto cruel death on a cross. Knowing and serving God means walking in this way of self-emptying.

How does one do that? This is particularly difficult for those of us who've learned to cherish our achievements and defend hard-won turf. Hearing the call of the Passion liturgy isn't about somehow rehearsing the events of the Crucifixion; it is about actively engaging the suffering of the world—its fears and anguish—and interceding with our words and with our actions. And yes, this gospel tells us the truth. Having the mind of Christ means sacrificing, loosening our grip on our achievements and positions. Can you imagine that not as burden or deprivation but as an invitation to a new level of freedom? If you believe that this is the way of God, then you can trust the journey that Holy Week sets before us.

Gracious God, help us to find your way of freedom in lives of service. Amen.

Throughout the Passion narrative we hear witness to God's gift and call. Today I invite you to meditate on Luke's version of the institution of the Eucharist. Here it is more First Supper than Last because his commandment—"Do this"—is tied to promises about sharing it in the "kingdom of God," and the presence of this story in the Gospel speaks to its continuation among the people of God. Nevertheless, we're still trying to figure out how to do it right.

The Eucharist was not simply a new ritual that Jesus invented and gave to the church. It stands in continuity with the Passover and the banquet practices of the ancient Mediterranean world, and it seeks to subvert and convert them. Those banquets marked and enforced social hierarchies, to divide rich and poor, the socially acceptable from the unacceptable. Even on this night when Jesus was speaking about the sacrificial gift of his body and blood, the disciples just didn't get it. Rather, they argued "as to which one of them was to be regarded as the greatest."

Never mind what happened later that night when they fell asleep while he prayed. Their argument shows that they had already fallen asleep. Much of the time, contemporary disciples are no better.

So then, what?

We call this meal a "means of grace," but it's not some magic spiritual pill. Within our practice of the Holy Meal, the call to repent and turn toward God's reign is both expressed and implied. Given today's reading, that means letting go of disputes about rank and privilege so we will be free to enter Christ's profound generosity. Is it possible that you're tired of the argument anyway?

God of the Eucharist, thy kingdom come, and thy will be done.
Give all of us this day our daily bread. Amen.

Palm/Passion Sunday

The Passion narrative is filled with violence: Judas's plot; a corrupt legal system; public humiliations of Jesus, along with a beating administered while in custody; and public torture and execution. Reading all this, one might conclude that such violence is inevitable or even God's will. But Jesus' arrest offers another possibility.

After Jesus has finished praying, we hear that Judas came leading a band of officers "with swords and clubs." Even Judas's kiss was a new means of violence. The disciples asked, "Lord, should we strike with the sword?" but did not wait for the answer. That sword was used, injuring "the slave of the high priest." Here continued a tragic cycle that seemingly never ends, extending all the way from Cain and Abel to our day. But notice that Jesus did something else. He commanded his disciples, "No more of this!" and then healed the one who had been injured, even though he was part of the mob that had come to arrest him.

I hope you see Jesus' words and actions as more than a rebuke of his first-century followers. Had the brawl erupted, of course, they would've been no better than the others. But there is a word to us as well. In the midst of strife and hatred, Jesus shows another possibility for those who've perpetrated violence.

Jesus never condones violence, but notice what he says later in the narrative to the (violent?) criminal who died beside him: "Today you shall be with me in Paradise" (Luke 23:43).

Lord, form our imaginations toward visions of reconciliation and peace. Amen.

Walk in Jerusalem, Just Like John

APRIL 11–17, 2022 • STEVE HARPER

SCRIPTURE OVERVIEW: The readings for Holy Week focus our attention on the sacrifice made by the Messiah. The prophecies in Isaiah speak of it. Psalm 22 tells of confidence in God even in the midst of betrayal and suffering like that experienced by Jesus. In First Corinthians Paul describes crucifixion as the center of our teaching as Christians. We follow these events through the eyes of the Gospel writer John. Jesus foreshadows his death in multiple ways, but even his closest followers struggle to understand and accept its meaning. Why would the Son of God experience such alienation and suffering? It is all for us, the ultimate work of love. But then he conquers the grave! Praise be to God!

QUESTIONS AND SUGGESTIONS FOR REFLECTION

- Read John 13:21-32. When have you noticed darkness planting seeds of betrayal in your heart? How did you follow Jesus' light?
- Read John 13:1-17, 31b-35. What status symbols do you hold on to that keep you from following Jesus' example of humble service?
- Read Isaiah 52:13–53:12. On Good Friday, God enters into human suffering. When have you felt God's presence in your suffering?
- Read John 20:1-18. How has Christ found you?

Retired seminary professor and retired elder in the Florida Annual Conference of The United Methodist Church.

John's Gospel has always been my favorite. It was the first part of the Bible I read after professing my faith in Christ in 1963. I have read it many times since, preached from it repeatedly, and for several years I used the Gospel of John as the basis for a course I taught in seminary about inductive study methodology. This week's Gospel readings (except for Saturday) are from John's Gospel. They give us the opportunity to "walk in Jerusalem, just like John," and to observe this Holy Week through his experience. In doing so, his words can lead us into a fresh experience of these days.

In today's reading, John begins the day before Jesus entered into Jerusalem on what we now call Palm Sunday. The passage begins in Bethany with Mary, one of Jesus' dearest friends. During dinner, or perhaps at the end of it, she anointed Jesus' feet with expensive perfume—valued at a year's wages. Judas complained, but Jesus put him in his place, honoring Mary's act of devotion.

When we think of Holy Week, we easily think of God's extravagant love offered to us through Jesus. But John reminds us that there is a corresponding extravagance that can come from us to Jesus. God spared no expense in the gift of Jesus. Similarly, we are invited to respond to God's love with exuberant generosity. Holy Week is not a time to be calculating (as Judas was), but rather to be "lost in wonder, love, and praise" as Charles Wesley wrote in his hymn text, "Love Divine All Loves Excelling." Holy Week is not only the story of how great God's love is for us; it is also the testimony of how great our love can be for God.

Dear God, work in me during this Holy Week so that I can live exuberantly in response to your amazing love. Amen.

Jesus' final week was, among other things, a great Summing Up—his way of emphasizing one last time what really matters. In today's reading, Jesus linked *life* (the seed) and *light* to describe himself, the same two words John used in the Prologue to his Gospel (1:5). It is a linkage that began in Creation, where light engendered all of life, across the spectrum, from the smallest particle to the farthest star.

Light enlivens. As the light of the world (John 8:12), the Word was the light of all people (John 1:4). The desire of the Greeks to meet with Jesus is John's way of pointing this out. As the incarnation of God—as the universal Christ—Jesus did indeed draw all people to himself.

We live in a God-saturated cosmos. The light gives life to everyone coming into the world (John 1:9). No one is bereft of this light. Nothing in all creation is without it. And because the light is in us, we are drawn, as the Greeks were, to light wherever we find it.

Light also exposes. In the verse just before the beginning of today's reading (12:19), the Pharisees are deeply troubled that "the whole world" has gone after Jesus—instead of after them. As light, Jesus exposed the failures of the religious/political system they had built—a system that worked to their advantage. Jesus' light exposed all that, and they didn't like it—not one bit. System builders never do like it. They push back whenever light reveals that their status quo has become a sacred cow.

To walk this Holy Week journey just like John is to walk in the light as Jesus did (see 1 John 1:7), and, like Jesus, it is to become light and life for others.

Dear God, bring us into the light to the extent that we become light. Amen.

Today's reading from John inspires multiple reflections, falling as it does in the section unique to John's Gospel where Jesus met with his disciples on the brink of his betrayal. The five chapters (13–17) encapsulate what I named yesterday as Jesus' great Summing Up. Through Jesus' words and actions with his disciples, John's Gospel invites us to become part of the story.

In addition to Jesus' teaching and example in this larger section, today's reading takes us into his heart, a broken heart. When he said, "One of you will betray me," he was referring to Judas. Much has been said about Judas in meditations like the ones I write for this week of *Disciplines.*

But today, I want to keep the focus on Jesus and what it must have been like for him to realize that the final piece of the betrayal puzzle would be inserted by the hand of one with whom he had journeyed for several years. The Gospels make clear that Jesus was under attack early on in his ministry. The religious/political leaders formed plots and made plans to destroy him. (See Mark 3:6.) But it was one from his own fellowship who did him in. The underlying emotions in today's reading are palpable.

Yet Jesus offered Judas the same bread and wine that everyone else received! Judas ate and drank at the Lord's Supper! Of all the examples of inclusion offered to us by Jesus in the course of his ministry, none is more powerful than this. Radical love. Amazing grace.

Some of us know the heartache of being "turned in" by our friends. We know the pain of being rejected by those who have known us the longest. In such times, we must recognize and express this piece of Jesus' witness—the piece that refuses to exclude or withhold grace.

Dear God, give me a tender heart toward everyone, including those who no longer want to have anything to do with me. Amen.

MAUNDY THURSDAY

Jesus' words and actions with Judas seen in yesterday's reading occurred in a larger context—the context of serving love. Jesus made it clear that he was giving his disciples an example that they were supposed to follow. Simply put, he said, "Love one another."

Jesus called it a new commandment. But on the surface, that was not true. Loving others was at the heart of the first covenant (see Leviticus 19:18), and Jesus had previously identified loving one another as the second great commandment (see Matthew 22:39). He went on to teach the radical nature of this love in the parable of the good Samaritan (see Luke 10:30-37).

So, what made his commandment new? We see it in the words, "as I have loved you." In the context of the Gospel of John as a whole, here is the pinnacle of the principle, "the Word became flesh" (John 1:14). Love acts. In today's reading, John connected the cosmic and the concrete, making clear that faith is always behavioral. Jesus expected his disciples to wash the feet of others and to offer grace even to those who turn on us (see John 13:18-30).

Walking in Jerusalem with John includes embracing a fact that James later emphasized: Faith is realized in works, and, without action, faith is dead (see James 2:14-26). This truth is also emphasized in 1 John 3:17-18. The world says, "You are what you do," and there is truth in that. But the deeper truth is this, "You do what you are." Or, to say it simply: If we say we have faith, we must show it.

In today's reading this is the new commandment, shown to us in the example of Jesus: A profession of faith must result in an expression of faith.

Dear God, work in me so that my faith is enacted, not just affirmed. Amen.

GOOD FRIDAY

In 1999, my wife, Jeannie, and I took a trip to the Holy Land. We discovered that it is true that visiting the Holy Land changes the way you read the Bible. Indeed it does, including how you understand the events portrayed in today's reading.

Of all the passages that I now read in a new light, the one that stands out is the gap between the events of verses twenty-seven and twenty-eight in chapter eighteen of John's Gospel. Tradition says that Jesus spent the night in Caiaphas's house. He was tied with a rope and let down into a circular dungeon. (Without light or corners, prisoners would go insane more quickly.) Jesus spent the night in a cell designed to drive him crazy. We descended a stairway into that dungeon, and the experience turned out to be the most moving one of my trip.

The two chapters we read today are jam-packed with pain and suffering—too much to capture in a brief meditation on the main elements of the Good Friday story. Without minimizing any of these details, I only report that it was the dungeon in Caiaphas' house that moved me most. The darkness of that dungeon draped my soul in a momentary sense of the suffering Jesus might have endured there.

The movement from Thursday to Friday is absent in the text but not in the experience of Jesus. He had been betrayed, arrested, and denied. He would soon be mocked, beaten, and crucified. In our Christian experience, we can find ourselves alone and in seemingly unbearable suffering. In those times we can feel totally abandoned. But we are not because God is there.

Dear God, thank you for being with me when I cannot tell up from down. Amen.

HOLY SATURDAY

I wish the Gospels said more about Holy Saturday. Except for today's reading from Matthew and one verse in Luke (23:56), nothing is written. Yet, it was a full day as much as any other day we have looked at. It is not only the day when Jesus was entombed; it is also a symbol for the days when we feel numb and lifeless—the day between loss and gain, between sickness and health, between a problem and a solution. It is a day we are all familiar with—one we revisit over the course of our lifetimes.

The reading from Matthew is clear about one thing: It is a day (a time, a phase) of insecurity. John shows it to us in the experience of the disciples and then in the conversation between Pilate and the chief priests. He shows that no one was confident, much less certain, about what was happening. Between darkness and light, we never are.

We have the benefit of knowing how things turned out in the Gospel story. But we need to read this passage from Matthew with the same mindset as those mentioned in it—insecure, fearful, not having any idea where things are headed.

We must not omit Holy Saturday from our spirituality. We cannot get from Friday to Sunday—from Jesus' death to his resurrection—without the tomb. Neither can we get from defeat to victory, sadness to joy without in-between numbness.

Holy Saturday teaches us that insecurity is part of the spiritual life. The psalmist cries out to God from that very place: "God, why have you forsaken me?" Holy Saturday is a stark reminder that spirituality includes being entombed as well as being enlivened.

Dear God, thank you that your grace enables me to live through the insecure times in my life. Amen.

EASTER

Two thousand years down the pike, it is hard for me to wait until today to say, "He is risen; he is risen indeed!" Since the first Easter morning, disciples have had the benefit of knowing how things turned out. As others have put it, we are Easter people, so that every day we can say, "He is risen; he is risen indeed!"

Walking in Jerusalem this week with John (and yesterday with Matthew), we have had the opportunity to consider more deeply what it meant for the first disciples to move toward Sunday with no idea that there would be a resurrection. Our experience parallels Mary Magdalene's in today's lesson: As does she, we stand weeping outside the tombs of our lives. We mourn the loss of many things, including sometimes the loss of the presence of Christ in our lives. Our first response is to ask, "Where has he gone?" Like Mary, we even ask this of the risen Christ himself.

Walking in Jerusalem with John keeps things real. Spirituality is reality—always. Reality is where the ingredients of life are mixed so that something new can emerge, just as it did for Mary when she heard the risen Christ call her by name.

And maybe that is the message of Easter this year for many of us. It is to know that Jesus is risen, risen indeed, and that the risen Christ wants nothing more than to call us by name. Without diminishing Jesus' resurrection itself, Mary's experience in the garden is the reminder that there is a resurrection awaiting us each day of our lives and when the days of our lives are over!

Dear God, because you live, I can live also. Thank you! Amen.

The King of Kings

APRIL 18–24, 2022 • DAVID RENSBERGER

SCRIPTURE OVERVIEW: After the resurrection of Jesus, the disciples are unable to remain silent. They go to the Temple to proclaim the gospel. Some people receive the message, while others do not. This causes turmoil within the community, but the apostles stand firm in their testimony, inspired by the Holy Spirit. Psalm 150 might be on the lips of those early apostles. Everything that has breath should praise the Lord! The author of Revelation recounts a vision that he receives from the risen Jesus Christ, who one day will return as Lord of all nations. In John we learn more about the source of the confidence of the apostles. They have experienced Jesus in the flesh, and this experience gives power to their proclamation of the reality of his resurrection.

QUESTIONS AND SUGGESTIONS FOR REFLECTION

- Read Acts 5:27-32. When has your faith compelled you to rise up, stand up, or kneel down in obedience to God rather than earthly authorities?
- Read Psalm 150. When have you praised God with great celebration? When have you praised God with quiet service to creation?
- Read Revelation 1:4-8. How do you see peace arising out of violence in the Bible and in the world around you?
- Read John 20:19-31. How have your experiences of witnessing violence or the results of violence helped you to understand that violence does not have the last word?

Retired seminary professor; scholar and writer on the Bible and on Christian spirituality; workshop and retreat leader; member of Atlanta Mennonite Fellowship and Oakhurst Baptist Church, Decatur, GA.

I'm writing this to you from a difficult moment in the past. Creating a book like *Disciplines* takes time, and I'm writing in the United States in 2020, the year of the COVID-19 pandemic and the Black Lives Matter movement, with a difficult election still to come. I have no idea how these crises affected you; but I know this week's scriptures shed light on them. May what you've learned since 2020 also shed light on these reflections.

Revelation begins magnificently with greetings from the One "who is and who was and who is to come" and from "the Alpha and the Omega." We are immediately in the framework of eternity, where the crises and triumphs, kindnesses and injustices, even the lives and deaths of earth seem insignificant. Yet they are significant, for we are also greeted by "Jesus Christ, . . . the firstborn of the dead, . . . who loves us and freed us from our sins by his blood." The Eternal One took notice of our wrongs and tragedies and sent us a Redeemer to share in them and overcome them, to overcome even death itself.

I don't know who comes to your mind when you think of resurrection and eternal life. I know there may well be someone special. When we celebrate the feast of Easter with flowers and trumpets and glorious hymns, there may be someone in particular whom you long to think of sharing life with the risen Christ. It may be someone lost to COVID-19, to an act of violence, or just to the hardships and hazards of life on earth. I invite you to hold that someone in your heart and think of Jesus reaching out his wounded yet warm hand to them.

Alpha and Omega, we are grateful beyond words that you took notice of us in our needs and sorrows, sent Jesus to share them with us, and in him gave us life and victory over death. Amen.

The King of Kings

John, the author of Revelation, begins with greetings from the Eternal One and the seven spirits, and from "Jesus Christ, the faithful witness, the firstborn of the dead, and the ruler of the kings of the earth." God's universal sovereignty is now exercised through the risen Christ. He will return, John says, and "every eye will see him, even those who pierced him; and on his account all the tribes of the earth will wail."

Throughout the history of Christendom, Christian kings have prayed to the King of kings to help them defeat other Christian kings. American Christians have not been immune to this thinking. But John does not say that the God of one mighty nation will help it rule over others. No. The King of kings is the one who was pierced, and all the peoples who seek to conquer one another will be dismayed by him.

In John's drama, every earthly ruler is responsible for Jesus' piercing. But it is the slaughtered Lamb that receives power. The kings, the wealthy, and the mighty still oppose him, but in the end their Babylon, enriched by trading in luxury goods and in human lives, comes to nothing. It is the One, and all the ones, victimized by those in power and authority whom God will vindicate (see Revelation 5:6-12; 6:15-16; 18:1-24).

Where do you picture yourself between the mighty and the slaughtered? Perhaps, like me, you are somewhere in the middle. But I wonder whether I am so innocent. The home where I've lived since 1981 is in a neighborhood developed in the 1950s for whites only. Only now is it slowly integrating. Who assembled the computer I'm writing on? Were they fairly paid? Are their lives secure? The middle is no safe place to be when the Lamb upends the mighty.

Slaughtered Lamb, have mercy. Give me courage to share in your reign of justice, humility, and compassion. Amen.

Though the John of the Gospel is probably not the John of Revelation, here too Jesus is the one who is pierced and wounded. Here too he is a witness to truth (see John 18:37), whose followers bear witness to him.

Even after his resurrection, Jesus remains wounded when he appears to his disciples. Indeed, it is by seeing his wounds—not his halo—that Thomas expects to believe that he is alive. Is Thomas "doubting"? Despite some modern translations, the word used in verse 27 is not "doubting" but "unbelieving." It's not that Thomas had trouble believing; he just didn't believe. But he was no more unbelieving than the other disciples; he was just not with them when they saw Jesus. They also remained fearful behind closed doors even after Mary Magdalene brought them the good news that Jesus is alive. They too needed the sight of Jesus' wounds in order to believe Jesus was alive.

Jesus' sharing of our suffering is the surest sign that this is the real Jesus, the one who makes God known (see John 1:18; 14:7). Thomas's confession "My Lord and my God" takes us back to the beginning of John: the Word was God, yet became human flesh and lived as we live. Jesus' wounds attest to God's willingness to dwell among us.

Jesus blesses those who have not seen and yet believe. How do they come to believe? Through the testimony of the disciples who are sent as Jesus was sent, and through the books written about him. These believers who have not seen become witnesses themselves, and they too are without halos. Our most faithful testimony to the wounded Giver of life is our own life-giving deeds (see John 14:12). It is those who suffer loss who manifest God's universal reign; in their suffering they let Jesus shine through them.

How have you borne witness to Jesus? In what ways have his wounds appeared in you?

During the COVID-19 pandemic, we learned that we don't need to be gathered in a public space to celebrate Easter or have the risen Christ come to us. This story in John was often mentioned. A group of people—disciples of Jesus—are fearful. They have shut themselves in and won't go out because there is something out there that might hurt them, even kill them. In this narrative from John 20 they are afraid of "the Jews." They are Jews too, of course, but in this Gospel, "Jews" means leaders and authorities. Jesus' followers fear punishment if they persist in his radical ways.

They are also in shock, closed in on themselves, unable to believe that good news can be true news. So when Mary Magdalene, apostle to the apostles, tells them that she has seen Jesus, they do nothing. The Gospel of John loves face-to-face encounters with Jesus: It's good to hear about him, but it's better to meet him. That was Mary's experience. Likewise, only when Jesus himself appears is the male disciples' fear replaced by renewed trust in God, the faith that Jesus had taught them.

The disaster of Jesus' crucifixion was not the end. God still had an ace to play. The shock of Jesus' return breaks through the inner barriers that the shock of his death had put up. The worst had happened, but it wasn't the end. The best thing, the thing beyond all imagination, not only can happen; it has happened. The trust in God shattered by Good Friday comes rushing back at the sight and touch of Jesus.

God really does reign over all, and Jesus' return to life from a brutal death proves it. Now, with trust in God restored, they are sent out to bring the good news of peace and forgiveness.

Risen Christ, when trauma has shocked us into fear and despair, come, stand by us, and give us your peace. Help us believe your good news. Amen.

Speaking to the authorities, Peter summarized the message of the earliest church this way: "God exalted [Jesus] at his right hand as Leader and Savior that he might give repentance to Israel and forgiveness of sins. And we are witnesses to these things, and so is the Holy Spirit."

Why does this message of forgiveness bring persecution? Luke says the Sadducees (a priestly ruling group) were jealous (see Acts 5:17-18). As has been true in later reforms in Christianity itself, the religious authorities disliked having unofficial centers of spiritual power offering divine forgiveness apart from the established rituals.

This was not just a call to individual penitence but a repentance and forgiveness movement. It called to mind other unauthorized reforms, like those associated with John the Baptist and the Essenes. To modern individualists, repentance and forgiveness sound purely personal. But such a movement had wider implications in the ancient setting. It aimed at the reformation of the entire religion and society. That was what got Jesus into trouble, and now it is his followers' turn.

Note that Peter did not speak of Jesus as a "personal Lord and Savior." Instead, he saw him as the head of an entire renewed people of God. Zacchaeus exemplified this renewal (see Luke 19:1-10). Forgiven for collaborating in unjust taxation, he expressed his repentance by undoing the harm he had done. But then he could not go back to his old ways. Enough penitents like Zacchaeus would have undermined the system that benefited those at the top at the expense of the working poor. Zacchaeus's personal salvation was one piece in a reform that was spiritual, societal, and political.

Have you ever sought forgiveness for sins that were structural as well as personal? Have you ever led others to such repentance?

"We must obey God rather than human beings!" (NIV). How do we discern the relation of Christian belief and spirituality to human authority?

Jews in New Testament times already wrestled with this question. Peter expected the high priest and council to agree with him. But people in their position might have held that obeying them equaled obeying God. Not surprisingly, they resisted Peter's claim that the resurrection of Jesus embodies a direct message from God that is independent of their authority. On the other hand, some of them might have willingly obeyed God rather than Roman authority a few years later when Emperor Caligula ordered a statue of himself placed in the Jerusalem Temple.

In Christianity, the question has been answered differently in different traditions and social circumstances. Established churches with long histories of social status may look askance at claims of direct instructions from God. "Free" churches—Baptists, Quakers, Mennonites, and others—have occasionally undertaken radical acts of nonconformity and civil disobedience. For me personally, Peter's assertion helped me decide not to cooperate with the draft during the Vietnam War, leading to a short prison term.

In all denominations, however, white Christians mostly see the church as aligned with social and political order and authority. In communities of color, the church may have to defend believers against authorities, or at least mediate between them and the police and courts. It is no accident that African American churches and ministers have held central roles in the Civil Rights and Black Lives Matter movements. Obeying God can mean creative spiritual resistance to oppressive human systems.

Jesus, King of kings, guide us when we must discern where your risen power directs our allegiance. Amen.

L et everything that has breath praise the LORD!" (NIV).
        In 2020, the year of COVID-19 and the killing of George
Floyd, "having breath" became an unexpectedly urgent issue.
Floyd said that he couldn't breathe more than twenty times.
Many COVID-19 patients needed a ventilator to breathe. My
daughter, a nurse anesthetist who puts patients on ventilators,
often must wear an N95 mask at work. She says, only half jok-
ingly, that you know when the mask is properly fitted because
you can't breathe.

Victims of crucifixion often died not of blood loss but of
asphyxia, unable to keep pushing themselves up against the
nails in their feet so they could breathe.

"Let everything that has breath. . . ."

But Jesus breathed again on Easter morning. He took new
breaths for all who cannot breathe because of illness or violence
or a job where breathing is hard. Imagine the first breath Jesus
drew outside the tomb, in the cool dawn air of spring. Did he use
that breath to shout "Hallelujah"? "Hallelujah" is the "praise the
LORD" that frames Psalm 150. When Jesus had breath again, did
he join in the chorus of praise with all else that breathes?

The risen Jesus, "ruler of the kings of the earth" (see Revelation 1:5), also reigns over all creation (see Philippians 2:9-10 and
Hebrews 1:3), receiving the praise of everything that has breath.
The glorious beauty of the creatures in spring reflects divine
glory, inviting us to join in their praise.

I hope your breath in 2022 is not beset with the choking
crises of 2020. I hope you are able to draw your breath freely
and can join the whole universe in praise and worship of the
One whose reign of compassion, love, and justice gives us hope
when our breath is short. Praise the Lord!

*God of resurrection, breathe your breath in us, and accept our
praise. Amen.*

Extraordinary Vision

APRIL 25–MAY 1, 2022 • GEORGE R. GRAHAM

SCRIPTURE OVERVIEW: Saul is one of the primary obstacles to the early spread of Christianity. The death and resurrection of Jesus does not fit his paradigm for the Messiah, so it cannot be true. It takes a miraculous intervention by Christ himself to change his mind. Psalm 30 reminds us that the light will always chase the darkness. We experience true suffering and true loss, but God can turn our mourning into dancing in God's own timing. In Revelation, John takes us to the throne room of God, where angels and creatures proclaim the glory of the Lamb of God who has defeated death and reigns forever. Returning to the Gospel of John, we read more about Jesus' post-resurrection appearances, which here include a seaside breakfast and a quiz for Peter.

QUESTIONS AND SUGGESTIONS FOR REFLECTION

- Read Acts 9:1-20. Jesus' resurrection calls us to an embodied faith. How do you bear the gospel?
- Read Psalm 30. Recall a specific time when you depended on God.
- Read Revelation 5:11-14. Have you ever worshiped the Lamb with your whole body? What keeps you from falling down to worship God?
- Read John 21:1-19. The author reminds us that Jesus calls us to be shepherds and sheep. Which role do you most often fill? How can you take on a new leadership role or allow others to lead you?

Ordained minister in the United Church of Christ; vice president of the Council for Health and Human Service Ministries; editor of *Alive Now* magazine from 1992 to 2000; lives in Lakewood, OH, with his family.

"Can we go fishing?" my thirteen-year-old daughter, Ellen, asks quite often. Her requests are usually last-minute ones, but I try to go whenever possible. I am her ride, the one who buys the bait, and the helper with twisted lines. Typically I just sit and watch, and usually she doesn't catch anything. But it's a great way to spend time together.

Simon Peter tells the disciples, "I am going fishing." They go too.

We don't know why Simon Peter was going fishing. Was he just taking a break? Was he hoping to provide food? Was he going back to what he knew?

The passage also raises other questions. How is it that the disciples do not recognize Jesus when he has already appeared to them several times after the Resurrection? Why does Simon Peter, who is fishing naked, put clothes on before he jumps into the water to swim to Jesus?

Commentators tell us that this story is an addition to the Gospel of John and should be read as an epilogue. This story serves as a kind of bookend to the calling of the disciples early in the Gospel. Simon Peter's strange act of dressing himself before jumping into the water to swim to Jesus somehow reminds me of Adam and Eve hiding from God in the Garden of Eden when they realized they were naked.

While this passage provokes many questions, there is no question that Simon Peter and the other disciples finally recognize Jesus. The same impulse that drives Peter to go fishing impels him to jump in the water when he recognizes Jesus. In hearing Jesus' voice, following his directions, and hauling in the catch, the other disciples recognize him too.

Loving Jesus, help us to recognize your voice when you call to us. Amen.

Waking up in my grandparents' house to the smell of breakfast cooking is a favorite childhood memory. My grandparents lived in Philadelphia, where scrapple is a regional breakfast food. This pan-fried pork and cornmeal mush is not something I would have normally eaten. But to me it smelled like love cooking, and so I ate it.

Eating fish for breakfast, as we read about in today's verses, would be an acquired taste for me too. I am guessing it was a normal breakfast for the disciples. They didn't have aisles of sweetened cereal to choose from like we do.

Peter had been so eager to get to Jesus that he left the disciples to do the heavy lifting of bringing in the fishing net. Now Peter runs back to the boat to bring some of the whopping haul to Jesus, who invites them, "Come and have breakfast." In an action that echoes the Eucharist, Jesus takes bread and gives it to them. Then he does the same with the fish.

None of the disciples asked Jesus who he was; they knew (21:12). They had seen him on the shore and heard him calling directions. But I wonder if it wasn't the smell of the fire and the fish roasting that clinched it for them. I wonder if they had smelled it before—if Jesus had fixed breakfast in the years they followed him. I wonder if they often woke up to the smell of love cooking.

Even after his resurrection, Christ was caring for the disciples, loving them so they would know how to love others. Christ is still present, teaching us how to continue the chain of love that started with those who followed him.

What actions remind you of God's care? When do you recognize you are in the presence of Christ? What does love smell like to you?

Wake us up, Jesus, to the smell of your love cooking in our lives. Amen.

Jesus' appearance in John 21 encapsulates his teaching about what it means to follow him. He has given the disciples instructions about how to fish, and then he cares for them by feeding them breakfast. Now Jesus focuses naturally on Simon Peter—the disciple who was eager to be first—to teach the importance of feeding others.

In this interaction, Jesus does not call him Peter, the name Jesus gave him when he called him to be a disciple. Jesus goes back to calling him Simon, the name he had until Jesus renamed him. Perhaps Peter, the *rock*, was a kind of public persona. Or perhaps Jesus wanted to take things back to where they began.

Jesus asks Simon Peter three times if he loves him. In part it seems to be a response to Peter's having denied knowing Jesus three times as Jesus faced death. By the third time Jesus asks, his question feels painful and awkward to Peter. His feelings are hurt. Jesus wants to make sure that Simon Peter's responses are not just eager ones, like jumping from the boat to swim ashore or running back to grab some of the fish that the other disciples had hauled in. He wants to confirm there is depth, commitment, and understanding in Simon Peter's response.

Following Jesus does not just mean hauling in a load of fish or being cared for by Jesus. It also means feeding Jesus' lambs and sheep—the poor and vulnerable who were the focus of Jesus' ministry. Jesus teaches that feeding and caring for those who are vulnerable are what it means to love him. Jesus asks Simon Peter three times to remind him—and all those who hear, including us—about the demands of this work and the depth of commitment that is necessary.

Jesus feeds us so we become willing and able to feed others.

Good Shepherd, help us show our love by feeding your lambs and tending your sheep. Amen.

After Jesus directs Simon Peter to care for his lambs and sheep, Jesus concludes his conversation with some straight talk about the likely outcome. Simon Peter might die as a result of following Christ.

I cannot hear this scripture without thinking of the summer my ninety-three-year-old father fell and broke his hip. To move my father from bed during rehab after his hip surgery, the nurses used a piece of medical equipment known as a Hoyer Lift. This device is a bit like a human-sized crane that can lift a patient from a bed using a belt and a pad.

Seeing my father having a belt fastened around him and being hoisted with the lift was an image of vulnerability and dependence. My father, who had once been so independent and energetic, looked incredibly frail and helpless. I fought back tears. He did not want to be confined in a nursing home. This is not where he saw life taking him.

My father recovered from the fractured hip but died the following year. For me, however, seeing him in the lift was harder than being with him in the final days before he died.

We are fortunate if we are able to live out our lives fastening our own belts and going wherever we wish. We are less likely to experience the religious persecution that Jesus warned Simon Peter about, but at some point infirmity, illness, loss, or injustice may lead us somewhere we do not want to go. Whatever the cause, faith and the examples of those who have gone before us—from Simon Peter to our parents—can help see us through.

Risen Christ, give us assurance that you are with us, even when life leads us where we do not want to go. Amen.

At the beginning of today's reading, Saul is breathing threats and murder. He is hunting followers of Christ to take them as prisoners to Jerusalem. (Saul's plan sounds eerily similar to Jesus' warning to Simon Peter in John 21:18.) But Saul has an encounter with Jesus on the road to Damascus that leaves him flat on the ground, losing his sight, and hearing Jesus ask, "Why do you persecute me?"

The scene quickly shifts to Ananias, a disciple and a follower of the Way, who has a vision in which Jesus directs him to find Saul and lay his hands on Saul to heal his eyes. Ananias knows Saul's reputation and that Saul has the power to bind him and lead him away. But God has other plans for Saul. Ananias follows the vision and goes to Saul. Scales fall from Saul's eyes, his vision is healed, he is baptized, and he recovers his strength.

The story of Saul and Ananias makes me think about contemporary stories of people who have walked into the face of danger, whether as part of civil rights struggles or encounters with hate groups. John Lewis led lunch counter sit-ins in Nashville as a young leader in the Civil Rights movement in the 1960s; had his skull broken as he attempted to cross the Edmund Pettus Bridge in Selma, Alabama; served in the final decades of his life as a member of the US Congress. In a letter published after he died in 2020, he spoke about the importance of "ordinary people with extraordinary vision" getting in what he called "good trouble." I admire John Lewis's courage, which was clearly driven by an extraordinary vision of justice for all God's people. May this vision inspire us to work for peace and justice in our world.

God of justice, give us courage to get in "good trouble" to help bring about your vision of love and peace. Amen.

In Psalm 30, the psalmist weaves from illness to healing, from divine absence to presence, from individual to community and back to individual. This personal testimony of deliverance and healing leads to a communal sharing and celebration.

There is a kind of dance and reasoning with God in this psalm, in the style of Wisdom literature in the Hebrew Bible. The psalmist attempts to goad God into responding by asking question after question: *If the psalmist died, what would the benefit be for God? Who would be left to praise God and tell of God's faithfulness? Would the dust praise God?* The final image of the supplicant putting on the clothing of joy in order to dance affirms that God has acted and responded to the prayer.

Before becoming ill, the psalmist was prosperous and felt secure. But it was true then as it is now that prosperity does not necessarily protect us from illness or from experiencing God's absence. Though we may be established as a "strong mountain," we are not invincible. We still call and depend on God for healing and comfort.

Praise is our response to God's action. Even when we experience God's work in our lives as individuals, the psalmist reminds us that we are to share our praise in community: It is meant to be seen and heard. While we can do it alone, we are really to dance in community. Changing out of sackcloth is also meant to be seen by the community. Finally, "not [being] silent" means we are to make sure others in the community hear the praises of our soul.

Clothe us in joy, O God, so that we can sing and dance your praises. Amen.

The book of Revelation delivers messages of judgment, but the passage that we read today offers a vision of peace, not only among humans but for the entire creation.

This peaceful vision involves the voices of "myriads of myriads and thousands of thousands" of angels, "every creature in heaven and earth" joined in song in praise of Christ. It brings to mind images of the peaceable kingdom (see Isaiah 11:1-9), but also adds the element of song.

What would this sound like? During the lockdown for the COVID-19 pandemic, recordings circulated of mass choirs of thousands of voices created virtually through computer technology. If we could add angel and animal voices, perhaps we would have a soundtrack for this passage.

Whatever the sound, all beings gathered together around the throne and the Lamb provide a powerful image. For us Christ is both Lamb and Shepherd. He is the one who suffered and who saves. He is the one who feeds us and invites us to feed others. The extraordinary vision presented in this passage is as inclusive of all creation as any passage in scripture. At a time when earth's resources and habitats are being destroyed at an alarming rate— not as a result of God's judgment but as a result of human sin and greed—may this vision of all creation praising God inspire us to commit ourselves to the preservation of God's creation.

May we join our voices with every creature in heaven, on earth and in the sea, proclaiming, "To the one seated on the throne and to the Lamb be blessing and honor and glory and might forever and ever!"

We join all beings in a song of praise to you, Creator. Show us how to care for your creation. Amen.

Pastoral Landscapes

MAY 2–8, 2022 • NICOLA VIDAMOUR

SCRIPTURE OVERVIEW: The imagery of sheep plays a prominent role in three of this week's readings. Psalm 23 uses the relationship between the shepherd and the sheep as its guiding metaphor. The Lord is our shepherd and leads us to safe and fertile places. Even when we pass through a dark valley, the Lord is there protecting us with a shepherd's weapon, a staff. In the Gospel reading, Jesus describes himself as a shepherd who calls his sheep. Because they are his, they hear his voice. In Revelation, Jesus becomes the sheep—or more specifically, the Lamb that was slain on our behalf. Those who endure will praise the Lamb forever. Acts is different in that it focuses on a resurrection story, a manifestation of God's power working through Peter.

QUESTIONS AND SUGGESTIONS FOR REFLECTION

- Read Acts 9:36-43. How can you be a witness and a vessel for God's activity?
- Read Psalm 23. Reflect on the questions the author poses in Tuesday's meditation. Allow God's guidance and correction to be comforting.
- Read Revelation 7:9-17. How does knowing Christ as both Lamb and Shepherd help you work to bring about things not yet seen?
- Read John 10:22-30. How does your faith allow you to hold your convictions without needing to grasp tightly to certainties?

Methodist minister in the Woughton Ecumenical Parish, Milton Keynes, England.

As a city girl, I sometimes get frustrated by the rural imagery that is used in our worship. I agree that green pastures and still waters can be good for the soul. But I also believe that bustling streets and glistening skyscrapers can give us a powerful sense of connection with God.

If I were to write a psalm beginning, "The Lord is my _____," *shepherd* would not be my first choice to complete the sentence. I would want something more urban, like *subway driver* or *security guard* or *night-shift worker*.

I do, however, like the idea of the Lord being my *pastor*—the word that is used to translate *shepherd* in many languages. Pastoral care is clearly not restricted to pastoral landscapes. People everywhere need someone who can revive their soul.

It is, therefore, important to explore what "green pastures" and "still waters" mean for people in their particular context. Where can they lie down and feel safe? What enables them to feel refreshed and restored?

Pastors, like shepherds, have a responsibility to lead and guide others to such places and even to "make" them lie down! Such directive instruction may feel uncomfortable to both shepherd and sheep. It is, nevertheless, a helpful reminder to pastors that it is important to enforce rest. Encouraging others (or themselves) to sit on another committee or sign up for a new volunteer rotation is not always what a pastor should be doing.

David, who wrote this psalm, was a shepherd. I imagine that seeing the Lord as his shepherd helped David to be a better shepherd himself. Daily he sought to offer to others what God was providing for him. By seeing the Lord as our pastor, we will deepen our understanding of what it means both to receive and to give pastoral care.

Pastor God, lead me to those places that nourish my soul. Amen.

On a pilgrimage to the Holy Land, we stopped off en route from Jerusalem to Jericho at the place known as the Valley of the Shadow of Death. Though probably not so named when the psalmist was writing, the valley's name captures in a poetic way the journey of grief and loss.

As we looked down into the valley from a hot desert hill, it was easy to imagine robbers hiding behind the large rocks and attacking solitary travelers, like the man helped by the good Samaritan (see Luke 10:25-37).

No doubt people walking that road would have recited Psalm 23 to bring them courage and an assurance of God's presence with them.

Perhaps the good Samaritan also had these verses in his mind and heart as he anointed the man with oil and left more money with the innkeeper than was immediately required. This enabled the injured man to dwell in goodness and mercy for as long as he needed to.

"The shadow of death" is a phrase that also occurs in two of my favorite scripture passages:

"The people that walked in darkness have seen a great light: they that dwell in the land of *the shadow of death*, upon them hath the light shined" (Isa. 9:2, KJV).

"By the tender mercy of our God, the dawn from on high will break upon us, to give light to those who sit in darkness and in *the shadow of death*, to guide our feet into the way of peace" (Luke 1:78-79).

All these passages involve a journey—from the shadows into the light, from hurt to healing, from death to life. And that journey is not just a beautiful metaphor. It is an actual path that each of us must walk day by day.

Lord, lead me from falsehood to truth, from darkness to light, from death to immortality. (An ancient Sanskrit prayer)

"Please come to us without delay." I wonder if you have ever received a message like that. For me, it brings back memories of being called to the hospital because a church member was dying. I can still feel my heart beating faster as I dropped whatever I was doing and set out, never quite sure what I would find when I got there, but desperately wanting to offer whatever support I could.

Peter's response to the news about Tabitha is a master class in deathbed pastoral care! First, he responded immediately. Even though she had already died, he recognized the importance of going to be with those who were walking "through the valley of the shadow of death."

Second, he allowed the mourners to share with him what Tabitha meant to them. They held precious memories that were important for them to talk about.

Third, he spent time alone with Tabitha, and he prayed. I imagine this privacy also enabled him to express his own grief.

Obviously, what happened next has never been my experience! However, Peter's use of Tabitha's name, his making sure that she knew that he was there, and the touch of his hand are all valuable ways of ministering to people on the threshold of life and death.

Peter then "showed her to be alive." A proclamation of our Easter faith to those who are grieving is crucial, particularly when we have to believe without seeing. Finally, Peter "stayed in Joppa for some time." He did not rush away as quickly as he had come. His pastoral care was ongoing.

Eternal God, stretch out your hand to those who are walking through the valley of the shadow of death and lift them into the light of your presence. Amen.

I have spent eight years of my life in Russia, so I have a strong reaction to the phrase "it was winter" in this passage. I immediately begin to feel cold! I think of snow (and more snow); frozen rivers; short, dark days; and being so wrapped up to go out that only my eyes are visible.

Winter is mentioned here to explain why Jesus is walking in Solomon's portico, a covered cloister of the Temple. He is enclosed first by the building and even more by the Jews who were "gathered around him." The time when he will be stripped and shiver with fear and then be swaddled tightly in the cloister of the tomb is getting closer.

I am reminded of the "winter of our discontent," referred to in the opening line of Shakespeare's play *Richard III*. There is political turmoil and rivalry for the throne and a strong feeling that things are about to change.

The questions put to Jesus reveal the impatience and growing anger of his interrogators. "How long will you keep us in suspense?" They are desperate to discover what lies beneath the layers of mystery that conceal who Jesus really is.

I was once told by a patient I was visiting in a psychiatric unit that I was too buttoned up. I was indeed wearing a dress that had a lot of buttons, but she was really commenting—quite accurately—that I was difficult to get to know. Boundaries are crucial in pastoral (and all) relationships, but that patient taught me an important lesson. I may get an icy reception if I always clothe myself in protective winter gear!

Jesus, your loving gaze enables us to see ourselves as beloved children of God. Whatever season our lives and our relationships are experiencing today, may our hearts be warmed and refreshed by your grace and your peace. Amen.

Which comes first for a Christian disciple: believing or belonging?

I believe that belonging is the starting point. Jesus calls his disciples to follow him long before he asks them about who they believe him to be.

In today's passage, Jesus tells those wanting to know who he is that "you do not believe, because you do not belong." They are not among his sheep. They are not part of his flock.

Becoming one of the flock involves three stages. First, the sheep "hear my voice." There is some kind of call. Then, "I know them." The sheep are known by Christ, even if they do not realize who Jesus is. Finally, "They follow me." This calling provokes a response and a desire to belong.

Are these three elements embedded in our church programs? Do our worship, our pastoral care, our discipling, our mission, our evangelism enable people to hear the voice of God, to realize that God knows them, and then to follow Jesus?

Jesus goes on to say, "I give them eternal life," and this sums up the message of the entire passage. Our belonging and believing are gifts from God. We hear God's voice before we respond. We are known before we know. We follow because we have been given a path and a Shepherd to guide us on our way.

We belong to Christ and to Christ's flock—the Christian community—locally and globally, on earth and in heaven.

Good Shepherd, may I be attentive to your voice today. May I be aware of what you know of me and alert to where you are leading me. Deepen my sense of belonging to you and to the people you have given me. Amen.

This is a heartwarming passage for a city girl! Heaven is multicultural and densely populated.

The palm branches—a symbol of victory and thanksgiving—remind us of the crowds who sang praises as Jesus rode into the city of Jerusalem at the beginning of Holy Week.

This passage also reminds me of the Taizé Community in France where the brothers (who wear white robes for worship) are joined by a great multitude of people to offer the songs and prayers in many different languages. Being in Taizé is always a heavenly experience for me!

Every Friday, evening prayer in Taizé takes place around the cross. A large icon of the cross is brought into the center of the church, then all the brothers turn toward the cross and fall on their faces before it. Afterward, the young people line up on their knees, sometimes for hours, to offer their own prostration and prayer at the cross.

The description of heavenly worship in Revelation gives a sense of a well-choreographed and planned liturgy, with everyone doing the same thing at the same time and reciting the same words. And yet, within that—as in Taizé—each individual's expression emanates from his or her own intimate relationship with God.

I believe that is what heaven will be like! We will be caught up and held within that great multitude of people from every tribe and tongue, and we will also feel a deep sense of personal communion with God. I treasure worship experiences I have had here on earth that have given me a glimpse of the heavenly city.

Sing your prayer today using a Taizé chant, a hymn, or a song that enables you both to feel part of a worshiping community and to express your own relationship with God. You might also try praying in a different posture—standing, sitting, kneeling, prostrating, or dancing!

The final part of this passage echoes Psalm 23. There will be no more hunger or thirst or pain. The shepherd will provide shelter, protection, nourishment, refreshment, and comfort.

There is, however, a significant shift from the psalm. The Lamb is the Lord. A sheep has become the shepherd.

I once went to a seminar on models of leadership in the church that rejected the idea of pastors being shepherds because it drew too sharp a distinction between the leader and the flock. Real sheep can never become shepherds.

It is also true that every pastor was once a member of a flock and seeks to follow the example of Jesus, who is both sheep and shepherd. It can be a difficult balancing act for pastors to hold these two aspects of themselves in tension. I know that I haven't always gotten it right!

I don't want to be put on a pedestal, and I try to be honest and open about my own vulnerability and "sheepishness"! At the same time, I recognize that members of my flock look to me for leadership and need me to be strong. I can only do that because Jesus—the Lamb who shared our human hunger, thirst, and pain—is also the Shepherd who knows what we need and leads us from death to life.

I have learned to be attentive to my hunger, my thirst, and my tears because they reveal what is truly life-giving for me. This daily practice then helps me to guide others on their own pilgrimage to eternal life.

This awareness of my own need is also the reason that I stand "before the throne of God, and worship him day and night within his temple." Whatever language I use—Lord, Shepherd, Lamb, or something else—the beginning and the end of my day, my life, my ministry, and my prayer is God.

Eternal God, you are my beginning and my end. Amen.

A New Commandment

MAY 9–15, 2022 • WEN-LING LAI

SCRIPTURE OVERVIEW: Change can be difficult. It is easy to get comfortable with what is familiar. In Acts, some in Jerusalem criticize Peter for having fellowship with the Gentiles. Peter explains that his actions are not his own idea but are inspired by a vision from God. This change leads to the spread of the gospel. Revelation speaks of a new heaven and a new earth. God cares for the earth that God created, but at the end of time everything will be changed and made better. In John, Jesus gives his disciples a new commandment, namely that they should love one another as he has loved them. This is how others will know that they are truly Jesus' disciples. Psalm 148 is not about change but is pure praise for the works of the Lord.

QUESTIONS AND SUGGESTIONS FOR REFLECTION

- Read Acts 11:1-18. God calls Peter to initiate change. How do you respond to changes in your church's culture? How do you discern what changes are from God?
- Read Psalm 148. The next time you sing, focus on praising God and sharing God's love through your words and melody.
- Read Revelation 21:1-6. How do you live a full life while waiting for the new heaven and new earth?
- Read John 13:31-35. In the wake of betrayal, Jesus calls his followers to sacrificial love. When have you needed to heed the call to this type of love?

Ordained minister serving the world as her parish, grateful to have found her theological home with the Alliance of Baptists in her pursuit of God's justice and partnership in mission; a sincere helper, a chaplain, a wife to Pastor Dave, and the mama to Anna and Geoffrey.

Psalm 148 is a thorough source of guidance for anyone who ever wonders why, when, where, or how to praise God. Whether down in the pit or up in heaven, everyone is to join all creation in celebrating the One who created all.

The psalmist describes how praises manifest in diverse forms. Through their mere presence to all, the sun, moon, shining stars, highest heavens, and waters above the heavens praise! In their established roles in the universe, sea monsters, fire, hail, snow, frost, stormy wind, mountains, hills, fruit trees, and cedars all praise! Regardless of human status, age, or gender, ALL are to praise God.

Although we all are created and commanded to exalt the Lord with our lives, voices, and actions, we have times when we struggle to bless and accept blessing. What then are we to do? The last verse in our reading suggests that we should listen for the sound of the horn that the Lord has raised. God is calling the beloved to recognize and then do something about our own lackluster connections with the Divine! God is calling us to release what is meaningless or dead and to make room in our lives for what is eternal and alive.

What, then, is eternal and alive? Love! In the end, we praise God not because God needs to receive praise but because we need to give it in response to God's love for us. We need to love because God-like love for God's people brings us closest to the abundant living God desires for us.

So then, if our praise of God is our recognition of God's sovereignty, then our praise is really thankfulness for God's eternal faithfulness and love. Praising God is loving God; loving God is obeying God's command to love all God's creation.

God of abundant mercy and patience, help us to praise you with both our words and our actions. Amen.

Who would not want God to wipe every tear from their eyes and remove causes for mourning, crying, and grieving— even death—from their life?

The visions that the narrator describes include the previous heaven and earth that have "passed away" before the new can be experienced and received. In the new dwelling place, God does not just visit but lives with human beings. As Eugene Peterson writes in *The Message,* "Look! God has moved into the neighborhood." God no longer merely watches or intermittently engages but participates in all aspects of human lives. I imagine that people who cohabit the world with the Divine will then face death and losses of all kinds so differently that we will not mourn, cry, and suffer pain as we do now. Perhaps the seer of these marvelous visions is trying to help us imagine how we can experience such new blessings here and now, as long as we are willing to make room for God. We do not need to wait any longer if we are willing to see how all things and people can be made new.

In addition to imagining, it is essential to trust in the Alpha and Omega for power and provision. While readers receive no details about how the Almighty will eliminate human suffering, we hear that we will receive a taste of satisfaction like the thirsty receiving water from the spring of life. When Yahweh says, "It is done," we can trust that all things are made new, most especially our lives. The challenge to us all is to be ready and willing to trust and accept with confidence the new and great blessings God offers us.

Dear God, creator of all that is past, our present, and our future, give us the courage to let go of what is familiar but draining so we can see and harvest the fruits of your new heaven and earth. Amen.

A re you kidding us, Peter?" The circumcised early Christians criticized Peter and demanded he explain why he dared to eat with "those Gentiles," who might have accepted the word of God but were not yet circumcised. Peter answered by describing in great detail his experiences that led to his otherwise unthinkable actions.

First, Peter saw a vision while praying that spoke to his heart about reframing and reconsidering what is clean and acceptable to eat. The repetitive frequency of three times (v. 10) indicated the possibility of God's determination and persistence in making sure that Peter heard and changed his thinking and behavior. Soon after the teachable moment in Peter's dreams, the Spirit gives Peter an opportunity to practice what he has just learned. No doubt he struggled with whom to believe—his "Christian" friends who spoke of "those Gentiles," or God, who had told him not to consider anything or anyone unclean whom God had called clean (see v. 9). Then, when he and his friends arrive at the home of Cornelius, a captain in the Roman army, they learn that Cornelius had been told by an angel to send for Peter, who would bring a message that would bring salvation to Cornelius and his entire household.

As I write these devotional thoughts during the COVID-19 pandemic, I am astounded at the possibility of inviting perfect strangers into my home for a message that could save my family! The blessed assurance and comfort to us all is that in times of great trials God still and always sends the good news through messengers of love and grace. Perhaps the words from Acts 11:9 concerning clean or unclean people are what we most need to hear in this day of judgmental and divisive rhetoric.

O God, you have cared and mourned with us throughout the COVID-19 pandemic. We thank you for your faithfulness to us and for your steadfast participation in our lives. Your love keeps us strong. Amen.

The period between Easter and Pentecost is referred to by some Christians as the Great Fifty Days. It is often a time for followers of Jesus to contemplate and practice how they might live to glorify God as Easter people in a community.

In four brief scripture verses, Jesus encrypted some hard to decipher messages about the glory of God with one new, yet simple and straightforward, commandment: "Love one another." Jesus leaves specific instructions with the disciples and directs them to focus on who he is as the Son of Man and what they are to do when Jesus is no longer physically present with them. Most of them might now finally understand what Jesus is giving them as the seeds they would need to grow and blossom into true Christ followers. Some of them might not have given full weight to Jesus' words until they experienced Judas's kiss, Peter's denials, and their own fear as they returned to the upper room after Jesus' sacrificial act of love for them on the cross.

So, how much weight do we give to these last words of Jesus? It's powerful to see how God ushered into history the command Jesus gave in this passage from John. It began as far back as the book of Leviticus. There, God gave as part of the law these words: "You shall love your neighbor as yourself" (19:18). Then, Jesus quoted those words as part of the Great Commandment: a combination of the *Shema* from Deuteronomy (to love God) and the command to love neighbor (see Mark 12:29-31). Finally, though, here in John's Gospel, Jesus gives added emphasis and clarity to the commandment: "I give you a new commandment, love one another . . . just as I have loved you." We are to love others the way Jesus did, the way he would, the way he will—if we are able to live out truly what he commands. After all, loving as Jesus loved is the true praise of God and the only way "everyone will know you are [Jesus'] disciples."

Loving and patient Guide, teach us to love as Jesus loves. In his name. Amen.

A New Commandment

The Bible is not a novel or a mystery story that is ruined by reading the ending first. Nearly everyone now knows the story of Jesus before they read the Bible, but even the earliest Christians proclaimed "Jesus is risen" before they passed out a Bible. Even if someone does happen upon a Bible with no prior knowledge, Matthew's ending gives away the surprise at the end of Mark. Knowing the ending is the reason we return to the Bible every day.

Today's reading from the very end of the Bible is foundational for our understanding of everything that comes before. We know the new heaven and new earth are coming, and the chaos and turmoil of the sea will go away. We live today with the unjust systems and human betrayal described in the Gospel of John, but the ending we see in Revelation undergirds Jesus' new commandment to love everyone (see John 13:34). When the Gentiles begin to accept the word of God (see Acts 11:1), we know because of Revelation that this is an early, small sign of the coming new earth.

God knows that our ways of seeing, seeking, and praising the Almighty are limited. Therefore, God patiently reaches out over and over again with the good news, telling the story forward and backward. Using all that we have received to praise God and share God's love fulfills not only the command to love others but also brings about glimpses of the new heaven and new earth.

Maker and re-maker of our world, help us embrace the opportunities you give us each day to bring about the new heaven and earth with our love. Amen.

Have you ever read a Choose Your Own Adventure book? As the name suggests, you make decisions along the way that determine how the story ends. Sometimes it is clear what the effect of a decision will be, but the implications of a choice are usually hidden and are sometimes comically unpredictable.

As you read today's scriptures—in any order you choose— consider each verse by itself and then in conjunction with the others. A natural order begins and ends the readings from John, Acts, and Revelation with the very last verse of Psalm 148: "Praise the Lord!"

No matter how the news seems—good, bad, or strange—we can praise God, knowing there are grace and blessings embedded in what we have just learned. We might wonder how and why God "has given even to the Gentiles the repentance that leads to life," especially if we replace "Gentiles" with "people not like us." We might struggle to love one another so we can be known as the disciples of Jesus. And we might wonder how long it will be until those who are dying without clean water or are thirsting to know the love of God will be given water from the spring of life. But we do know the choice to make.

The first and last thing is to praise God. Whatever path we find ourselves on, we are to praise God with our worship and our actions. We praise God by following Jesus' new commandment to love all people. We praise God when we show love for others by providing food and water—literal and metaphorical— to people who are hungry and thirsty for the love of God.

Lover of all, thank you for creating us to sing praises to you for all that we see and in all that we do. Amen.

Right before Jesus' farewell discourse to prepare the disciples for his death and departure from the community (John 14:1–17:26), Jesus gives them a deceptively simple commandment: "Love one another." He doesn't stop there; his additional instruction about *how* to love one another—"just as I have loved you"—suggests that there is more to this loving than might first appear. Jesus essentially wraps the essence of who God is and why humans are created into this "new" commandment, "Love one another."

By this point the disciples—and the readers of the Gospel of John—have learned from Jesus by watching him love, teach, heal, and interact with people. The disciples know how Jesus has loved and cared for them, but can they now love like Jesus? Would they wash one another's feet as Jesus has? Would they break and serve bread while sharing the cup in remembrance of him as Jesus has? Would they calm one another's fears as Jesus did on the sea to Capernaum? Would they die for one another?

Jesus has modeled how and whom to love; now he explicitly asks his followers to love "just as I have loved you." To love like Jesus means to be present and empathic to people in times of need, as Jesus was for Mary and Martha after the death of Lazarus. To love like Jesus is to feed the multitudes by working for the equitable distribution of food. To love like Jesus is to heal by ensuring that everyone has access to medical and psychiatric care. To love like Jesus is to offer mercy to the penitent thief by reforming our unjust justice systems. And to love like Jesus is to receive as siblings in Christ all seekers of the good news. By these works of compassion everyone will know we are his disciples.

Lord Jesus, Son of God, have mercy on us as we strive to love one another as you have loved us. Amen.

Transformative Blessings

MAY 16–22, 2022 • ROSE SCHROTT

SCRIPTURE OVERVIEW: As we near the end of our Easter celebration, we begin to wonder: *What do we do when the party is over?* God meets us in this place of uncertainty by offering transformative blessings through this week's readings—a word that grounds us in our God-given identity while calling us to a greater purpose in the world. This divine mystery asks us to hold in tension the grace of God, who gives us gifts we do not earn, and the call of God toward action. Psalm 67 bestows on us the blessing and call of God's radiance. John reminds us of the blessing of peace and the call of integrity. The conversion of Lydia in Acts invites us to create space for mysterious interplay between the divine and human action. Revelation reminds us of the blessing of life and reconciliation. Holding all these things is made possible through the Holy Spirit, who plays a prominent role in many of the readings this week.

QUESTIONS AND SUGGESTIONS FOR REFLECTION

- Read Psalm 67. How do I radiate the blessing of God? How do I share this light and experience the brilliance of others?
- Read John 14:23-29. Think of a time when you were able to hold peace and pain together. How did you recognize the Spirit's presence with you?
- Read Acts 16:9-15. What does it mean to you to be sent by the Holy Spirit?
- Read Revelation 22:1-5. How do you experience the blessing of living water? Who do you believe is beyond saving? How do you think of them in light of the blessing of reconciliation promised in Revelation 21 and 22?

May 2021 graduate of Pittsburgh Theological Seminary with a master of divinity degree; a native of Pittsburgh, she is interested in the intersection of writing, spiritual formation, and public theology.

One of my earliest memories from the church is the pastor standing in front of the congregation in his black preaching robe, billowing sleeves swaying beneath his extended arms, reciting the benediction from Numbers 6:24-26: "The LORD bless you and keep you" (Num. 6:24). To this day, these words bring me comfort whether I find them in Numbers or reinterpreted in Psalm 67.

The passage in Numbers marks Israel as God's chosen people, and Psalm 67 edits the language to argue that Israel's purpose extends beyond election. Building upon the Abrahamic covenant (see Genesis 12:1-3), the psalmist invites Israel to see that they have been blessed in order to share God with the nations.

The God who blesses Israel is the source of all order and meaning, judging and guiding the people of earth. This divine, righteous order was central to the Mesopotamian worldview. It was one of the reasons that many regarded the sun-god Šamaš as the guardian of life. The psalmist claims this role for Yahweh, who shines God's divine face upon the beloved.

It is this God of divine order, of the sun, that blesses Israel. And to be blessed by Yahweh is to be made holy. So, when we know God, we too glow—perhaps not literally but in truth. And the radiance that comes with God's blessing cannot be contained or controlled. Like a lamp at night, we begin to stand out in a way that others notice. And, as Psalm 67 tells us, no one lies beyond the invitation of this light—not even the "nations" or those who are perceived as idolatrous, dangerous, and perverted.

God whose brightness eclipses the sun, help me to see all the ways that you bless me and make me holy. Open my heart to see the radiance of others and share your goodness with them. Amen.

As someone intimately familiar with anxiety, I always feel a bit defensive when it comes to Bible passages like John 14. They remind me of how scripture has been weaponized to shame those with mental health issues. Jesus' peace also seems so impractical. After all, fear is a response that allows us to survive.

My qualms are soothed by turning to the language of first-century Israel-Palestine. While the word *peace* in English typically communicates some kind of absence—of violence, of noise, of confusion—its counterpart in Hebrew, *shalom*, connotes total and complete well-being bestowed by God. Similarly, the word for peace in New Testament Greek, *eirene*, goes beyond absence to communicate harmonious relationships with God and others.

The peace Jesus offers, therefore, is not blissful ignorance. It does not minimize our emotions. Rather, it creates a safe space, a home where we are never alone because the "Advocate, the Holy Spirit," is with us. In Greek, the Holy Spirit literally is the "one who comes alongside." Jesus' peace is the comfort of sitting in silence with a friend. It is the security of knowing that when you are too sick to get out of bed, there is someone else in the house. It is the reassurance found in holding your mother's hand while you are in labor: someone else has felt a similar pain and survived; you are not alone.

Jesus' peace offers a secure identity where we know ourselves as the beloved children of God. Through the Holy Spirit, this peace blesses us with the perspective of knowing that we are never alone. When we hurt or fear, we can hold on to this peace without dismissing our emotions and know that God is still good.

> *God of peace, thank you for sitting with us. Help us to be aware of your presence in our lives. In all situations, grant us the blessing of perspective, knowing that we are never alone. Amen.*

While John 14 graces us with a blessing of peace, it also holds us accountable. Before Jesus speaks of peace, before he promises the Spirit, he reminds his followers that truly knowing and loving God cannot be separated from actions: "Those who love me will keep my word."

So, as we near the end of our Easter celebration, we see a glimpse of the answer to our question, "What's next?" It is not an easy answer, but it is an answer nonetheless: We, the church, are to be the incarnational presence of God in the world. We are to love God and love one another—not just with our words but with our actions.

This is not easy work. There are constant temptations and setbacks. But it is inescapably our work. As Jesus teaches us in John 14, this means that our words and actions must be in sync. We cannot believe in the love of God and act out hate, even of the smallest kind. We cannot believe in God's grace and withhold grace from others. We cannot believe Jesus came for everyone but exclude a person or group.

Love means love. And love cannot be compartmentalized. To love God is to love others. To love others is to love God (see John 13:34-35).

Thankfully, we are not left alone under the weight of this call to integrity. We have the Holy Spirit to teach us and encourage us. As Jesus reminds us, when we proclaim our love for God in harmonious word and deed, the Trinity abides in us in the person of the Holy Spirit. And perhaps, with the Spirit's help and God's grace for our failures, we can hold together the gift of God's grace with the call to act it out.

God of love, we give you our attempts and failures at living lives full of integrity. Transform us, abide in us, that we may be your loving presence. Amen.

We jump into the Acts narrative shortly after the Council of Jerusalem where, guided by the Holy Spirit, the early church agrees to include Gentiles in its community of Jewish Christians without requiring them to keep Jewish law. As a result of this decision, Paul and Silas set out to strengthen established churches by sharing this radical decision.

Throughout this journey, readers see the mysterious interplay between the Holy Spirit and human initiative. For instance, right before today's reading, Paul and company are "forbidden" by the Holy Spirit to reach their desired destination of Asia (see Acts 16:6). Then a vision tells Paul to go to Macedonia. Paul's company responds by crossing the Aegean Sea and making the strategic decision to walk nine miles inland to Philippi, an important city situated along the Via Egnatia thoroughfare.

Once there, Paul and his group of missionaries make another strategic decision to seek out Jewish practitioners on the Sabbath, which leads them to a group of women worshiping by the river outside of town. Paul speaks to Lydia, and Lydia decides to go to worship and listen to Paul. But it is ultimately the Holy Spirit who opens Lydia's heart and inspires her to accept the gospel.

The question of why the Holy Spirit opens some hearts but not others is not answered. What we do learn is that we exist in a mysterious interplay of divine intervention and human decision, the spiritual and the material, call and response, strategy and trust. While we have a role to play, we learn that it is ultimately the Holy Spirit—who is surely in us all before we ever know it—who prompts, stirs, calls, and blesses us.

Holy Spirit, help us to be like Lydia today and pay attention to the ways we are prompted, called, and blessed. Through this blessing, may we bless others. Amen.

It appears that Lydia was an immigrant and former slave. To begin with, she shared her name with a region of Asia Minor known for her occupation: the production of purple fabric. Whether named for her homeland or known as a woman of Lydia, it seems Philippi was not Lydia's home. Second, animal urine was used in the dyeing of purple cloth to give the color greater shine and endurance. Therefore, it was seen as dirty work limited to slaves and former slaves. The Hellenistic world would have looked down on Lydia for her occupation, citizenship status, and gender. Additionally, her religion as a proselyte to the monotheistic Jewish faith would have served as a negative marker in the religiously pluralistic world of the Roman Empire.

Yet despite the social realities of Lydia's world, God chooses her and opens her heart to begin the congregation at Philippi. The status markers of society do not matter. She is freed to be her truest self: the beloved of God.

Once baptized, Lydia demonstrates her faith immediately by putting the gospel into action and offering shelter to Paul and companions, who were facing the hostility directed toward Jews in Roman colonies like Philippi. Lydia offers Paul and the group protection in her house and bases her argument for them to stay on the maxim of being true to Christ.

Lydia teaches us, therefore, that our God is the God who liberates—giving the freedom of true life to those restricted by the principalities and powers of the world. And accepting this freedom translates into acting in solidarity with others. Just as we read in John 14 and Psalm 67, love and action come together. God blesses us with a freedom that we cannot keep to ourselves.

Liberating God, help us to embrace your blessing of freedom. May we be transformed by this gift and empowered to act in solidarity with others. Amen.

Transformative Blessings

Water is essential to embodied life: Not only are human beings 60 percent water, but we last only three days without drinking it. For those who lived in the semi-arid world of the Mediterranean basin, the reliable water of rivers was a valuable resource.

This passage tells us that the water flowing from the divine throne of God the Father and Jesus the Lamb is remarkably pure and "bright as crystal." Further, it is found splashing up and out of the center of the street—available to all, unlike clean water in the Roman Empire and in many places today.

Water language describes God's presence throughout the Bible. For instance, Ezekiel 47:1-12, Joel 3:18, and Zechariah 14:8 all depict water flowing from the future Zion—that perfect kingdom in which God dwells with God's people. Jesus describes himself as the water of life throughout the Gospel of John (see John 7:37 and 4:14). And the Holy Spirit is poured out and fills people like water.

But there is perhaps a deeper meaning to the symbolic biblical language of water. To know God is to be connected to the source of all life. By God's grace, we get to drink the living water—in eternity, yes, but also here and now. We get to taste what it means to be alive. We get to bathe in divine waters and know that God, like water, sustains us, cleanses us, and comprises our very being.

As we are reminded in the sacrament of baptism or even by a hot shower, cool glass of water, or a walk by the sea, the physical and the spiritual are not separate. God gives us the blessing of life through the living water. And we are constantly reminded of this grace if we have eyes and hearts to see.

God of living water, thank you for sustaining us. Amen.

Scholars call the book of Revelation a work of apocalyptic literature. It is not the genre of zombie wastelands but—from the Greek—the genre of "uncovering." Revelation works to reveal the truth about the Roman Empire for an audience in Asia Minor. What everything ultimately comes down to, the author explains with symbolic language, is a choice between empire and God. You cannot serve both. And there are real, dire consequences for supporting an empire that encourages hierarchy, violence, and corruption.

However, today's passage suggests that God's love might just be enough in the end. While other biblical texts written in different contexts foretell the demise of the nations (see Isaiah 17:13-14; Jeremiah 25:3-32; Joel 3:2, 10-19), Revelation 21 and 22 promise healing and reconciliation. Ultimately God's grace overwhelms not just death but the sin that causes it. Perhaps we all have a place in God's "book of life."

Whereas Psalm 67 prays for God's radiance in order for Israel to minister to the nations, everyone in the New Jerusalem gets to see the face of Yahweh and bask in its light. However, as our other passages this week have shown, this promise of ultimate unity and fulfillment should not make us complacent. We have work to do.

In life after Easter we must somehow hold together the muddled mass of grace-filled blessings and calls for action. And so we wait and work and learn from the Spirit as we hold on to this tension. All the while we bask in the light of God's presence with Yahweh's love written on our foreheads like name tags, the brilliance of God's blessing radiating from us for all to see.

Revealing God, reconciliation is possible in you. Help us to hold on to this hope and to put it into action with your Holy Spirit's presence and power. Amen.

Jesus and Life Together

MAY 23–29, 2022 • TOM ARTHUR

SCRIPTURE OVERVIEW: How did you first hear about the gospel? Was it from your family or a friend? Or was it from a completely unexpected source? This week's readings remind us that God uses many different techniques of revelation. Paul and Silas are in prison in Philippi, and the guard of the prison has no idea that he is about to encounter the power of God and come to faith. The psalmist says that creation itself reveals God's glory and power. In Revelation, Jesus speaks directly about his future return and reign, as attested by his messenger and by the Spirit. Jesus prays in John for his followers, because through their unity the gospel will be proclaimed to others. Although Jesus ascends to heaven, the revelation of his plan and purpose does not end.

QUESTIONS AND SUGGESTIONS FOR REFLECTION

• Read Acts 16:16-34. Recall a difficult time in your life. Were you able to continue to praise God through this time?

• Read Psalm 97. Write your own word picture of what it means to be a child of God, who is in control.

• Read Revelation 22:12-14, 16-17, 20-21. How has Jesus' invitation to partake of the water of life changed you?

• Read John 17:20-26. What signs of division do you see in your community? How can you work toward the oneness to which God calls us?

Pastor of Sycamore Creek United Methodist Church, a multi-site congregation in the Lansing, MI, region; leads the Reach Movement team for the Michigan Conference helping churches grow and multiply; he and his wife, Sarah, have two children, Micah and Sam.

In our story today, Paul and Silas encounter an enslaved girl who has a "spirit of divination" that is making her owners a lot of money. The spirit in her would cry out that Paul and Silas were "slaves of the Most High God." They get so annoyed with being constantly shouted at—even though it's true—that Paul commands the spirit to come out of her.

She is now free from her spiritual slavery. With this freedom go her divination skills, and her owners are not happy. They're no longer making money from her, and they lodge a complaint against Paul and Silas: "These men are disturbing our city . . ." This is code language for "we're losing money because they're setting our slave free." It turns out that salvation disturbs unjust economic systems.

In the same way that these slave owners made money from their enslaved girl, the United States built its wealth with the labor of enslaved Africans. The economic impact is still felt today in the Black community. Christian sociologists Michael Emerson and Christian Smith, in their book *Divided by Faith,* state that the median net worth of Blacks is just 8 percent that of whites.

How can salvation disturb this unjust economic system? One answer became clear to me when I inherited money after my parents died. My wife and I decided to prioritize three things with this money. We tithed to our church, used half of what was left to set up college savings accounts for our boys, and gave the other half to create seminary scholarships for future Black pastors. Following Jesus meant for us that when we inherited wealth, we were given an opportunity to disrupt unjust economic systems around intergenerational wealth. Did this one act solve every problem? Absolutely not! But it was one way we could help undo centuries of economic enslavement.

How can your financial decisions this week help build a more just economic world?

Yesterday we read about how salvation disturbs unjust economic systems. Today the story continues, and we learn that salvation also disrupts unjust power dynamics.

Paul and Silas are thrown in jail. The jailer is charged with making sure they stay there. At midnight during a prayer and praise service, an earthquake breaks the locks of the jail. The jailer sees the jail cells open and assumes the prisoners have escaped. He takes responsibility for their escape and attempts to kill himself. Having failed to fulfill the responsibility given him by his authorities, he knows that same authority will require him to pay with his life.

What he doesn't anticipate is that Paul and Silas have not used their freedom to escape from prison. They recognize that they have a higher calling than just getting out of jail; theirs is a spiritual calling for the salvation of souls. So they let the jailer know they are still there.

The jailer is flabbergasted. He knows how these things work. Prisoners don't voluntarily stay in jail. He demands to know why they haven't left. Once they tell him about Jesus, he is so moved that he wants to exchange his current authority, which requires him to take his life, for the authority of Jesus, which requires him to lay down his life for the freedom of others.

The jailer asks Paul and Silas how he can be saved in this way. They tell him to "believe on the Lord Jesus, and you will be saved, you and your household." This means trusting that Jesus' counter-cultural way of life really is Life. It means trusting that Jesus' rescue mission in the world is worth giving your life to. It means using your freedom to serve others so they can know the love of God in Jesus Christ.

Where can you use your freedom this week for the salvation of souls?

I grew up in a conservative evangelical church in the holiness tradition, and I have a deep appreciation for this tradition's emphasis on personal holiness and evangelism. The key questions were the following: Where are the impurities in my life? What are the idols I pursue more than I pursue God? How can my life be a witness to the love of Jesus for everyone?

I became more familiar with justice traditions in college and found myself thinking about how systems and structures in our society privilege certain groups, either intentionally or unintentionally. And I started to consider how my individual choices were playing into these systems and structures. This is sometimes called the social gospel or social holiness.

For some reason these two emphases are often set against each other. One side of the Christian tradition looks with skepticism at the other. But I've never liked that split. I don't want Jesus without justice. I don't want justice without Jesus. I want Jesus and justice!

When I read John Wesley's forty-four standard sermons in seminary, I found a spiritual home in Methodism. Wesley emphasized both personal holiness and social holiness. Jesus and justice! He took sin seriously and understood that it comes in two forms: personal sin and corporate sin. We need the personal gospel to root out personal sin and the social gospel to root out corporate sin.

We see this same pairing together in today's psalm. Verse two says that righteousness (personal holiness) and justice (corporate holiness) are the foundation of God's throne. The foundation! You can't build anything in the kingdom of God without taking into account both righteousness and justice. They are foundational. If we are missing either one, we've got a lopsided spirituality. We need both to have perfect Christian love.

Do you tend to focus on personal holiness or social holiness, Jesus or justice? How can you seek both this week?

ASCENSION DAY

Today we celebrate Jesus' passing the baton of his mission to his disciples, the church. It's a period of transition that reminds me of the first week of July in the United Methodist Church, the week many appointed pastors begin work in a new church. The baton is passed from one leader to the next.

Jesus gives his disciples directions that have always seemed contradictory to me. He tells them that the gospel is to be proclaimed to all nations, but then he tells them to stay in Jerusalem. Jesus is giving them a Great Commission but telling them to hold still.

Why does Jesus give this seemingly contradictory guidance? The reason becomes clear. The disciples are to wait for the power of the Holy Spirit before heading out on the mission. They are to pause in prayer to make sure they've got what they need from God before they attempt to accomplish the mission God has put before them. They need to fill their tanks with the power of God before they head out on the long journey.

I make the mistake all the time of trusting in my own power to accomplish the mission God has given me. I don't pause long enough to make sure I'm pointed in the right direction. I don't pause long enough to take stock of my own motivations. I don't pause long enough to gather companions for the mission. My impatience pushes me to go. RIGHT NOW!

Where are you tempted this week to act before taking the time to seek the power of God? What do you need to do to seek God's power for God's mission this week?

Let's stay with the story of the Ascension one more day. Why? Because Luke does. He ends the Gospel of Luke with the story of the Ascension, and then tells the story again at the beginning of Acts. Why does he tell and then retell this moment in the life of Jesus and his followers?

I think Luke decides to tell the story of the Ascension twice because it's an absolutely crucial moment, a leadership transition moment. Here we find the passing of the church plant off to the second pastor.

I know something of moments like this because I'm a second pastor. I followed the founding pastor of Sycamore Creek. The church went from having a grandma as their pastor to having a thirty-three-year-old who didn't even have any kids as their pastor. That's a whiplash moment for any church, even a strong one.

These moments are important because being off by even a small amount can lead to really challenging events over time. If a rocket heading to the moon is off course by one degree, then it will miss it by over four thousand miles. Transitions and new beginnings are that important!

There are at least two things that are essential to get right at this moment in Luke's story: the mission and power of the church. First, the followers of Jesus have to decide whether they will focus on themselves and "restore the kingdom to Israel" or whether they will be a community focused outward to the world around them. Second, they must be empowered to accomplish their mission by the Holy Spirit.

During moments of transition, be sure to get those two things right. Otherwise you might be off by more than four thousand miles!

Where do you have a transition this week that could result in your focusing on yourself? Ask for the power of the Holy Spirit to stay focused outward.

When we think of heaven, we usually think of some place in the sky. But in John's vision, heaven is a new city. I love this image. We can easily imagine a new set of city gates leading to a downtown that supports all the city's residents to the glory of God. Let's take a stroll through that city and see what we find.

First, the tree of life is present in this city. The last time we saw it was in Genesis when Adam and Eve were banned from ever tasting its fruit. But in this new city the damage that was done by humanity's first parents—and then replicated by all of us over and over—is healed. We are able to live in the presence of God and one another for eternity. This is because our metaphorical robes have been washed by the gift of grace in Jesus' life, death, and resurrection.

Jesus sends an angel to declare that he is the rightful ruler descended from king David, but even more than that he is the "bright Morning Star." His presence declares a new day. He is a light that guides our every moment in this new city.

All who wish to drink the water of life and receive it as a free gift are invited to come into this city. The thirsty will thirst no more. Perhaps this is more than just a physical thirst. Perhaps it is also a thirst for love and mercy and justice. All of these things we now only experience in part. In this city we will experience them in full.

The author of Revelation ends the book with a prayer we all can pray: **Come, Jesus, and be our Lord. Do not tarry any longer. Let us no longer sit in the shadow of harm and injustice and the lack of love that we experience in the cities and towns and countrysides where we live today. Come, Jesus, and remake our life together according to your will. Amen.**

How can you begin to help build this kind of city, this kind of life together?

Our church has been involved in a movement of anti-racist churches in Lansing, Michigan. As the COVID-19 pandemic was beginning, and following the deaths of Ahmaud Arbery, Breonna Taylor, and George Floyd, a Black gospel singer in the area reached out to us to help organize a "Prayerdemic." The Prayerdemic included an open letter from Christian leaders in the region taking a stance against racialized violence.

The letter was carefully written to garner support across a broad theological spectrum of Christian traditions. Mainline denominational progressives signed the letter as well as evangelical conservatives. White, Black, and brown Christian leaders signed it. I'm not sure I've ever seen a local document signed by so many diverse Christian leaders.

Despite this overwhelming consensus, I received one email from a local pastor who told me that while he agreed with 99 percent of the letter, he couldn't sign it because he disagreed with one sentence. How much do you have to agree with a fellow follower of Jesus to partner together in mission?

My list of required agreements has gotten very small: Jesus and love. I'm not saying certain disagreements aren't important, but I can overlook a lot if we agree on Jesus and love. I've taken my cue for this shrinking list from Jesus himself.

In our reading today, Jesus prays that we would be unified in our love for one another as Jesus is unified with the Father and the Spirit in love. He prays that the world would know the unique nature of who he is by the unity of love that his followers have for one another. That seems like a big challenge some days. Thankfully, Jesus is praying for us to accomplish it!

Where do you need to overlook a disagreement with another follower of Jesus for the sake of shared mission?

The Gift of the Spirit

MAY 30–JUNE 5, 2022 • ELAINE EBERHART

SCRIPTURE OVERVIEW: In preparing for Pentecost, we focus again on the work of the Holy Spirit. Acts 2 recounts the famous story in which the disciples are miraculously able to speak in other languages in order to preach to the crowds in Jerusalem. The psalmist states that God creates and renews creation through the Spirit. According to Paul, if we are led by God's Spirit, the Spirit confirms that we are children of God. In the Gospel of John, Jesus promises to send the Helper, the Holy Spirit, who will teach us how to love him and to keep his commandments. In some branches of Christianity, fear of excess causes hesitation about the Holy Spirit; however, we must never forget that the Spirit is central to God's redeeming work.

QUESTIONS AND SUGGESTIONS FOR REFLECTION

• Read Acts 2:1-21. The miracle of Pentecost is not only in the multitude of languages but also in the act of listening. How can you experience worship in many languages or offer deep listening this Pentecost?

• Read Psalm 104:24-34, 35b. How do you witness God's experience woven through all of creation?

• Read Romans 8:14-17. The author reminds us that spirit also means breath. When have you felt led by the breath of God?

• Read John 14:8-17, 25-27. How has fear kept you from trusting God?

Vice chair for the Department of Development at Mayo Clinic in Rochester, MN; associate at Green Bough House of Prayer in Scott, GA.

Following John Lewis's death in 2020, commentators cited often his urging to get into "good trouble." Good trouble put him in harm's way often as he worked to end segregation and drive racial justice, and it guided him in making difficult decisions during his political service. As his life showed, the advancement of God's love and justice sometimes requires getting into good trouble.

As adopted children of God, we are led by the Spirit, an instigator of good trouble in the advancement of the gospel. Without the Spirit's urging, would we raise our hand at a meeting to question whether the church offers enough support for members living with dementia? Would we advocate for a shelter to be built in our church for persons experiencing homelessness? Would we put aside our trepidation to volunteer as the adult sponsor for the youth lock-in? Would we respond enthusiastically when asked to share our faith at a prison Christian fellowship meeting? Would we have the courage to sing hymns at the bedside of a friend as she dies?

We know, however, that there are a thousand reasons to resist the Spirit's urging to good trouble. We might hurt someone's feelings if we point out an injustice or suggest a way to improve our church's care for others. Following the Spirit's leadings may bring discomfort or compromise our safety, as it did for John Lewis. As for the youth lock-in, a host of reasons including the guaranteed loss of sleep may cause us to ignore the Spirit's urging. Even if we are stuck in hesitation and fear, however, the Spirit is calling to us to remember the good trouble we have witnessed in Jesus, and to follow.

God, I hear you calling me to good trouble. Guide me with wisdom and courage as I seek to follow you. Amen.

The Gift of the Spirit   185

Each of us faces fear, and rarely do we know long periods of time without suffering. These experiences are parts of the human condition that come as surely as the changing of seasons. But usually they affect us as individuals or small communities.

Sharing deep pain and uncertainty with almost everyone we know does not happen often, but an extended time of shared suffering began early in 2020 as the COVID-19 pandemic entered our world. The unfolding of the pandemic and its health and economic impacts were everywhere, on the news, and shared in the virtual conversations to which we transitioned for contact. There was no place to escape it, no refuge from worry about what would next emerge.

Does the knowledge that one is a child of God make a difference when we are struck with the sure knowledge that we are not in control? Does our birthright as God's own provide just a moment of calm when the newscaster reports an uptick of virus cases in our region? When we receive the late-night call informing us that our child has been picked up by the police, do we know that our desperate pleading for God's help is an affirmation that we are connected to the source of love through the Spirit? Does that connection soothe and sustain us when we hear a bad diagnosis at the doctor's office? Can we find meaning in whatever pain comes our way by remembering the betrayal and suffering of the Christ with whom we share an inheritance in God's reign?

Not only can we trust that God is with us in whatever suffering we face, but our status as God's adopted children promises that we will know God's glory amid our pain. Both are promised: the hardship we all will endure and the glory of being related to God through the Spirit, who assures that we are never alone.

Consider with gratitude when you have experienced God's presence in suffering.

After four years of living within shouting distance of the ocean, I moved back to the prairie in the upper Midwest. The great expanses of sea and grasslands bring distinct images to mind when reading and reflecting on this psalm.

I loved the feeling of waves breaking over my feet and watching the sun move in and out of clouds, creating new patterns of light on the water when I lived in Florida. Even if my head was full of thoughts of work, the magnitude of the sea and sky grounded me again in gratitude for the gift of creation.

And the prairie is no less extravagant in displaying God's glory. Snow-covered fields tinged with the blue from the reflection of the sky fill me with thankfulness for the ability to see such beauty. I am reminded by those same fields covered in corn in summer that what I most appreciate in nature is change. I am renewed along with the landscape as the tight bud opens to a flower and the leaf that was the brightest green in spring changes to brilliant red in a matter of months.

Recent scientific studies have recommended time in nature as good for mental and physical health, but watching the Spirit renew creation through the seasons is more than support for my well-being. It is a reminder that I am connected to creation through the One who orchestrated it and sustains it. It is the Spirit's call to recognize that others lack not only the beautiful vistas I take for granted, but safe water, clean air, and arable land—the essentials of life on this planet. It is our obligation to safeguard this gift for our children and their children so that they may behold God's glory in creation and praise its maker.

I am blessed to enjoy your creation, O God. Guide me as I partner with you in stewarding and protecting it. Amen.

Philip has walked with Jesus, heard the teachings, and witnessed lives transformed. He has been as close to God incarnate as anyone could hope to be, but he still needs a sign as Jesus prepares the disciples for life after his departure. "Show us the Father," Philip says. "And then we will understand. You will not need to do anything else. We will believe" (AP).

When I read this passage, I half expect the next verse to be, "Then Jesus rolled his eyes." Instead, Jesus again makes the case for his identity and his mission. "How can you demand to see the Father," Jesus asks, "when all that I have done has pointed you in the direction of the Father? I have shown you the Father. And if that does not work for you, Philip, believe simply because of the works I have done in my Father's name" (AP).

I like to think that I would have been the good disciple who paid attention and kept notes, the one who would have believed without requesting proof. Unfortunately, I know that is far from the truth; I would have merited many an eye roll. Though the Spirit has wooed me and testified to me about God's presence, I have demanded evidence even when I have witnessed the work of the Spirit right in front of me.

How often have I seen relationships restored when I was certain that there was no way through the division? I may have prayed, but did I dare to hope for healing, remembering that the Spirit always is seeking reconciliation? I simply would not believe in the Spirit of love's ability to penetrate a hardened heart and a closed mind, especially my own. But as Jesus' ministry among his disciples pointed toward his Father, the Spirit's movement toward restoration has always pointed to the undeniable existence of a loving God.

O God, I acknowledge my unbelief as I seek you today. Amen.

We often talk about our mission and values where I work. It is a hospital that was started by Franciscan sisters with a local doctor and his two sons. Because the mission and values are seen as inviolable even as innovation and change are constants, I know that when my supervisor leaves her position, her successor will be as committed to our mission and values as she was. The successor will advocate for us in our work and our lives outside of work. When we are discouraged, our new supervisor will remind us of our call to service, inspiring us to new commitment.

In his farewell instructions, Jesus announces a succession plan. His time with the disciples is limited, but the Spirit who will come after him will be with them forever. The Spirit will be their advocate and teacher and will cause them to remember Jesus' words and deeds so that they can set them as their touchstone. Enabled by the Spirit, the disciples will continue the work they have witnessed as they walked with Jesus. They will offer healing where there is brokenness. They will bring peace amid dissension. They will speak the truth that sets the prisoners free.

We have inherited our mission from the disciples, and the call they received from Jesus is the same one that comes to us through our baptismal vows when—through water and the Spirit—we are initiated into the priesthood of believers. Surrounded by our community of faith, we are charged with loving our neighbors as ourselves and with proclaiming the good news of God in Christ with our words and with our lives. As the cloud of witnesses between the disciples and our generation would attest, without the Spirit such a mission is unattainable. But with the Spirit, nothing is impossible.

I pray, O God, for a deepening commitment to your mission for my life. Amen.

Several years ago, I first learned about the Enneagram, a personality-typing tool that a friend described as helping her understand herself better. After reading about the Enneagram's nine personality types, I could not decide which fit me, so I registered for a class. In this class there were nine panels of persons with different personality types. The first panel was made up of persons who identified as Enneagram type one. Panel two was made up of type twos, and so on. The leader asked the people on these panels a common set of questions. Their answers revealed the characteristics of each type.

On the second day of the class, a panel took the stage to answer the questions. To a person, they answered the questions exactly as I would have done. I was so astounded by hearing my words come out of their mouths that I interrupted the leader to say that this was my Enneagram number, and these were my people.

I thought of that experience when trying to imagine how those gathered on the Day of Pentecost felt when they heard the message proclaimed in their native languages, whether they were home folks or visitors, those who were born into the faith or others who had been drawn to it as converts. The gift of hearing through Spirit-enabled translation must have been astonishing. How much more remarkable, however, was the message that announced a new age in which all hearers would be partners in God's mission of love and justice. Just as God's reign was proclaimed for the understanding of all, the call to participate was equally inclusive, issued without regard to status or age or gender. Even now, the Spirit speaks in a way that we can uniquely hear and understand, calling each of us to partner in the new thing God is doing in our world.

Thank you, God, for speaking to me in a way I can understand.
Amen.

PENTECOST

To those gathered in a room on the Day of Pentecost, Peter announces the inauguration of a new age, a transition marked by a mighty wind, by tongues of fire, and most important, by the gift of the Spirit. Peter promises that the Spirit will provide gifts of prophecy, dreams, and visions for all people. Though he does not describe the nature of the prophetic message, surely the Spirit will inspire dreams that align with the ministry of Jesus and visions that reflect the possibility of a world in which God's love pervades every human interaction.

Prophetic dreams and visions are not future gifts. They are gifts for here and now. Not a once-and-for-all event in the room in Jerusalem, the Spirit comes again to the community in every age, inspiring visions that propose how current realities can be transformed by God through us. They do not project some distant reality; dreams and visions are exercises in truth-telling. They name where relationships and institutions fall short of the example of Jesus, and they call us to new fidelity to the gospel of love.

With gratitude for their counsel, I witness prophetic truth-tellers frequently. I see on television a young woman barely in her teens who takes on heads of state as she describes the devastation of our planet and demands change. A colleague calls me from my place of privilege as he tells of his harrowing journey as a teenager from Somalia to Minnesota, and then names the needs of the immigrant community in our city. I read an article from the pastor of my church in which he reminds me that in spite of what is happening around us, we are at once waiting and working for a world transformed.

O Giver of dreams and visions, open my heart to the Spirit's leading so that I become emboldened to speak your truth in love to those who are in special need of it. Amen.

Resilience

JUNE 6–12, 2022 • PAMELA D. COUTURE

SCRIPTURE OVERVIEW: In our society we often privilege intellect and expertise. However, in Proverbs we read that God values wisdom. Wisdom has been present since the beginning, and some early theologians understand this Wisdom to be none other than the Son of God. Part of wisdom is understanding our place in the universe. The psalmist marvels at the vast display of God's power in the heavens yet also recognizes that humans are a manifestation of God's glory. The New Testament readings invoke the Trinity as we approach Trinity Sunday. Paul says that we have peace with God through Christ, and we are given the Holy Spirit. In John's Gospel, we read that Jesus Christ has received everything from the Father, and the Spirit will guide his followers into all truth.

QUESTIONS AND SUGGESTIONS FOR REFLECTION

- Read Proverbs 8:1-4, 22-31. When have you heard God calling out to you?
- Read Psalm 8. The author reminds us that our shortcomings are not because we are only human but because we fall short of our humanity. How do you strive to be more human—a little lower than God?
- Read Romans 5:1-5. How do you allow God's peace to calm you when you feel your life swirling around you?
- Read John 16:12-15. To which person of the Trinity do you feel "closest"? How can you develop your relationship with the other two persons?

Jane and Geoffrey Martin Chair in Church and Community, Emmanuel College; Executive Director, Toronto School of Theology, Toronto, Canada.

Meditating on these scriptures in November 2020, I try to imagine the world as it might be in the week of Trinity Sunday, June 2022. Eighteen months ago, I could not have imagined our world as it is today: holiday gatherings stilled by a global pandemic; a US president challenging the orderly transfer of power. More familiar catastrophes threaten joy and peace: violence from systemic racism, extreme weather events from climate change, and increasing polarities of wealth and poverty.

In February 2020 I received an email from Jane, a good student who had not submitted her assignment on time. "I am so distraught by what is happening in Wuhan that I haven't been able to study." This Chinese-Canadian Buddhist had a PhD in microbiology and had published articles on SARS. She was reading the Chinese websites and anticipated the devastation that COVID-19 could wreak around the world. After her initial distress, Jane gathered her resilience and presented the realities of what she was reading to the class. Her Buddhism strengthened her as she struggled with the pandemic. She brought warnings about the novel coronavirus that were emerging from the doctors in Toronto's emergency rooms.*

The Gospel of John spoke to sufferings that were too painful for the disciples to know in advance. For traumas we cannot anticipate, these words live for us too. Reading further in John, they are words of transformation, of restoration, of joy, of peace. John does not ignore the depths of our grief but promises words born of the Trinity—Creator, Redeemer, Sustainer—that meet us when we need them because the unimaginable happens.

*Jane's word of truth is published here. https://www.degruyter.com/view/journals/ijpt/24/1/article-p5.xml?language=en

We open ourselves to you, God, to hear the truth of the Spirit as you speak to the depths of our sorrows. Quietly we wait in the name of God who is Three in One. Amen.

How do we mourn our loved ones who have died? At an unexpected moment, we feel the gasp in our throat, we lower our face; tears erupt, then sobs. We hear—even mimic—the particular way they said our name, the special inflection in their voice that communicated connection, appreciation, hostility, demand. We ponder the shelves in the grocery store, looking for a particular brand . . . the overhead speakers bring a new song, and we walk to an unoccupied aisle, overcome with sadness we want no one to see. We pass a spot with a special fragrance; it takes us to a time when our loved one walked this spot with us. We see an object that our loved one used—one that is out of place for everyone else but is dear to us, and so it stays.

When we share the loss of loved ones with others, we tell stories. We relive endearing, awkward moments. Our mourning is touched with laughter and fond memories of some small craziness. We feel appreciation for the way our loved one gave meaning to our life. We regret things not said. We relive other close calls, times we took risks and felt the exhilaration of cheating death.

Like the paradox of particular pain that arises in ordinary moments or of grief that is touched with humor, we find the mystery of faith: Forgiveness and acceptance are bundled into justification, trust in the future rests in faith, and the promise of peace and hope endures in sharing God's glory. On these blessings, our deepest griefs are borne.

Holy God—Lover, Beloved, Love—share in our suffering, that we may share in your peace, hope, and glory. Let us mourn well as we live on. Amen.

Collective trauma occurs when a population as a whole is wounded. How can we respond to the long-term mental and spiritual effects of the tumult that the COVID-19 pandemic has brought? Children have not had adequate time for socialization; parents have been stressed into sleepless nights by constant work and family care; elders have been isolated from family and friends; church communities could not gather for worship, fellowship, or mission. How are we now experiencing the sustained effects of having to value the opposite of what we hold dear? Over the long haul, a community's capacity to function can be pushed to the limit. What if one questions whether one can endure suffering that seems to have no end? What if outward conditions change but the inward effects of what has been remain with us?

The sequence of effects in Romans 5:3-5 is often read as a spiritual demand, a moral ideal to be achieved. In difficult times, the promise that suffering will produce endurance, character, and hope may seem too much to bear.

Can we read this verse—originally written to early Christians—not as a demand but, rather, a comfort? Might we put away moralistic interpretations and read it anew as a nudge, a reminder, an opportunity to refocus, especially when the damaging effects of life seem too much to bear?

It is a reminder that when we pay attention to the evidences of God's love, we are reawakened to the truth that "hope does not disappoint us." Consider the small signs of God's love in creation: birds that migrate and reappear on our windowsill; spring animal babies born in the woods; the beauty of leaves in the fall. All these and more are reminders of life lived, hope sustained, and love renewed.

Notice one sign of God's love in your surroundings, and concentrate on that for a long moment. Give thanks for every sign of hope and love that appears to you.

Usually we think of wisdom as something that grows and develops as we age. As we accumulate experiences, we reflect on them, learn from them, and develop new understandings that we fold into what we know. We begin to look at circumstances from multiple perspectives. If we do this work, we become wise—or at least wiser—as we mature.

But the imagery in this passage suggests that human wisdom and divine Wisdom differ. Divine Wisdom originates before anything that is created. It is like the familiar verse of John 1:1, "In the beginning was the Word, and the Word was with God, and the Word was God." God's Word and God's Wisdom preexist water, earth, sky, and the form of the universe. God's Wisdom creates, gives birth, gives shape to otherwise amorphous elements. And in the end, the creation of humanity that can grow in wisdom is God's Wisdom's delight.

When an older, wiser person—parent, grandparent, aunt or uncle, teacher, mentor, spiritual guide, religious leader—truly enjoys us, when their eyes light as we come into their presence, when their voice warms with affection, we experience delight because we sense finite wisdom and glimpse Wisdom that is infinite.

Wisdom who brought us forth, make yourself known to us, that we too may grow in wisdom. As you delight in us, so may we delight in one another. Amen.

The campground near our Wisconsin cabin is deserted in the winter, but it begins to populate in mid-May. By Memorial Day weekend, people camp by the cool, tannin-colored water. They unfold their tables and chairs, light campfires, and launch canoes, kayaks, paddleboards, fishing boats, jet skis, and pontoon boats, filling the lake with activity. Children run from the beach into the water, splashing and laughing. On the nearby pier, they squeal in delight when they hook a small panfish.

Other seasonal migrants also appear. During the winter, a kiosk with empty hooks stands like a still sentinel at the access point to the lake. One day in early spring Lake Association volunteers fill it with free-to-use life jackets for boaters and swimmers to borrow and return. Through the kiosk, the local Lake Association communicates understanding, takes a stand, and cries to the campers this wisdom: "Flotation devices save lives." Throughout the summer, the kiosk interacts with the boaters: Some days it is filled with life jackets, some days it is sparse; occasionally it is empty.

In today's passage, Divine Wisdom is personified as a woman who stands at the city gate, actively seeking presence in our lives. She helps human wisdom mature. Divine Wisdom, like the life jacket kiosk, appears like grace. We do not earn grace; rather, Divine Wisdom and God's prevenient grace are present in our lives before we appear, even when we do not pay attention. God seeks us out; God invites us into relationship. Campers can ignore the life jackets, and we do not have to acknowledge Wisdom's presence. And yet, neither will go away. Rather, Wisdom calls to us, wanting to connect with us. Wisdom accompanies us. Wisdom is in our midst, calling us to herself.

Let us open ourselves to the ways Divine Wisdom is seeking a presence in our lives. In the name of the One who is Object, Vision, and Intention we pray. Amen.

Our children and grandchildren live in the four corners of the United States. In the summer of 2020, in a hedge against COVID-induced family separation, we bought a used red truck and our own pull-behind motel room with a queen bed, kitchen, bathroom, and shower. But when COVID-19 cases rose sharply, we canceled our plan to meet our family outside Yellowstone National Park. We opted instead for a three-day trip to an Ojibway-run campground on the shimmering waters of the lake the Ojibway call *Gichi-gami* (Lake Superior).

On our last evening, some new families had arrived. We sat in our old blue canvas folding chairs; as campfires lit the twilight, the lake turned its evening colors. At one picnic table, a group of teenagers played cards. In the center of the knoll, young girls turned cartwheels on gymnastic mats. Their mothers, some in hijabs, others bareheaded, watched and chatted. The beauty of their vacation soothed our souls.

We quip, "Out of the mouths of babes" when a child says something precocious. Yet the context implies that strength is derived from children when those around them are threatened. My colleague Judith Newman reminds me that Hebrew poetry is ambiguous. Quoting Robert Alter, she says the most innocent and vulnerable of children provide "a source of strength" against the "inhuman forces of chaos," no doubt bringing a smile to the face of God! Certainly, these children, teenagers, and their parents witnessed to this profound possibility in a summer we spent discerning an invisible but vicious threat.

God of all people, help us find strength in vulnerability and innocence. In the name of the One who is the eye of the mind, its expression as word, and the will that produces that expression, we pray. Amen.

TRINITY SUNDAY

Psalm 8 recounts one of scripture's most familiar contrasts. Two ideas cannot be separated: When human beings consider our place in the universe, we are nothing. Psalm 78:39 echoes the sentiment that human beings are "a wind that passes and comes not again." And yet God makes us "a little lower than God" to "have dominion" over the animals that fill the seas, the earth, and the air. Our place in the whole scope of the universe is minuscule, yet we make a huge difference to everything that lives. Humans are the stewards of all God's creation. And in so honoring humanity, God is glorified.

On Trinity Sunday, we are reminded not only how small we are in the scope of the universe but also how little knowledge we have of God. The early church experienced God as the Father in the prayer Jesus taught, as the Son who was the embodiment of God on earth, and as the Spirit who remained present in their lives. But later theologians explored further.

Augustine's treatise "On the Trinity" particularly impressed me when I first read it forty years ago, and it remains with me to this day. As summarized by Eugene Webb of the University of Washington, Augustine's Trinity is "lover, beloved, and love; the mind, the mind's knowledge of itself, and its love of itself; the eye of the mind, its expression as word, and the will that produces that expression; object, vision, and attention; memory, inner vision, and will; memory, understanding, and love."* On Trinity Sunday, we contemplate the mysteries of life: of humanity, of earth, and of God.

*https://faculty.washington.edu/ewebb/R428/Augustine.html.

Father, Son, and Holy Spirit, help us to love ourselves, love the earth, and love the mysteries begun in you. In the name of our Creator, Redeemer, and Sustainer, we pray. Amen.

Summer Epiphanies

JUNE 13–19, 2022 • PATRICIA RAYBON

SCRIPTURE OVERVIEW: The fact that we trust in God does not guarantee that life will be easy. Believers suffer discouragement as well. Elijah is a powerful prophet of God who faces profound discouragement. He looks around and sees faithlessness and desolation, as does the psalmist wrestling with his own sense of despair. In both cases the person's spirit is revived—by divine visitation to Elijah and by the psalmist's self-talk about the truth of God's faithfulness. The New Testament readings take us in a different direction. Paul speaks of the freedom we have when we are in Christ, heirs to all of God's promises. The Gospel writer tells of another kind of freedom, the freedom experienced by a man delivered from demon possession.

QUESTIONS AND SUGGESTIONS FOR REFLECTION

- Read 1 Kings 19:1-15a. Recall a time you ran to a silent place. How did God send you back into the world?
- Read Psalm 42. The author asks us to imagine the words of this psalm coming from the mouth of Elijah and the Gerasene man. Consider how these words might be yours as well.
- Read Galatians 3:23-29. How does your faith in Christ help you to realize that there is freedom in unity rather than to flee in fear?
- Read Luke 8:26-39. What true story do you have to tell to the world of what Jesus has done for you?

Essayist and author of *My First White Friend, I Told the Mountain to Move, Undivided,* and a historical mystery novel, *All That Is Secret*; member of the historic Shorter Community A.M.E. Church in Denver; loves movies, popcorn, gardening, biking, and watching college basketball with her husband, Dan, and family.

Dorothy Zellner knew Mississippi would be bad in the summer of 1964. It was a Southern state known for oppressive injustice against Black citizens, but her need to help reverse the problem was unrelenting. Thus, with one thousand other college students, she signed up with the Student Nonviolent Coordinating Committee, joining Black activists in the South to carry out voting-rights campaigns during "Freedom Summer." Too soon, however, the battle turned deadly. Three SNCC volunteers were ambushed by Klansmen and killed. As FBI agents searched swamps for their bodies, the remains of eight other Black males, apparently murdered, also were found.

Over the summer, dozens of SNCC workers were beaten. Scores of Black churches and homes were bombed or burned. Zellner, in an *American Experience* episode, described her dismay: "I knew it was going to be bad. I didn't dream for a minute that people would be killed. But it was always in the back of everybody's mind that something—bad things—were going to happen. So, it was terrifying."* How, then, did young volunteers respond? Many called on God.

Elijah did the same when Jezebel threatened his life. Fleeing for his life, Elijah "went on alone into the wilderness . . . sat down under a solitary broom tree and prayed that he might die. 'I have had enough, LORD,' he said. 'Take my life, for I am no better than my ancestors who have already died'" (NLT).

Such lament can seem pitiful and weak. Or, we can remember the strength in what Elijah and countless civil rights workers did. In their woe, they called on God. In a battle, it's a powerful first step.

American Experience: Freedom Summer. https://www.pbs.org/wgbh/americanexperience/films/freedomsummer/#part01

Inspire us, Lord, to call first on you. Amen.

Fannie Lou Hamer had nothing else to lose. Born the last of twenty children to sharecropper parents, she grew up in dire Mississippi poverty. She began picking cotton on a plantation at age six, and she left school for good at twelve to help her aging parents work the fields. After marrying, she and her husband wanted children, but during surgery for a uterine tumor, a white doctor performed a hysterectomy without her knowledge or consent—a common practice, many said, to suppress Mississippi's poor Black population. Deciding eventually to register to vote, Mrs. Hamer was challenged instead by her plantation's owner—a Mister Marlowe—"who told me I would have to go down and withdraw my registration or leave, because they wasn't ready for that in Mississippi."*

She left that night, eventually becoming a SNCC field secretary and evolving into an iconic folk hero in the civil rights movement. Enduring beatings in jail and gunfire from nightriders, she never wavered in her goal of helping Mississippi's poor people—Black and white. She held audiences rapt with her down-home, courageous oratory: "I guess if I'd had any sense, I'd have been a little scared—but what was the point of being scared? The only thing they could do was kill me, and it kinda seemed like they'd been trying to do that a little bit at a time since I could remember."

Such clarity in one's calling comes from hearing God. Thus, as Elijah fled his tormentors, hiding in a cave, the Lord himself spoke to him. "What are you doing here, Elijah?" (NLT). The question is asked of all who seek to serve God. What are you doing here? Is this your ministry? May we listen well as God directs and guides.

American Experience: Freedom Summer. https://www.pbs.org/wgbh/american-experience/films/freedomsummer/#transcript

Clarify my calling, Lord, speaking to my spirit in a clear voice that can only be yours. Amen.

As a young African American child, Anthony Harris, PhD, had few educational opportunities. This was by design. The Jim Crow laws of Hattiesburg, Mississippi, kept his elementary school underfunded and poorly supplied. Then came the summer of 1964. At a Freedom School set up by the Student Non-violent Coordinating Committee, Harris and friends read books and staged plays. Suddenly blessed with enrichment activities, Harris took guitar lessons from Pete Seeger, the renowned folk singer, who had come to Mississippi to volunteer.

Photos of young Anthony with Seeger show a dynamic that arises when humans engage in creativity and uplift. They show hope.

Freedom School "planted a seed in my mind that things are going to change, things are going to be different," said Harris in a 2014 documentary. "And Freedom Summer helped to give us that courage; it helped to give us that hope."*

Harris sounded like the writer of Psalm 42. Exiled far from Jerusalem and unable to worship in the Temple, the psalmist had moaned in lament, "Day and night I have only tears for food, while my enemies continually taunt me, saying, 'Where is this God of yours?'"

Recalling God's goodness, however, the psalmist realizes: "Why am I discouraged? . . . I will put my hope in God! I will praise him again—my savior and my God!" (NLT). The sons of Korah, a Levite killed while rebelling against Moses, surrendered their sorrow in songs of hope—a seed of emotion watered by praise. Seeger offered a young man the same. Then God, in his mercy, made hope grow.

---

*https://www.pbs.org/wgbh/americanexperience/films/freedomsummer/#transcript

In my distress, O Lord, plant in my heart a seed of hope. Then water it. Amen.

As the only Black student in my high school graduating class, I was accustomed to occasional snubs. Thus, at a recent class reunion, some who shunned me in high school did the same. Was it because of race? Why were they still not bothering to say hello? I wasn't sure. Yet I insisted on going. With my skeptical husband in tow, I vowed to take a hard look at my past—to pin my name tag on my sweater, my yearbook photo affixed, acting as if I belonged.

In fact, I did belong. I reminisced and reconnected with many old friends. To my surprise, I also made new friends. One varsity football player came over to talk to me about race, of all things. We'd never exchanged two words in high school, but he asked my opinion on how racial healing happens.

Listening to him, I marveled at how social taboos and racial awkwardness had blocked our friendship as teens. Then I considered that, in the 60s, my classmates and I had struggled to integrate a society while watching friends go to Vietnam and come home in body bags, our world still torn. Other classmates had left us too. Accidents, illnesses, and life came calling. We who were still here looked joyful and grateful. So, on the drive home, I confessed to my husband an unexpected epiphany. "God kept me." Despite the racism and more, "God sustained me." Indeed, God sustains us all.

The sons of Korah came to a similar conclusion. "For you are God, my only safe haven" (NIV). Despite the shame of their father's rebellion, these temple attendants each knew God as "the source of all my joy," their life and hope. Despite storms, may we discover God this way too.

In our storms, Lord, thank you for keeping us even before we know you are God. Amen.

Kalief Browder never should have been locked up. At age 16 he was jailed on charges he stole a backpack because his parents couldn't pay his $3,000 cash bail. Without ever standing trial, he was imprisoned for three years—nearly two years in solitary confinement. After an article about Kalief was published in *The New Yorker* magazine, New York City Mayor Bill de Blasio vowed to clear the backlogs in state court and reduce the youth-inmate population.

The effort was too late for Kalief. After release, he never recovered from prison's indignities, including multiple assaults and food deprivation during solitary. In 2015 he committed suicide at his parents' home. His tragedy illustrates the soul-killing costs of a criminal justice system that disproportionately confines America's Black citizens. As one author has described the mass incarceration of Black males in the U.S., it's "the new Jim Crow."

Our spiritual lockdowns, however, run across racial lines. During SNCC's Freedom Summer in Mississippi, leader Bob Moses observed that "white people are probably more oppressed, in terms of their ability to speak, than Negroes." By that he no doubt meant that white Mississippians were held captive by their own racist theology and culture.

As the apostle Paul describes such imprisonment, "Before the coming of this faith, we were held in custody under the law, locked up until the faith that was to come would be revealed" (NIV). As a "Hebrew of Hebrews," Paul understood this more than most. He knew the confinement imposed by a law no human could keep. "So the law was our guardian until Christ came that we might be justified by faith. Now that this faith has come, we are no longer under a guardian" (NIV). God's freedom is freeing, indeed.

Jesus, we thank you for paying the price to unlock our heavy spiritual chains. Amen.

After my Army reservist dad visited a Maine church one summer Sunday during a two-week reserve hitch, he was followed to the parking lot by several church trustees who warned him never to return. Yes, to a church. Their worry? My dad was a Black man. Never mind that he was a decorated World War II hero who had been awarded three Bronze Stars, a Victory Medal, and an American Theatre Campaign Ribbon for his valor and service as an infantry unit commander during battles in the North Solomons, Netherlands East Indies, and Bismarck Archipelago. In America's segregated Army, my dad had distinguished himself and still was serving in the US Army Reserves.

At the Maine church, however, the white men there declared their own decree: You're not enough. Not white enough; thus, not right enough. So leave. And don't come back.

The apostle Paul faced similar tensions during the time of his letter to the churches in southern Galatia. Topping the list of controversies was the relationship of new believers, especially Gentiles, to Jewish believers and the laws that some still passionately practiced.

Calling instead for post-law unity, Paul wrote, "So in Christ Jesus you are all children of God through faith" (NIV). Then came the real challenge: "There is neither Jew nor Gentile, neither slave nor free, nor is there male and female, for you are all one in Christ Jesus." Driving the point home further, Paul added, "If you belong to Christ, then you are Abraham's seed, and heirs according to the promise."

During America's Jim Crow era, some churches chose bigotry instead of inclusivity. Sadly, some still do. May all finally learn that, in Christ, we're humbly all his, all in Christ, all together. Forever.

Jesus, we are one in you, and, by your Spirit, we agree to act like it. Amen.

Can the demon of racism be dislodged in an instant? A Birmingham pastor said yes. While watching a young couple unload their car on the street across from his church, he decided to invite them to his church. Then, halfway across the street, he realized they were Black. In the blink of an eye, he knew the Lord was calling him to minister to precisely that couple—in fact, to all people—not just white people. In that instant, he vowed to start a multicultural church serving the poor, and he kept his vow. A similar epiphany transformed John Newton, the slave trader turned abolitionist, whose hymn, "Amazing Grace," famously declares, "I once was lost, but now am found, was blind but now I see."

Jesus' power to break our spiritual shackles can be found in the Gospel of Luke. As Luke tells it, Jesus arrived in the region of the Gerasenes, a Gentile area, when he was met by a demon-possessed man from the town. But, in fact, all of us meet Jesus when we're burdened by spiritual demons like bigotry, jealousy, unforgiveness, naked ambition, and anger. Like the shackled man, we may waste our lives among dead things— lies, conspiracy theories, hard-hearted disobedience, idolatry, and racism.

Racism is a pervasive spiritual brokenness. It replicates itself like a deadly virus, infecting legions as it rages through a body. But not even racism stands up to the Lord's authority.

Thus, John Wesley's pamphlet "Thoughts Upon Slavery" has inscribed on its cover the convicting words of Genesis 4:10: "And the Lord said—what hast thou done? The voice of thy brother's blood crieth unto me from the ground" (KJV).

Indeed. Now freed, confess and tell others that Jesus saves.

Lord, heal my heart now of racial sin. Amen.

The Path of Discipleship

JUNE 20–26, 2022 • LYDIA WYLIE-KELLERMANN

SCRIPTURE OVERVIEW: This week's readings open with the dramatic scene of Elijah's departure. As the prophet is taken into heaven by fiery chariots, his cloak falls to his successor, Elisha—symbolic of the continuation of God's prophetic work. The psalmist praises the Lord's mighty works of the past and finds encouragement in them. Paul reminds us that freedom in Christ comes with responsibility. We cannot live to satisfy our fleshly desires. If we live in the power of the Spirit, then our manner of life should stand out and bear godly fruit. In the Gospel reading, Jesus challenges his followers with the cost of discipleship. His statements here may seem extreme, but he is pointing out that we can be tempted to find excuses for not proclaiming the kingdom of God.

QUESTIONS AND SUGGESTIONS FOR REFLECTION

- Read 2 Kings 2:1-2, 6-14. When has fire—real or metaphorical—changed your life? How have you seen God working in this change?
- Read Psalm 77:1-2, 11-20. Recall a time when you needed God's help. Where did you look for God's encouragement?
- Read Galatians 5:1, 13-25. Along with our freedom, we are given a responsibility. How do you use your freedom to serve others?
- Read Luke 9:51-62. When have you heard Jesus' call to follow? What have you had to leave behind to follow the one who has "set his face to go to Jerusalem"?

Writer, editor, activist, and mother from Detroit, MI; editor of *Geez* magazine, which sits at the intersection of art, faith, and justice; editor of *The Sandbox Revolution: Raising Kids for a Just World* (Broadleaf Books, 2021).

Stories have the power to help us see another way, to shake up our imaginations, and even to transform our lives. I give thanks for being able to hold this sacred book that is filled with stories from a multitude of times, cultures, perspectives, and traditions. I particularly love the stories that force us out of our logical brains and into the fertile ground of mystery and power.

We are given one such story today. Elisha walks beside Elijah in his final days. As they approach the Jordan, Elijah rolls up his cloak and strikes the water with it. The water divides, and they cross on dry land. Then a chariot of fire and horses of fire appear, and Elijah is swept up into heaven in a great whirlwind.

What a story! Does it not sound like a childhood bedtime thriller? Or a tale of magic? Or a dream no one understands when we try to retell it the next morning? It is tempting to dismiss stories like this or turn the page in befuddlement, skipping to the next reading.

Stories are not always factual, but sometimes that makes them even more true.

What a gift it is to be called to sit in messy absurdity without a clear answer. Scripture needs not just intellectuals and scholars but artists and dreamers. Again and again we are offered moments to call upon the places inside of us that can find truth and meaning beyond logic.

As we open scripture, we find an invitation calling upon our paintbrushes and poetry, our right brain and inner dreamer, our ancestral memory and our prophetic imagination!

O God who dwells in stories and mystery, breathe life into our imagination. We trust that in this messy, fertile place we can dream a world that does not yet seem possible. Amen.

The story of Elijah and Elisha illuminates the intergenerational nature of our work and faith. The Spirit moves through us from generation to generation. Mentorship is offered. Leadership transitions.

We too are part of such stories in our own time and place. My heart is stirred up remembering the ancestors who now live in picture frames and on the edges of my memory. It was in ordinary walks by their side where I was taught the gentle and powerful lessons of what it means to be human.

Elisha begs me to seek out the elders in my life before they cross the river or their chariots swing low. These are the days to ask for stories and histories, to offer thanks, to listen, to be formed and transformed, and to hold their hands and feel the Spirit move between us.

When Elijah has gone, Elisha picks up the mantle and continues the work. With holy gratitude, may we each pick up the mantle that lies before us, even if it is just for a short while. Let us run our fingers across each stitch. Breathe in the smells that still linger from the ones we loved. Notice the holes and recall the stories of the places it has been. Pull it over our shoulders feeling the weight of history. Find a needle and thread and mend the tears. Give it new stains and carry it on new paths until, one day, we take it off again and lovingly wrap it around someone younger and wiser.

O God, we give thanks for this cloak that reminds us of our belovedness, smallness, and belonging in the great cloud of witnesses. Amen.

Amid the cries to God, the land rises up. The elements come alive as signs of the intimate connection between Creator and creation. The waters tremble, and the skies echo God's voice.

The land matters to our faith.

As we read scripture, we can't help but learn the contours of the land. We feel the dry path under our toes as we cross the Jordan. We carry the dampness in our bones during the endless rain on a wooden ark. We stand in awe of the height of the cedars of Lebanon. We smell the fish in the Sea of Galilee. We know the dusty road on the way to Jerusalem. The geography of the land is crucial to the stories of our faith.

God dwells in the beauty and the pain that are visible in our earthly siblings. God is reflected in the chickadee out my window and the opossum who lingers in the alley. God is present in the soil next door that is poisoned with lead because of years of industrial abuse. God weeps in the increasingly powerful hurricanes and the fires of the west.

We tread in dangerous theological territory if we ignore our sacred and small place in the grand ecosystem of life.

The psalms call us to be attentive to the landscape. It is a calling to pledge allegiance not to the arbitrary borders of countries but instead to all life that depends on the same rainfall.

God who breathes life into this world, empower us to become disciples of this land. The earth is crying, and we are listening. Amen.

When I see terms like "flesh" and "sexual immorality," my stomach tightens and grief rises in my throat. I know I'm entering scriptural territory that has been used for generations to exclude and hate. Sermons on texts like these have forced so many LGBTQI folks to leave churches, carrying trauma in their bodies, wondering if there is a God and if they are loved and whole.

Years ago as a teenager I attended a gathering focused on feminist, womanist, and queer theology. I didn't yet know I'd end up falling in love with a woman and be called in spirit and body to a vocation of marriage.

At this gathering, a group of young activists and seminarians asked for a conversation with Catholic Worker and scripture scholar Laurel Dykstra. They were tired of having Bible verses condemning their sexuality spewed at them and wanted to know what Bible verses they could use to fight back.

Laurel listened to the pain and then responded, "The Bible should never be used as a weapon." That was it. The conversation was over. Yes, we were receiving vicious attacks on our humanity, but we were not to return a shot with another shot.

So often, scripture is used as a weapon to harm, exclude, or deny another's humanity.

So, friends, as we open these pages this week and every week, let us scrutinize the text to understand its historical and cultural context. But let us also take the words that summon justice, liberation, and community, while laying down our weaponized words by the riverside to study war no more.

O God, you know the power of words and the ways they can become flesh. Be with us as we speak out of these ancient, sacred texts. May they honor you and all of creation, calling us to justice, communion, and wholeness. Amen.

A dozen years ago, I stood on the hillside of the village of Sarra in the West Bank. I was there with Meta Peace Team doing third-party nonviolent intervention. The Israeli military had put a roadblock on Sarra's main road out of town. A couple hundred folks had gathered to protest.

After some negotiation with heavily armed Israeli soldiers, a leader of the protest called out: "We have seven minutes to vacate or they will begin shooting."

I thought, *All right, that's it. Time to pack up and go home.*

But then I saw five boys younger than ten climb the mound of dirt. They wore traditional Palestinian dress and began to dance the Dabka. Immediately, the tension evaporated in clapping, laughing, and singing. It was a feast of joy set before a display of weapons.

Moments later the air that had just held the sounds of laughter and pride filled with tear gas and sound bombs. The land was trampled by feet in fear. But for seven minutes there had been courageous resistance in the form of joy, and that can never be taken away.

As I read this letter to the Galatians—written in a time of conflict—I am struck by the addition of the word *joy* to the fruit of the Spirit. Discipleship is hard work, and too often we lose sight of joy. Amid pain, unrest, and a historical moment aching with injustice, joy can feel like the hardest thing of all to find.

I believe living joyfully is a calling—not to happiness that is ready-made or store-bought but to the kind of joy that is birthed only after (or only when) we have touched and known deep pain.

O God of our tears and laughter, give us the courage to stand up before the powers and play, sing, laugh, and dance justice into being. Amen.

I can never read this text without my anger showing toward Jesus. The disciple can't pause long enough to bury his father?! Doesn't discipleship include the work of burying the dead? After all, Jesus said, "Blessed are those who mourn" (Matt. 5:4).

I was nineteen when I fell on my mom's body, weeping and clinging onto the warmth that still lingered in her skin. The dirt under my fingernails as we buried her ashes taught me more than anything else about who I want to be and what discipleship looks like.

So, yes, part of me still wants to yell at Jesus.

However, stories change on the page depending on our perspective. Years have passed since I buried my mother, and now my life is filled with the clutter of crayons and caterpillars and children crying in the night. When I read the scripture text, I am no longer the disciple being called but the parent who is being left behind.

I look at my four- and seven-year-old and wonder what I would want for them in that moment. I think I would want to sing out, "Leave my old bones and go dance along the road you were born to travel!"

My prayer for my children echoes the gospel and the work I have to do as I tend and nurture their hearts: Trust your conscience and discernment. Do not be afraid of urgency or risk. Do not depend on security, but put your trust in love, joy, and a cry for justice along the journey. And always know that there will be family and community ready to love you when the dusty roads lead back home.

O God, let your embryonic waters flow through us as we grab one another's hands and join in the great journey of discipleship. Amen.

Well, dear friends, Jesus has set his sights on Jerusalem. The path is clear. The time is now. Our invitation waits.

It will not be easy. There is no safety or security. There is nowhere to lay our heads. Normal life must cease. Business as usual is no more.

But there will be community: mentors to walk alongside, stories to learn, and mantles to pick up. There will be children full of life who are wiser than you or I.

There will be space for dreaming, for mystery, for imagining new ways of living when the walls come crumbling down.

There will dirt under our feet and palm branches in our hands. There will be stars and wind and songbirds along the journey who carry a love of God and this world.

There will be those along the path who sit in pain because they have been hurt by words, laws, codes, and disciplines. They will be ready to receive our hands and loving invitations to join the journey.

When we reach where we are going, there will be pain and grief brought on by a system that deals in death and fear. But we will keep going. With spices and oils, we will go to the body to love and honor and pick up the cloak. And in that place, there will be dancing, joy, and mystery.

O God, we give thanks for this day, this call, and this life. Bless the dirt under our feet and the life that is to come after us. Amen.

Humility and Healing

JUNE 27–JULY 3, 2022 • MELISSA TIDWELL

SCRIPTURE OVERVIEW: The readings from the Hebrew scriptures describe what can happen when our own strength fails us. Naaman is a great military commander from Syria, but he has no power to heal himself. The psalmist, traditionally David, has become too comfortable in his prosperity. Both men must humble themselves before they can experience healing and restoration from God. How often do we let our pride stand in the way of our healing? Paul admonishes his readers to carry themselves with humility and to build up one another. What they do will always come back to them; what we sow, we reap. The story in Luke warns against being proud even of the gifts that God gives us. Our greatest joy is not that we can do things for God but that God has already accepted us.

QUESTIONS AND SUGGESTIONS FOR REFLECTION

- Read 2 Kings 5:1-14. When have God's instructions been more involved than you expected? How did you respond?
- Read Psalm 30. How can you continue to praise God during dark, lonely, and hopeless times?
- Read Galatians 6:1-16. When has your faith community struggled with members' lack of humility? How did you resolve the situation so that you could welcome and nurture new Christians?
- Read Luke 10:1-11, 16-20. When have you misconstrued God's accomplishments as your own successes? How did you refocus your life or ministry on serving God?

Presbyterian writer and pastor; serves as pastor of Trinity Presbyterian Church in Stockton, CA; author of *Embodied Light: Advent Reflections on the Incarnation*; former editor of *Alive Now* magazine.

In this story of a miraculous healing, we see the powerful and the humble drawn together, as God uses persons and circumstances to reveal the divine will. Naaman, who is the victor in battle, is helpless against the disease of leprosy. The king of Israel, powerful within his kingdom, is suspicious of Naaman. In contrast, we see humble persons who act as agents for God's will. The servant of Naaman's wife, taken captive in war, could have been bitter about her status but seeks the good of those around her. She suggests that the prophet of her home country could provide healing. Naaman's assistants, also modest in power and status, urge their irritated boss not to reject the method of healing prescribed by the prophet but to give it a chance to work.

In the center of these two sets of characters, between the powerful and the powerless, stands the prophet Elisha, who makes it clear that worldly power is nothing compared to God's power. Elisha is the instrument of healing, but he does not need to make the act of healing extravagant or showy. What would be a magnificent feat for an earthly doctor is done simply by the divine healer. God's grace and mercy are there for those who are able to listen and humbly accept.

This healing is part of a longer story of the political power struggles in Israel's rise and fall. Within the larger frame, this moment can also be set apart as a timeless reminder of the power of God to bring us into relationship so that we may be made whole.

This week, try out some simple prayer actions as a way to practice humility. Try washing your hands slowly and meditatively, seeking the wellspring of every blessing, asking for its mercy to flow toward all those in need of healing.

Naaman wants to be healed of his leprosy, but he also seems to need to be recognized as an important person. Naaman wants Elisha to perform some complex ritual, not just prescribe a simple bath in a not very impressive river. Naaman's ego almost gets in the way of his healing, until his assistants point out that he would have gladly performed a difficult task if the prophet had assigned it. So why not take a simple path?

Naaman is not a sympathetic character, so we might be reluctant to identify with him. But I can imagine feeling slighted and skeptical if I traveled to a respected hospital for relief from an ongoing illness, only to have the doctor send someone out to the parking lot to tell me just to wash my hands each day.

Naaman needed for his healing to be complicated to satisfy his sense of importance. Sometimes we want a recognition of how serious our problems are. But what if what we need is not complexity but humility? Humility is often the first step toward being able to accept help, to be human. As long as we are insisting on our own agendas, we miss the signs that God is working through something or someone we do not expect.

A prayerful posture that begins with gratitude for our lives and the world around us can help us step back and find our place in God's intentions. We might realize we are standing deep in the flow of a healing river.

What's the most humble task you do regularly in your household? Taking out the trash? Cleaning the cat box? Do a chore today with gratitude, and notice how such seemingly menial tasks can become pathways to prayer.

This psalm is a song of gratitude, a praise offering in response to healing. The author seems to have been someone who was wealthy, even powerful, who thought prosperity made persons untouchable, unmovable. Consider this prayer as if it were Naaman's prayer, the prayer of a powerful military leader who knew victory and wealth.

When things go our way, we might feel that we cannot be moved. But, of course, every human will experience suffering. We encounter natural disasters. We age. We get sick. Our pets die. Our loved ones die. In these times of grief and suffering we can become more compassionate, more open to receiving consolation and hope.

The psalmist grapples with the idea that suffering is caused by God's anger. I don't accept that as the last word on a theology of suffering, but it certainly can feel that way. That kind of painful admission is part of the beauty of the Psalms, where every human emotion gets poured out in raw honesty and in ultimate praise of God.

One of the most quoted thoughts of this psalm is that "joy comes with the morning." If you have ever lived through a long night of worry, pain, or grief, you know that is seems as if the night will never end. The simple fact of the sun rising from the horizon can feel like a sign of hope, showing that we are not alone and can find the strength for another day. While we might long for miraculous healings like Naaman or the psalmist received, we give praise for the mornings we have seen and will see in our lifetime of testimony to God's grace.

Wake one day this week in time to watch the transformation from dark to light.

Paul's letter to the Galatians is beloved for its bold appeal to oneness in Christ. The specific context of the letter, an argument about Gentile Christians, seems archaic now. Underneath the specifics of the issues, however, is a message for us that goes to the heart of the gospel.

The issue in Paul's day had to do with forming the new and exciting church of Christ. The debate was about who belonged and who would be welcome. Paul began preaching to Jewish believers in Christ, but then he attracted many Gentile converts. Did these new believers need to undergo a conversion to traditional Jewish customs? Did the men need to be circumcised before they could become fully Christian?

Paul declared that circumcision is an outward sign, but what is needed is the inward change of heart.

Reading our Bibles every day is an easy-to-spot outward sign, and we feel satisfied by the progress we make in reading through a book. But the inward sign of our progress would be noticing that the message of the Bible is growing in our lives—maybe in more patience as we deal with a thorny relationship, or a welling up of joy at a beautiful sunset. These things are signs of the fruit of the Spirit that Paul wrote about in the passage just before today's text (see Galatians 5:22-26). You might take a moment to look over that list and compare it to your own spiritual progress from the outward to the inward, from the old creation to the new.

How many outward signs of faith do you have around you? Think of items like crosses, Bibles, or clothing. As you take note, give thanks for a corresponding inward gift.

You reap what you sow" has become a casual saying that means something like, "You will get what's coming to you." It carries a bit of menace, a warning of divine payback, a bill coming due. But the message Paul is sharing with the Galatians is less about a transaction and more about how we use our freedom in Christ to live out the newness of redemption.

Sowing is an intention, a hope. If I stick a Christian symbol on my car but drive around town in a venomous rage, cursing at other drivers, is my drive truly Christian? Was my intention to be Christian or to *appear* to be Christian?

Paul has gained something greater than respectability. He gave up a life of status and reputation to answer a call from God that led him to be jailed and scorned. That call also caused him to experience the wild freedom of trusting God and letting everything else go, of being reconciled into this wonderful mystery of God he calls the new creation. He urges us not to grow weary in doing what is right, even though at times our efforts seem futile.

We can express our hope through small actions of generosity, like helping a friend who struggles with addiction or depression, or speaking up against injustice. We may not see the final results of these actions because the harvest is not always immediate. But if our intention, our hope, is to sow the seeds of the new creation, then what we will reap is far beyond anything we can imagine.

Keep track today of all the places you are sowing seeds of the Spirit—situations you are working and praying for in hope. Imagine the faithful harvest in each intention, and give thanks. Make an effort to sow seeds of peace somewhere today.

As Jesus prepared to go on a preaching tour, he sent seventy followers out before him. They were sent in both vulnerability and power, and Jesus explained the risks. He spoke honestly of the lambs going out among the wolves and warned that some people would not accept the message that the seventy were bringing.

But Jesus also gave these believers the ability to heal and bring the kingdom near. The instructions he gave were simple: Carry no bags, accept whatever food is given, offer peace, and move on from those who don't accept the offer. Perhaps it is in the simplicity of lifestyle that the power of offering peace in God's name is so apparent.

That contrast between simplicity and power makes this passage a good complement to our Hebrew Bible passage for this week. Where healing is done, it does not need to be flashy or hyped. The power of God is available, and the peace of God can be given as a gift to those who are willing.

This humble way of working may seem foreign to our ideas of ministry or of healing. We tend to build big churches and fill our services with many words and loud music. There is nothing wrong in praising God with everything we have. But sometimes what matters more than anything is the gift of presence, of quiet contemplation, of a hand held, and a burden shared. When we humbly offer ourselves as vessels by which God's will is done, something powerful and lasting happens. May we know vulnerability and power as we continue walking in Christ's way.

Take a walk today and bless each home or other place you pass. Where do you see signs of the kingdom of heaven brought near? Where do you sense a need for healing?

In an earlier part of Luke, Jesus sent out believers to heal, but they came back discouraged. This passage has a positive result and is likely less familiar. Maybe that is because we think of the disciples as clueless. They often don't get what Jesus is about and are distracted by their own desire for greatness. But here they follow the directions to live simply and offer healing, and they report their success eagerly: "Lord, in your name even the demons submit to us!"

Jesus responds with an enigmatic statement about seeing Satan fall from heaven like lightning. Biblical commentaries offer varying theories. Some speculate that Jesus feels the power of the disciples' work from a distance, and some suggest that Jesus is talking about a cosmic event that happened before Creation. Some hear the words of Jesus as commendation, while others think Jesus is warning the disciples against comparing their power to the immense power of God.

These are just hypotheses and not very satisfying ones at that. Maybe that is not a bad thing. We speak often of spiritual things as mystery. By the word *mystery* we don't mean a riddle or an illusion or a cold case we have to solve. Mystery is a fount of meaning that offers truth and grace beyond our knowing.

Our best approach to mystery is grateful humility. We can't know everything that Christ knew. We can't even understand everything he said. But we can know that Christ's power is sufficient, and we live with a comfort that all the powers in the universe do not compare to the peace he sends us to share.

Write a brief progress update about the mission to which God has called you. What amazing spiritual revelations have you witnessed? What moments of healing and grace have you shared? What else would you like to explore?

The Fruit God Desires

JULY 4–10, 2022 • LYNNE M. BAAB

SCRIPTURE OVERVIEW: Amos is a farmer called by God to deliver a message to Jeroboam, the king of Israel (the northern kingdom in the divided monarchy). Because the king has not listened to the warnings from God, judgment will come. The psalmist also warns of judgment, in this case for those who oppress the weak and needy and fail to protect them from the wicked. Such heartless people will surely be brought low by God. The opening to the letter to the Colossians is a prayer of thanksgiving for their faith in Christ and the spiritual fruit they are producing in the world. The parable in the Gospel reading challenges our human tendency to ignore need. Jesus teaches that mercy should overcome any reason we might find to harden our hearts.

QUESTIONS AND SUGGESTIONS FOR REFLECTION

- Read Amos 7:7-17. Look for God's plumb line in the world. In what ways is the ground you stand on askew?
- Read Psalm 82. If you sit on the council of the Most High, how does this change your perspective on the world?
- Read Colossians 1:1-14. Prayers of mere words are just the beginning of prayer. To what prayerful actions do your prayerful words call you?
- Read Luke 10:25-37. The author writes, "Even those trying to be faithful walk askew." Consider how you live out Jesus' call to love your neighbor.

Author of numerous books and Bible study guides, including *Sabbath Keeping* and *Nurturing Hope: Christian Pastoral Care in the Twenty-First Century*; served as associate pastor in two Presbyterian churches in Seattle, WA, and has taught pastoral theology in several seminaries; visit her website: lynnebaab.com.

When I was fifteen years old and disillusioned with church, God spoke to me through Mount Rainier. The mountain seemed to be saying, "There's more to life than what you can see and feel and touch. The supernatural is real." That mental picture of Mount Rainier speaking about God's existence helped me navigate my tumultuous high school years. God speaks to the prophet Amos in a mental picture too: a plumb line.

Early in Amos, the prophet proclaims God's judgment on Israel because the people "trample the head of the poor into the dust of the earth" (2:7) and "crush the needy" (4:1). Amos expresses God's desire: "Let justice roll down like waters, and righteousness like an ever-flowing stream" (5:24).

While he faithfully proclaims God's judgment on Israel, Amos also argues with God, saying that this small nation needs God's care and support, not God's judgment of locusts and fire. Amos describes God's reply, beginning with the picture of a plumb line, a tool used in construction to make sure walls are perfectly vertical. The picture of the plumb line implies that God is evaluating Israel against the standard of justice and righteousness that Amos has mentioned throughout his prophecy. Is Israel bearing the fruit that God desires?

No! Israel's walls are crooked, and Amos speaks that truth. The high priest tells him to be silent, but Amos cannot. Amos, like many other prophets described in the Hebrew scriptures, has a strong call to speak God's truth to the people of Israel (7:14-15). God's words of judgment in Amos 7:16-17 reinforce the significance of this picture of the plumb line God gives Amos.

God of the plumb line, straighten the walls of our lives. Help us embrace your call to justice and righteousness. Guide us into your truth and your values. Amen.

The writer of Psalm 82, named as Asaph at the beginning of the psalm, opens with a picture of God presiding over the council of judgment. Asaph brings his complaint to God in the heavenly council room: "How long will you judge unjustly and show partiality to the wicked?" How long, God of justice, will you let the wicked prosper? How long do we have to wait until you rescue the weak and needy from the hand of the wicked? How long can we bear seeing orphans, the lowly, and the destitute suffering?

Asaph is drawing on the concerns and values of the God he worships. Throughout the Hebrew scriptures, in the words of the law and in the prophets, God has revealed the fruit God wants to see in the lives of the people of Israel. The prophet Amos describes that fruit vividly: "Let justice roll down like waters, and righteousness like an ever-flowing stream" (Amos 5:24). Asaph is appealing to God's own values and character. "When," he asks God, "are you going to take care of the evil around us, so that justice and righteousness—care for the weak, orphan, lowly, destitute, and needy—can flourish in the land?" (82:3-4, AP).

Through the words of this psalm, God invites us to sit for a few moments with our anger at the fact that vulnerable people always bear the cost of selfishness. Some of that selfishness comes from the strong and powerful, but some of it comes from ordinary people like us. We are such a mix of generosity and stinginess, kindness and self-focus. Only God can sort it all out and help us bear good fruit.

God of mercy, help us to grieve with you at the suffering of the weak, lowly, destitute, and needy. God of truth, help us to confront our self-focus and self-absorption. Help us long for the fruit of justice and righteousness. Amen.

I was in midlife before I realized that God's judgment could be good news. God's judgment will be righteous and based on truth. We don't have to worry that God will be capricious. Because of Jesus' death on the cross, we know God's love will cover us. We stand before God today, and we will stand before God at the time of judgment, confident in Jesus' righteousness and sure that all will be made right. All evil will be purged.

"Rise up, O God, judge the earth; for all the nations belong to you!" In the earlier verses of the psalm, Asaph tells us why he wants God to exercise judgment: The weak, orphans, lowly, destitute, and needy are being oppressed by the wicked. Asaph's sense of what is right and good is violated by what he sees. He knows that the wicked will die like other mortals. But why are they getting away with oppression now?

Asaph rejoices that one day God will judge all forms of evil. People will no longer make unwise and unkind decisions that imperil others. Self-seeking, self-justification, self-absorption, and self-deception will come to an end. Destructive viruses and catastrophic natural disasters will be no more. All forms of violence will burn away.

In addition, all the evil inside me will be removed, and I will stand before God clean and pure. No longer will my mind be tossed about with fears and catastrophic thoughts. No longer will I battle the inner voices that speak lies to me. No longer will I be tempted to act in unkind ways. What a wondrous day that will be!

Judge of the earth, we long for human life on earth to be made right and for your good creation to be restored. Until then, cleanse us of selfishness and self-seeking. Help us rely on your great love and kindness to live fruitful lives. Amen.

Jesus was a master teacher. In this passage, he uses the classic teaching device of answering a question with another question. This incident occurs when a lawyer wants to test Jesus.

The lawyer asks how to receive eternal life. Jesus refers him back to the Hebrew scriptures, and the lawyer quotes from Deuteronomy 6:5 and Leviticus 19:18. Jesus affirms the answers. Eternal life is rooted in love for God and love for neighbor.

The lawyer expands the ways of loving God in his quotation. Deuteronomy 6:5 commands that we love God with our heart, soul, and strength. The lawyer adds "and with all your mind." These four sources or expressions of love have helped me pray about my own life. Sometimes I focus my prayers on those four areas of life and commit those parts of me to God. Some days, I might need to confess my shortcomings to God in one or more of those areas. Sometimes I ask for God's help to be more fruitful in each of those parts of myself.

Our entire being belongs to God. We are called to use our whole self to love God and our neighbors. At times God gives us power like the disciples received, but all power must be used in love.

God of my heart, soul, strength, and mind, help me love and serve you with my whole being. Help me to bear the fruit of love for my neighbor. Amen.

Sometimes the lawyer in this story irritates me. Luke 10:25 says that the lawyer wants to test Jesus, and verse 29 describes the lawyer's desire to justify himself. I want to believe that if I had been there, physically present with Jesus, I would have hung on every word and rejoiced in Jesus' amazing presence. However, I have to admit that I might actually have been adversarial and combative like the lawyer.

Jesus answers the lawyer kindly and straightforwardly in a way that has stood the test of time. How many Christians over the past two thousand years have been challenged by the story of the Samaritan who went out of his way to help someone who belonged to a culture and religion at odds with his own?

The key moment comes in verse 36 when Jesus asks the lawyer who in the story acted like a neighbor to the man who was robbed. We can think of "neighbor" here as a verb in order to paraphrase Jesus' question: "Who neighbored the man?"

The Samaritan, in his acts of neighboring, bandaged the man's wounds, carried him on an animal to an inn, cared for him, paid the innkeeper for further care, and promised to come back to pay for any additional costs. These extravagantly caring actions, motivated by the pity in the heart of the Samaritan, show the kind of love involved in neighboring.

Take some time to consider the various people in your neighborhood—at church, at work, in sports clubs, book groups, Bible studies, and the many other settings in your life. Ask yourself what it means to neighbor them as a form of fruit that comes from love of God and love of neighbor.

Jesus, our Savior and friend, help us receive your teaching with open hearts. We want to love you with our whole selves. We ask that our love for you flow into the fruit of true neighboring. Amen.

The apostle Paul had never met the Christians in Colossae when he wrote to them. His friend Epaphras had visited their city in Asia Minor and told the Colossians about the gospel of Jesus Christ. As he opens the letter, Paul identifies himself as an apostle called by God's will, and he connects himself with his partner in ministry, Timothy. After grounding himself in his relationship with God and his partner in ministry, Paul thanks God for the faith of the Colossians and for the way their faith has flowed into love. This faith and love come from the hope of God's future that Epaphras told them about.

Then Paul uses the metaphor of fruit. The gospel, Paul says, has been bearing fruit and growing through the whole world, just as it bears fruit and grows among the Colossians. Paul's prayer of thankfulness makes clear the fruit is grounded in faith and love, based in hope. As Colossians 1:8 describes it, the fruit is "your love in the Spirit." Paul indicates that when the gospel is at work in people's lives, growth and fruit are natural outcomes.

This introduction to Paul's letter shows some of the ways that Paul views the gospel as profoundly relational. Paul grounds his own identity in his relationship with God and his partnership with Timothy. Paul reminds the Colossians that Epaphras brought them the gospel, and the fruit of the Colossians' engagement with the gospel is love, both for God and for each other. The Holy Spirit is equipping them (and us) for love. We do not bear fruit in isolation, but only as we are supported by and giving to others. And our love for others is the fruit.

God, you use the growth and fruitfulness of nature to teach us about yourself and your call to us. Remind us of the connections to others and the reliance on the Holy Spirit that make good fruit possible. Amen.

Paul prays for more fruit and growth among the Colossians. Specifically, Paul prays that the Colossians will be filled with the knowledge of God's will, grounded in spiritual wisdom and understanding. The effect of that knowledge will be to "lead lives worthy of the Lord, fully pleasing to him, as you bear fruit in every good work."

This is knowledge that doesn't stay in our heads. It flows into our hearts and hands and feet, enabling us to live in a way that pleases God. In Paul's prayer of thankfulness in Colossians 1:3-6, we see that God's fruit includes "love in the Spirit," closely connected to God's priorities of justice and righteousness that are expressed in the prophets and the psalms.

Leading lives worthy of the Lord and bearing fruit result in increasing knowledge of God, which in turn leads to fruitful lives. We can pray for this pattern of knowledge/fruit/knowledge for ourselves and for those we love.

If we want to praise God sincerely as Paul does, our best strategy is to act faithfully on what we already know of God. As we know God and act in ways that reflect God's character, we will know more of God. We will increasingly draw on God's power and patience, and we will be able to thank God joyously and sincerely for all that God has done for us in Jesus Christ.

God of love, justice, and righteousness, we need your help to act on what we already know about you. Through your Holy Spirit, help us bear good fruit so that our knowledge of you can grow and our lives produce more of the fruit you desire for us. Without you, we can do nothing. With you, we can be co-creators of peace on earth. Amen.

A Justice Journey

JULY 11–17, 2022 • JUAN CARLOS HUERTAS

SCRIPTURE OVERVIEW: This reading from Amos provides more indication of the reasons for God's coming judgment. Too many in Israel have been oppressing the poor. They cannot wait for religious festivals to end so that they can make more money through corrupt trade, including what we now call human trafficking. If we understand the psalmist to be David, the warning he issues in this passage concerns Saul. Because Saul has turned to evil, God will not allow him to remain in power. While God is love, God also sometimes brings judgment. The author of Colossians extols the elevated status of Christ, who has reconciled us to himself through his death. In Luke, Mary prioritizes spending time with Jesus, while Martha focuses on working for Jesus. It is Mary who receives Jesus' praise.

QUESTIONS AND SUGGESTIONS FOR REFLECTION

- Read Amos 8:1-12. Who in your community has been left behind? How can you care for them?
- Read Psalm 52. How do you remain rooted in God's steadfast love when you cry out against injustice?
- Read Colossians 1:15-28. What do you need to let fall away to reveal the mystery of Christ in you?
- Read Luke 10:38-42. How do you focus on Christ even as you attend to the necessary tasks of daily life?

Husband, father, spiritual director, and the Minister of Proclamation and Practice of Justice at First Plymouth Congregational Church, Lincoln, NE.

We are not used to hearing these kinds of words. Doom and gloom, judgment and punishment are not the inspiring words we prefer to hear from scripture. You may be wondering, *What has happened here? Why these words? Why this time?*

Scripture reminds us often that we all have a tendency to forget. We make promises we fail to keep both individually and as communities. Sometimes we merely forget, too busy with our own lives to pay attention to caring for our neighbor. There are other times when we do not respond because it will cost us something—it will require sacrifice, a giving up, a change of life.

The people of Israel had become opportunists, selling out their own for profit, forgetting the neediest among them for gain. God was angry at their lack of attention to the obvious hunger, need, and desperation of their brothers and sisters.

Too often we claim to follow Jesus but ignore the plight of those around us. Sometimes we claim to be "too busy." Sometimes we are afraid that paying attention and hearing the needy around us will cost us something. But ignoring them will cost us the abundant life that God promises.

Pay attention and look around; God is speaking. Today be attentive to your patterns of living, spending, consuming. Do they reflect God's call to simplicity, sharing, and abundance? Do they reflect care of neighbor?

God of abundance, help me to hear your voice calling me to bring good news to the poor. Amen.

It is easy to ignore the obvious, especially in difficult times. It is easy to think only about ourselves and to assume that everything is fine as long as we are well. It is easy to turn away at the struggles of others whom we see on our screens or hear about on our phones.

Imagine having to live in the day-to-day struggle to survive; to live in constant anxiety, uncertainty, and fear; to live with no hope of getting ahead no matter how hard you work! Imagine living in a context where those who have much get more every day, and yet you who have little seem to have less—less of everything, including hope.

I have often wondered what it would take to get our attention. It has been my experience as a pastor that as much as I would like to think otherwise, preaching does not really get people's attention. Preaching is easily filtered through our own ways of seeing the world. Preaching is also easily dismissed with a simple "I disagree with you, pastor." Preaching has its limits. So do Bible study and other practices that we hope will help people wake up to the realities of their neighbors.

Justice seems fleeting.

Today the prophet proclaims that we are about to pay attention! Creation will groan in ways that we will not be able to ignore. We will be directly affected by our inattentiveness to the neediest among us. God is about to do something that will guarantee our response.

God is calling us, shaking us, reminding us over and over again of the consequences of our unjust and uncaring ways but also that solidarity with God's other children is difficult but possible by the power of the Spirit.

God, open my eyes, take away my excuses, help me be in solidarity with those who are hurting, suffering, and struggling. Amen.

Give us justice! Give us justice! Give us justice! I can hear it as a chant for our days. God once again is sitting at the head of the divine council looking over our neighborhoods. What does God see?

I have to admit that on most days I do not know. I am too focused on my own family life: getting kids to school, leaving on time for work, cooking dinner, and paying bills. People in my circles of influence and friendship have lives very similar to mine. Seldom do I encounter someone who is that much different from me.

Studies show that I am not alone. Most of us have friendships, relationships, and connections within our own small circles. We are enmeshed with people of similar classes, ethnicities, races, and places in life. An echo chamber of sameness keeps us from seeing those who are different.

Justice is about doing what God does. It is about making things right in the world; it is about equity, peace, reconciliation, and care for all people. It is a restoration to God's original intention for the world. But it is difficult to do justice if we live in ways that protect us from even seeing injustice.

Today the psalmist invites us to open our eyes. We are being called to see as God sees—which can be overwhelming; many of us purposely avoid it. Yet if we are to be God's people, we must embrace such an awakening so that we can participate in God's work of rescuing, delivering, freeing, and saving.

God of justice, open my eyes to the many ways that the places where I live, work, and play fall short of your vision of equity for all of creation. Amen.

Who are we? Who is Jesus? What do the two have to do with each other?

These are some of the questions that capture my imagination often. I have lost count of the sermons I have preached on those questions and the conversations I have had about them.

These are questions of identity that press us to think deeply about key values, ways of looking at the world, and the place of faith in our lives. It is easy to sing about Jesus, to hear about Jesus, and to claim to believe in Jesus. It is much harder to follow Jesus.

The apostle Paul wrote some of the most stunning verses in all of scripture about who Jesus is: "the image of the invisible God," "the firstborn of all creation," "the head of the body," "the beginning, the firstborn from the dead."

God's incarnation makes reconciliation possible. God in the flesh paves the way by self-sacrifice, by humility, and by a willingness to meet us where we are.

We humans are "estranged and hostile in mind." We are the ones who ignore the commands of God: the ones who break covenants, who are prideful, who fail to live into God's ways.

The Spirit of God invites us into the awe and wonder of who Jesus is and the awe and wonder of being a reconciled people. The Spirit invites us into the recognition that by the power of the Holy Spirit we too can be agents of reconciliation.

Remember that going on this reconciliation journey means that we'll follow Jesus' model of sacrifice, humility, and struggle. If we choose this way, the hard way, it will in the end make us rooted, hopeful, and connected with our true selves and with all of creation.

God, awaken in us the awe and wonder of who Jesus is and—through him—who we can be. Amen.

As I write this we are in the midst of the COVID-19 pandemic. Our world has changed before our eyes, uncertainty is in the air, divisiveness abounds, and hope is becoming harder to find. Where is the good news that we so desperately need?

Jesus came for such a time as this!

God came into the messiness of our lives and our world. God showed us that all things will be reconciled in the end. God reminded us of God's creative power from the beginning of time to today. God reached out to us so that we could see God's face in our humanity and re-member a world that seems dismembered.

It turns out that suffering, struggle, and pain are part of what it means to be human in this broken world. This brokenness becomes a recognition of our desperate need for healing, for completion, for salvation. God's coming in Jesus shows us that God is wiling to enter into our messiness, into our suffering, alienation, and pain in order to restore, renew, and reconcile us.

Though God has not caused our suffering, God redeems it, transforms it, and recreates it so that we can become more like Jesus—more filled with hope, more able to be agents of God's reconciling power, no matter what season we are in, no matter what season the world is in.

I am not sure where we will be when you read this. I am not sure what might come a week from now as I write this. I do know that the God who created all things is with us; I do know that God gets it; I do know that we have seen God's face in Jesus. For this is a God who becomes one of us and takes up our struggles and sufferings. That's good news indeed!

Creator God, help us see you in the faces of those I encounter who live with suffering, pain, and uncertainty. Amen.

It all looks perfect and delightfully curated. A simple picture communicates having it all together: options, jobs, financial resources, and opinions. Each social media post drips with humble-bragging self-righteousness.

But we know better. We too are tempted to boast, tempted to show off the perfect response on social media, tempted to stretch the truth a bit to make ourselves look better, feel better, maybe even *be* better?

The psalmist reminds us that God is not impressed with our showboating. How does our posture model humility? Are our motives rooted in love? Are the words we speak or write coming from compassion? Are our eyes cleared by grace? Do we see as Jesus sees? On whom do we depend? In whom do we trust?

It would be easy to look away and ignore the realities that plague us and keep us from embracing this journey into a more Christlike life. It would be easy to fall into the trap of using social media harmfully. It would also be easy to simply walk away and not engage the world of social media at all. Yet the hope of life in God is the hope of Spirit-led awareness that leads us into continued transformation.

Today as you browse through social media feeds, remember to live humbly, trust in God, practice gratitude, and surround yourself with community. These pieces of luggage are the perfect ones for the justice journey.

God, help us not be distracted by the appearances of others; instead, help us grow in deeper awareness of our need for your grace. Amen.

My brain has a tough time shutting off. I try hard at night to slow down and relax. If I do not, my insomnia emerges with a vengeance. My brain will not stop making connections and coming up with ideas for making the world a better place.

I am sure that I am not alone.

We live in a culture that values productivity. We love stories of hard workers who have become wealthy from their work. We place a high value on being busy, staying busy, and being seen as someone who is always busy.

I get it! I am a recovering workaholic. But it is odd that we have such trouble resting, since the story of our faith begins with a God who, after busily creating the world, takes a break. Still, even as I get ready to go to sleep I find myself having to give myself permission to slow down and let my body rest.

Much work is needed in the world. Much work is needed in our homes, neighborhoods, and cities. The list is truly endless. And that list is important; it does matter! Martha's tasks must be done. And yet . . . those tasks are not to become our gods, the center of attention in our waking and in our sleeping.

Seeing God requires sabbath, slowing down, connecting with our deeper selves and those we love. It requires us to get out of the machine of production and into the space of a God who comes and visits us, sits with us, and wants to heal us. Put down the towel and sit. Jesus is waiting!

God, forgive me for my busyness that keeps me from relaxing in your presence. Slow me down and hold me close. Amen.

Longing for Reconciliation

JULY 18–24, 2022 • JEANNIE ALEXANDER

SCRIPTURE OVERVIEW: Hosea can be a difficult book with trouble-some metaphors. This prophet is called to live with an unfaithful wife as an image of how Israel is unfaithful to God. Yet even in this initial statement of judgment, God includes a promise of restoration. Psalm 85 appeals to God's steadfast love. God has become angry with the people for their unfaithfulness, and the people appeal for God's mercy, which they are confident they will receive. The Colossians reading warns against replacing or even supplementing the simple truth of the gospel with human wisdom, religious rules, or anything else. We have fellowship with Christ through our faith. Jesus teaches us to ask God for what we need and for what we want just as we would ask a human parent.

QUESTIONS AND SUGGESTIONS FOR REFLECTION

- Read Hosea 1:2-10. How is God reminding you of your covenant relationship?
- Read Psalm 85. When have you needed to pray for restoration in your life, in your relationships with the wider community, or in your relationship with God?
- Read Colossians 2:6-19. Paul teaches us the value of community. How can you help make the community more just?
- Read Luke 11:1-13. How has praying regularly changed you? If you do not pray regularly, start a practice now. Look for the ways it changes you.

Executive director of No Exceptions Prison Collective; co-founding resident of Harriet Tubman House, an intentional community in Nashville, TN, dedicated to works of abolition, liberation, and food sovereignty; loves bees, bogs, and all things wild.

Reconciliation and redemption are constant themes of the biblical narrative because we so often need them. We see individuals, families, tribes, and nations turning away from the path of justice and love and toward their own destruction again and again. It's easy from our distanced perspective to think these people are foolish or unwise. But this ignores the truth we know from our own experience: Turning away from justice and love is often done with the best of intentions. Understand this as we look at our own lives and the evil that confounds the world around us. We sacrifice justice and wholeness for negative peace—the absence of violence, tension, or discomfort. We silence the will to love because we want to live unbothered by the needs of others.

This is where our fault so often lies, not in a desire for evil but in a desire for incomplete, malfunctioning good. We avoid confrontation at the cost of justice, vulnerability, and uncomfortable truth.

Today's reading reminds us that the difficult path does not end without hope. It ends on a reminder that even if one generation, one people, one tribe, or indeed one individual fails, those that are "not my people" can again be called "Children of the living God." Reconciliation is there, waiting on a turn back to the difficult road of righteousness. It is that turn that reconciles us to the love and justice we have left by the wayside. Let us not wait until judgment. May we repent now of our desire to live lives of negative peace.

Spirit who knows the secret thoughts of my heart, who knows my weakness and my strength, show me the ways I seek negative peace rather than the fullness of righteousness. Deepen the desire of my heart for a world made in your image, God of justice, Spirit of love. Amen.

What drives us? What motivates us to take up the path of reconciliation and turn our hearts toward this difficult and holy calling? The answer is almost always the suffering of those we harm, of ourselves, of those we are close to, or simply of the world at large. When we witness suffering, we see the world as it is and not as we wish it to be. In that moment we are invited to join the work of reconciliation.

Suffering highlights the necessity of action, healing, and renewal. But instead of that renewal, we often turn to pity or paralysis. Rather than doing the deep introspection and hard work of self-analysis and redemption, we simply ask God to "turn us." But what good is pity or paralysis? Whom does it serve? It is cheap grace for an oppressor to sob over the realization of wrongdoing without embracing true transformation.

Pity tempts us with easy emotion rather than difficult growth. Paralysis tempts us with "not making things worse" instead of the transformative work of making things better.

We all like to downplay the ways we contribute to a world where evil holds sway; it can be overwhelming to recognize exactly how broken our world's systems are. Yet, as Christians, we simply cannot ignore our calling to participate in the redemption of all creation. We know we cannot fix all wrongs, but we are called to action. Reconciliation is an active process; we must enter into it as such.

How have I avoided actions I knew to be necessary? How can I change my inaction into a positive, loving response when faced with this choice again?

When we dream of a reconciled world, we may mistakenly think of "returning to the Garden," as if the history of the world will be erased and we will be placed new and naked before a snake and a tree. But this is not the blueprint of reconciliation. Reconciliation does not propose a clean slate but a justified one.

When we are looking to reconcile, we must ask not only what has happened and how things have been broken, but what the new relationship, new world, and new system look like. In today's scripture the psalmist longs for a time when mercy and truth meet. This is the vision of a place that has suffered greatly and has been renewed.

When we look for renewal, we must be as bold as the psalmist; we must dream of new systems and new relationships that have learned from the previous damage.

This newness amid a frank examination of history is echoed in the book of Revelation as John sees the New Earth and the New Jerusalem. Here at the end of all things exists a tree whose leaves "are for the healing of the nations" (Rev. 22:2). Even in New Jerusalem healing is still a work in progress. Reconciliation always is; it is a daily choice that sees the past not as an enemy but as a treasured teacher.

The language of this psalm reminds us that reconciliation at its core is growth and transformation to be embraced at the heart level. This is why systems like our own criminal punishment system thwart proximity. Our past cannot be anything but an enemy if our choices have left us no hope of learning, growing, and reforming.

O God, you know the truths I cannot speak even to myself. But I believe in your love and mercy, and I believe that you have made a way for me even through the wilderness of my own heart. You have created a sanctuary and spring within me, so that I can be whole. Amen.

Longing for Reconciliation

Think of how much more work it takes to reconcile with a family member than with an acquaintance. History can intrude into even the sincerest attempts to mend a broken relationship. That is one reason why we are tempted to think that we are better than the person we have wronged. This is especially likely when our apology is not accepted. We forgive ourselves for our sins because we have made the first—and often the easiest—step in reconciliation, and we hold the person we have wronged in contempt for stubbornly refusing our offer.

But the truth is that no one, not even a family member, owes you a relationship. No one has to forgive you; no one has to move past whatever wrong you have committed. While forgiveness may be ideal, it is simply not how the world works. The offer of reconciliation must come freely and without an insistence on a continued relationship. We must hold ourselves accountable and also give grace to those who simply cannot remain in the relationship.

"Thy will be done" cuts so much deeper than the cursory thought we give it when we mumble the Lord's Prayer. In the end we are fighting not only against our personal desires for justice, fairness, and acceptance but also against the powers and principalities that demand retribution rather than healing. Our transactional culture rejects evolution and reconciliation, the very conditions of the beloved community.

If we believe the words of Jesus and the invitation to full redemption without qualification, what does the kin-dom of God look like alongside human kingdoms?

Reconciliation sometimes comes only with persistence, but that does not mean belligerence. Rather, it is an unwavering dedication to the new path of righteousness. Often people are not ready to receive an apology or participate in the process of reconciliation; they are hurt and need to heal. Only with the constant display of new understanding can they risk accepting a new relationship.

When we look for signs of reconciliation, we can easily become discouraged. Our world is tumbling through ecological collapse while we labor under corrupt hierarchies, look for hope amid broken families, strive for justice with governments that cage other human beings, and keep the faith of God's love in the face of churches that preach hate. Reconciliation sometimes seems hopeless. But if we dare to walk this path, we will find that Jesus has cleared it and walked ahead of us.

The request for bread and forgiveness of debts is not merely metaphorical; they are the difference between life and death. Never forget that the everyday reality of Jesus of Nazareth was a world of domination and deprivation.

In today's scripture Jesus reminds us that we must press on, steadfast and unwavering. We must dedicate ourselves to justice, mercy, and love. When we pray for the earth to be as it is in heaven or for our debts to be forgiven as we forgive, we are not reciting a line that requires nothing of us. We are committing our entire lives to God's work.

As we dedicate ourselves and do the work day by day, we will see the Spirit working alongside us. When we keep seeking the new world, we will find it in the most unlikely places.

Creator of all life, justice, and a way forward, give us bread for today and the strength to create a system that forgives debts so that our children may be fed tomorrow. Amen.

As people who believe that all things are being made new, we can recognize—even in the brokenness of failure and in the hurt of people with whom we will never be able to reconcile—that we are not trapped in the worst things we have done. We can be better and are being made whole moment by moment. Reconciliation is in that hope of transformation.

Are we the worst thing we have ever done? Are we lost in the moments of our greatest sin? For some people, the answer isn't theoretical. We label them by their sin. To our society they will never be more or less than that moment. We cage them and try to retain that moment of guilt, spreading out one instant over decades and reducing a human being to a single act. Our labels strip their humanity and freeze them in time. In our devotion to a false justice and captivity to a false philosophy, we prevent them—and ourselves—from ever seeing reconciliation.

This endless existence in a point in time is diametrically opposed to the work of new creation. What is justice or reconciliation without growth, newness, and the transformation of not just the person but of the society that birthed them? The principalities and powers are terrified that we will truly believe and live into the truth that God "forgave all our trespasses, erasing the record that stood against us with its legal demands." To maintain power they perpetuate a system where the small gods of our world command our loyalties, and the brutalizing overseer of systemic racism separates us from our siblings in Christ. If only we could see the holy in the mundane, then we might see the face of God in our neighbor.

Dear God, help me see that we would stand in a garden of abundance if only our clenched fists were open hands. Amen.

The work of reconciliation is only sustainable inside the community of all who seek to be reconciled without exception. We need each other. We are a body of holy revolution and renewal, growing "with a growth that is from God." We need each other to see the work finished.

The new world is not complete without each of us, and it cannot be completed without all of us. To be reconciled ourselves we must truly embrace and enact a world where no person is thrown away or forgotten. This radical act of re-creation, renewal, and reconciliation can only fully mature in the midst of a people who have dedicated themselves to seeing it through.

The call of Christ in the world is to reconcile all people to each other. This does not mean that we must all get along, or that we must stay in community with everyone. Rather we must seek to live into these principles, fortified and supported by those around us, welcoming all who wish to join.

This new welcoming process is not simply, "We'd love for you to be a part of God's family in Christ. Come, be reconciled with everyone." Rather, we extend welcome as God has always extended it: by offering forgiving love to all. That is our work. Paul wrote in 2 Corinthians 5:19: "God was reconciling the world to himself through Christ, by not counting people's sins against them. He has trusted us with this message of reconciliation" (CEB).

The new world is not a prison; it is a garden. We that plant hope and water seeds of that which is to come stand together in joy—reconciled to a life abundant, without walls, in full knowledge of what came before, and ready to love the world as it is grows.

Where have we sought to weed out the "other" from the garden? What could an inclusive garden look like over the carefully manicured garden of empire?

God Is Enough

JULY 25–31, 2022 • DANIEL WOLPERT

SCRIPTURE OVERVIEW: Hosea relates a further message from God. Israel has repeatedly ignored God's teachings, even though God continues to reach out with love and kindness. A just response would be wrath, but God will respond with mercy to restore the people. The psalmist echoes this teaching about God's enduring love. Although some have gone through periods of distress, when they call out to God, the Lord responds with steadfast love. We then explore guidance for the life of a Christian. In Colossians we read that we should focus on heavenly realities, not the physical world. Rather than pursuing our own pleasure, we should put on a new self and behave more like God desires. The parable that Jesus tells reinforces this point. We should focus on storing up heavenly treasures, not earthly ones.

QUESTIONS AND SUGGESTIONS FOR REFLECTION

- Read Hosea 11:1-11. How have you suffered the consequences of turning away from God? How has God welcomed you back?
- Read Psalm 107:1-9, 43. What stories of God's goodness does your family tell to the next generations?
- Read Colossians 3:1-11. How has Christ renewed you? How do you see Christ in others?
- Read Luke 12:13-21. How has greed shown up in your life? How do you combat greed in all its forms to live out of a mentality of abundance?

Healer and student of the spiritual life; co-founder and executive director of the Minnesota Institute of Contemplation and Healing; spiritual director and Presbyterian pastor; author of several books and multiple articles on spiritual life, leadership, and healing.

In this first passage of the week, Hosea reflects on the beginning of the kingdom of Israel when the people were first called out of Egypt. The uncertainty of not knowing what the future held for them combined with the challenge of the wilderness caused the people to turn away from the invisible God of the universe to tangible gods made of wood, stone, and gold. Uncertainty does this to us; our anxiety wells up and makes us grasp on to things that seem solid but are not helpful.

Yet God, through Hosea, reminds the people that it is God who was always with the people, leading them with compassion and love, feeding them, and guiding them.

This is both the theme and the challenge for this week of reflection: God is enough. God's guidance, leading, and presence are enough for us as a people moving through the present moment into an uncertain future.

A spiritual life that practices prayer and justice makes this assertion of God's sufficiency real. We work together in community, turning to God to encourage and guide us.

Let us practice embodying the fullness of God's care.

God of the universe, help us to know that you are enough for us. We long to experience your care and compassion. Feed us with your presence. Amen.

I bet most people talk to themselves. I have extensive conversations in my head, mulling over the day and any challenging situations and interactions I have had. Sometimes these internal dialogues are not healthy; they can become a vortex for negativity, a place of habit where I'm trapped in old patterns of thought. But sometimes they permit healthy processing that leads to life-giving action or that reorients my heart and mind in a helpful direction.

This habit of internal dialogue may come from God, who is often shown talking to God's self in passages like today's reading. I have an image of God muttering, roaming the galaxy, ruminating over the challenge of dealing with us. We seem to give God endless material for self-reflection. And most of these instances are times and situations when God could lose God's temper and smash us!

Those of us who are parents know these moments. Your child has just drawn on the wall with markers for the fourth time in as many days, and part of your internal conversation drifts toward the possibility of lots of yelling. But if we are coming from a place of grounded awareness, we don't give in to that impulse. And that's what God also decides—*I'm not going to lose it*—and we see, as the passage unfolds, that God's compassion and presence allow the people to reform and return from exile. Once again, God is enough for the people to return home.

Our spiritual life helps us to experience God's compassion, God's turning toward us. In the quiet conversations of our mind we can find God roaring and leading us home.

God of endless patience, help us to listen for you. Help us to hear your roar. Bring us into your presence. Amen.

When we assert that God is enough, we should not slip into a spiritualized fantasy that dismisses the real challenges of life. These six verses of the psalm extol the blessings of God and the reality that God is enough. But we know that there are many who are hungry who do not get fed. There are those who get sick and do not get well. These tragedies unfold even as people cry out to God for help.

Many people have a transactional view of God and God's action in the world. I've known these people to turn away from God, angry and disappointed because they have suffered and their prayers have not been "answered." Yet if we look at the world with clear-eyed realism, the idea that God will give us everything we ever want and will prevent all suffering is simply wrong. This is an immature and inaccurate image of God.

The great spiritual teachers of our faith understood the realities of suffering. They looked to the life of Jesus to see that embracing faith means living hopefully in the midst of the suffering of the world. Any understanding of God's fullness must take into account that God is enough in both good times and bad. God comes to us in our suffering not necessarily to fix it but rather to help us with the endurance that leads to a deeper faith.

God's love endures forever no matter what happens. When we discover this truth, it is enough.

God of suffering and rejoicing, help us understand the mystery of faith and the mystery of you. Especially in our suffering, help us to know your love. Help us to experience you as a companion along the paths of our lives. Amen.

The final verse of today's psalm invokes Wisdom: "Let those who are wise give heed to these things." This is a nod to the biblical Wisdom tradition that focuses on how to live a life centered upon God. In Proverbs, Wisdom is personified as a brilliant woman; and as humans we are called to listen for her, to enter into her house and seek understanding (see Proverbs 9:1-12). In fact, as people of God our primary calling is to follow God's lead and commands, becoming wise in the process.

Jesus says that doing the will of his Father is his primary mission on earth, and, as such, he places himself at the center of the Wisdom tradition (see John 6:38). As Christ followers, we are to embrace this tradition of discernment which calls us also to seek God's will.

Although there are many techniques of discernment prayer, they all ask us to pay attention to what is "life-giving" and what is "death-dealing" in our experience. Since God is the giver of life, becoming more aware of the life-giving Spirit in our midst will enable us to move in accordance with that Spirit and find God in our day-to-day activity. This experience of God's constant companionship leaves us satisfied. God's presence is enough in every situation.

In the Christian spiritual tradition, discernment is not simply a tool for decision-making; it is, rather, a way of life, the way of Wisdom. That is the reason the original name for the Jesus movement was the "Way." These early communities and gatherings of disciples saw themselves as followers of the way of Jesus, followers of God's will.

Let us seek wisdom, so we will know God's sufficiency.

Loving God, grant us wisdom. Help us to orient our lives around you so that we may know your will and meet you wherever our life's path takes us. Amen.

A friend of mine was worried about his grandmother because she was living alone in their old family house in Mississippi. He called her and told her of his concern. She was in her favorite chair on the porch and chided him, saying, "Don't worry; I'm not alone. It's just me and ol' JC out here rockin'." For this woman, being "raised with Christ" wasn't some abstraction or vague liturgical phrase. It was a real and lived experience. Jesus was with her on the porch, her mind was set on things of Christ, and this gave her comfort. It was enough.

The beginning of this third chapter of Colossians uses the imagery from the three-storied universe cosmology: Heaven is above, Earth is in the middle, and Hell or Sheol is below. Today we know this isn't how the universe is constructed, but we can understand this image as a way of describing what is still true of God: God is invisible to us and non-material.

Jesus often talked about the kingdom of God being close by, drawing the attention of the disciples to a non-material reality that is always with us, even as it is unseen. This is the realm of the eternal, of the resurrected Christ. Our spiritual life trains our awareness such that we become grounded in that world rather than the material, ephemeral reality in which our physical body resides.

When my friend's grandmother said that JC was on the porch with her, she didn't mean that a material body was present but rather that she was attuned to the non-material presence of the Divine. From that vantage point, God is always enough.

God of eternity, help us to see you everywhere. Help us to know that we are never alone because you are always with us. Amen.

The scripture passages for these final two days discuss our response to the reality that God is enough. If God's presence, care, generosity, and life-giving Spirit are enough to sustain our lives, how do we respond to these amazing gifts? This passage answers that question by calling us to "put on the new nature" that recovers the image of God in which we were originally formed.

At its heart, the Christian spiritual life is the process of allowing this image of God to emerge from our selves. Sanctification, the theological term that describes the action of the Spirit on our being, is about everyone who is "in Christ" becoming Christlike.

Rather than seeing this sanctifying action of the Spirit as an impossible dream, Christians are asked to see it as the ordinary activity of our life of faith. Yet the world we inhabit is full of people who claim to be Christian but engage in all of the behaviors that this passage says we are to lay aside. We can see how the world co-opts our faith.

Becoming Christlike requires practice. Members of Christian spiritual communities pray together five to seven times a day, not because they think they are holy but rather because they know how much practice and help they need! God and the world groan for a time in human history when a significant proportion of humanity takes the process of sanctification seriously. When we do, the world that we all desire to see might emerge right before our eyes.

God, in your great generosity you have given us everything we need. Help us respond to your gifts through a wholehearted engagement of the life you want us to live. Amen.

This is one of my favorite Gospel stories. In one stroke, Luke challenges both the multi-billion dollar retirement industry and the personal storage shed industry!

We spend much time and energy building more barns to store up our excess, which is what our materialistic society tells us to do. It is a sad truth that many of our church institutions reflect the same values as the larger society. So much of the fighting in our denominations is really about the pension funds and who is going to get them.

Building a bigger barn or fighting over retirement funds are signs that we are struggling to believe that God is enough.

Once, as a joke, I took a picture of a pastor friend in his martial arts gear, printed it out, and wrote on it: "Jesus loves me, but just in case." I taped it to his door, and he got a good laugh from it. It is natural for us to hedge our bets.

Yet the cumulative effect of our laying up of treasure is that most churches are starved for the funds they need to be vibrant, mission-focused communities. There is an old church joke (or observation) about the council arguing and arguing about spending $10 before adjourning so everyone can go home in their $50,000 trucks. It seems that it continues to be difficult for us to be generous toward God. What will it take for us to be so?

God, as we come to the end of this week of reflection on your generosity, give us generous spirits. Help us embrace the truth that you are enough for us. Amen.

Sacrificing Certainty

AUGUST 1–7, 2022 • JENNIFER BAILEY

SCRIPTURE OVERVIEW: The prophet Isaiah brings a harsh message to the Southern Kingdom of Judah. Although they are performing sacrifices and observing feasts, they have lost their heart for God. God wants no more meaningless sacrifices but instead wants the people to repent. The psalmist proclaims a similar message from God. The people's sacrifices have become pointless because the people have forgotten God. The primary offerings that God desires are thanksgiving and ethical living. The author of Hebrews sounds a note of harmony, emphasizing that Abraham's faith in action—not his performance of religious duties—brings him favor with God. Jesus teaches that we cannot rest on our laurels of simply "having faith." Instead we should remain vigilant and continue to perform acts of charity, including caring for the poor, as a response to our faith.

QUESTIONS AND SUGGESTIONS FOR REFLECTION

- Read Isaiah 1:1, 10-20. Consider the author's difficult questions: Is there blood on your hands? Does your worship lead you to acts of mercy and justice?
- Read Psalm 50:1-8, 22-23. How do you "bring Thanksgiving as [your] sacrifice" and "go the right way"?
- Read Hebrews 11:1-3, 8-16. How do you demonstrate faith as a verb, not just a noun?
- Read Luke 12:32-40. God promises us a bountiful kingdom, but we cannot take our worldly possessions there. How do you work toward living as if you are already in God's bountiful kingdom? How do you help to create it?

Ordained itinerant elder in the African Methodist Episcopal Church; serves on the staff of Greater Bethel A.M.E. Church in Nashville, TN; founder of Faith Matters Network.

These days there seems to be very little of which we can be certain. The past several years saw a global pandemic take the lives of millions of beloved brothers, sisters, grandparents, and friends. The changes to our climate have made generational storms into annual weather events. People have become less kind, more certain of their own beliefs, and convinced that being right is more important than being in relationship.

In the midst of what sometimes feels like unending chaos, I have found myself leaning ever more on the practices and traditions of my faith that shaped me growing up. Leading the weekly prayer call at church became a way to mark time and ground myself in communal vulnerability and shared witness. Taking Communion kits and gifts to sick and shut-in church members became a highlight of ministry as our acts of service reminded people they are never alone.

The practice that has brought me the most comfort is singing the hymns my elders taught me. I often flipped through our church's hymnal as a child at Bethel A.M.E. Church when my pastor's sermon was a little too long or a bit over my head. These days the hymn "Hold to God's Unchanging Hand" is at the forefront of my consciousness. It begins simply, "Time is filled with swift transition, naught of earth unmoved can stand. Build your hopes on things eternal, hold to God's unchanging hand!"

In these words, I find solace. Change is inevitable, but so is God's steadfastness. Today's text defines faith as "the assurance of things hoped for, the conviction of things not seen." I have often heard this scripture interpreted to mean that faith is the absence of doubt. But perhaps "faith" could also be interpreted as trust in the absence of certainty.

Dear God, help us to hold fast to your steadfast loving-kindness. Free us to sacrifice certainty, and open our hearts to the new thing you are doing in our lives and in the world. Amen.

Growing up, I remember hearing family stories of ancestors who risked their lives in search of a better future for their descendants. These were the aunts and uncles who fled the terror of the Jim Crow South in the Great Migration—an exodus of nearly 6 million Black Americans from the rural South to the great cities of the industrial North. They left with the little they had, unsure of what would welcome them when they arrived. Yet they trusted God to make a way.

Hebrews 11 is full of examples of biblical ancestors who chose trust in the absence of certainty. Here we find the superheroes and superheroines of faith whose lives of service to God are revered in stained-glass windows, sermons, and liturgy.

Today's reading amplifies the story of Abraham and Sarah, two of the most important figures in the Jewish and Christian traditions. When God called Abraham, he set out without knowing where he was going or what was in store. He and Sarah were faithful but—and this is the good news for us—not flawless. They are examples we can hope to follow.

The glimpses of the humanity of Abraham and Sarah in Genesis show us how God holds our doubt, pain, and uncertainty as we move into the unknown. Abraham asked God why it was taking so long for God to give him the descendants that were promised (see Genesis 15:2-3). When Sarah overheard God saying that she would get pregnant in her old age, she laughed and then lied when she got caught (see Genesis 18:10-15).

God does not call us to perfection but to patience. God's view of time is much longer than our own. God holds all that ever was and all that will be. God is also empathetic. That is why, as we wait, God does not require us to be silent but opens space for dialogue.

What questions do you have for God today?

Irecently attended an intergenerational conversation between the women of a Catholic religious Order and young spiritual seekers. The community is called Nuns & Nones, and it seeks to foster relationships that create prophetic communities of care and contemplation that incite courageous action. The conversation I listened in on was focused on the three vows the nuns take when they enter religious life: poverty, chastity, and obedience. The younger community members lovingly inquired about the sacrifices the elder women had made to commit their lives to Christian service. To my surprise, the nuns in the group uniformly emphasized the ways that their vows had expanded and enriched their lives rather than limiting them.

Perhaps I should not have been so astonished by the conversations. Our reading from the Gospel of Luke points us toward the conclusion reflected in these women's testimonies. Verse 33 tells us to sell our possessions and give alms to the needy so that we create a treasure for ourselves in heaven that cannot be stolen or destroyed.

I have not yet reached the place of spiritual maturity where I am willing to give up all my material possessions. But God is, thankfully, still working on me. In the nuns and their young friends, I see living examples of how to reimagine what we consider precious and dream about the possibilities that can be opened up when our treasures align with our deepest values and convictions.

What treasures do you hold closest to your heart?

As we sacrifice certainty and attempt to discern God's will for us and our communities, how do we know we are on the right track? How can we rest assured that our efforts are pleasing to God?

In the early verses of Psalm 50, God is preparing to render judgment on the people. God summons those called faithful to account for their actions. It appears that the people are doing exactly what they have been taught to do, moving through the rituals and preparing burnt offerings. Yet this is not the sacrifice that God desires. Instead, God asserts that sincere gifts of thanksgiving are most desirable and pleasing.

One interpretation of this text is that a sacrifice that is pleasing to God holds at the center a spirit of gratitude. Today the term "thanksgiving" in the United States is most often associated with a holiday filled with family, food, and football. Yet, as the classic gospel song by Dr. Charles G. Hayes and the Cosmopolitan Church of Prayer reminds us, "Every Day Is a Day of Thanksgiving" or, at the very least, has the potential to be a day of thanksgiving. Scientists have long studied the positive benefits of gratitude and have found that the daily practice of expressing appreciation is correlated with better mental and physical health, improved self-esteem, deeper empathy for others, and even better sleep.

The writer of this psalm might have been onto something. Even in the midst of our sacrifice God desires for us to be whole and well. Placing gratitude at the center of our daily spiritual practice can and will improve our well-being.

For whom or what do you feel grateful today?

Gratitude is at the center of sacrifices that are pleasing to God. Of equal importance is how we express that gratitude in the world.

The book of Isaiah begins much like Psalm 50, with God rendering judgment upon the people and explicitly rejecting sacrifices grounded in rote rituals. Instead, God encourages the people to cease doing evil, seek justice, rescue the oppressed, defend the orphan, and plead for the widow. God calls us to challenge the systems that allow inequality and poverty to persist.

It seems that another quality of sacrifice that is pleasing to God is being of service to others. God invites us to be hands that heal the hurting and downtrodden. In doing so, we become co-creators with God of the Beloved Community—a state without poverty, hunger, and hate and in which everyone is cared for. In serving others, we find that we are also serving ourselves. It is through service that we become more fully aware that each of us has been and will be on the receiving end of needing help.

In the early days of my ministry, I often worked alongside college students who were discerning their vocational path. They were asking big questions about where God was leading them to serve. Each of us, they believed, has a "prophet purpose." We are all called to live in that space of grief and hope, so that we become partners in God's work of justice and reconciliation. Yet each of us also has a unique role to play. To find it, we must read the signs of the times for ourselves, and discern where the Spirit moves each of us to act.

What specific part of the world's brokenness most speaks to your own passions, griefs, hopes? Where do you feel most called to do the work of justice?

Turning on the news these days can easily be overwhelming, given the amount of suffering in the world. It seems that there is always a new tragedy and a new fear about what might happen next: a mass shooting here, a natural disaster there, and a moment of violent conflict just around the corner. If we are not careful, we can develop compassion fatigue: "an indifference to charitable appeals on behalf of those who are suffering, experienced as a result of the frequency or number of such appeals." In other words, being asked to care about every horrifying event can lead to emotional and physical exhaustion and a diminished ability to empathize with others.

So what are we as Christians, who are called to seek justice for the marginalized, to do? It helps to take a long view of time. As Bishop Ken Untener of Saginaw says in *A Prayer of Oscar Romero*, "We cannot do everything, and there is a sense of liberation in realizing that. This enables us to do something, and to do it very well. It may be incomplete, but it is a beginning, a step along the way, an opportunity for the Lord's grace to enter and do the rest."*

One of the beautiful things about being a Christian is that we are constantly reminded that it is not up to us alone to solve the great challenges of our time. During the time Moses was leading the Israelites to the Promised Land, he complained to Jethro about having to settle all disputes and answer all the people's questions about God's will for them. Jethro told him, "You can't do this alone. . . . Let me tell you how to do this so that God will be in this with you" (Exod. 18:18, THE MESSAGE).

---

*"Prophets of a Future Not Our Own," U.S. Conference of Catholic Bishops, https://www.usccb.org/prayer-and-worship/prayers-and-devotions/prayers/prophets-of-a-future-not-our-own, Accessed April 23, 2021.

Where do you go when your cup is empty? What are the practices that sustain you?

Stay ready so you don't have to get ready. I'm not sure when and where I first heard that phrase, but it has always stuck with me. Perhaps it was on the playground during a game of dodgeball. It may have been a line from a popular song or movie from my childhood. Regardless of its origins, it is a quote I think about often when I revisit today's passage from Luke 12.

The scripture finds Jesus among the multitudes using his favorite teaching tool, a parable, to offer guidance about how to prepare for the coming of the "Son of Man." Jesus uses the example of slaves (some translations say "servants") preparing for their master to return from a wedding banquet not knowing when he will return. Those who stay up and keep watch will be rewarded for their diligence.

I find this passage challenging. I am the direct descendant of enslaved peoples who came to the United States as part of the transatlantic slave trade. Any talk of the master-slave dynamic immediately makes me uncomfortable as I consider the unspeakable horrors my family was subjected to under the system of chattel slavery. Yet, I also believe that we are called, like Jacob, to wrestle with God as we make meaning of the biblical narrative and let it speak to us.

So what does this parable have to say to those of us sacrificing certainty today? Jesus' instructions provide us with a blueprint for action. While we patiently wait for God's revelation, our task is to go about the work of serving others with gratitude. The best way to prepare for the in-breaking of the kingdom of God is to practice by building the Beloved Community with one another right now.

And so we keep watch, knowing that change for the better is coming. We keep watch, sacrificing certainty for a new revelation of God's vision for a more loving world.

Believe It or Not

AUGUST 8–14, 2022 • BEN INGEBRETSON

SCRIPTURE OVERVIEW: Isaiah compares the people of Israel to a vineyard that God has planted. However, the grapes that grow there have become wild. There is no justice, no right living in the vineyard, so God is considering letting it be destroyed. The psalmist uses the same metaphor to bemoan the state of God's people. The vineyard has been overrun, burned, and cut down. The psalmist appeals to God to restore the vineyard. The author of Hebrews presents many more examples of people of faith in past times. All these exemplars now surround us and cheer us on in our life of faith. In Luke's Gospel, Jesus cautions that following the gospel requires full commitment. For some, this will mean tension in relationships, even within families. Following Jesus is not a commitment of convenience.

QUESTIONS AND SUGGESTIONS FOR REFLECTION

- Read Isaiah 5:1-7. Recall a time when you lovingly prepared a place. What would prompt you to destroy it?
- Read Psalm 80:1-2, 8-19. How has God restored you when you have been at your most vulnerable?
- Read Hebrews 11:29–12:2. Who makes up your personal Faith Hall of Fame? How does each person cheer you on in your spiritual journey?
- Read Luke 12:49-56. What does it mean for your life of faith for Jesus to have come to bring division?

Director of New Church Development for the Dakotas/Minnesota Conferences of The United Methodist Church; consults with the Reformed Church in America and the Moravian Church; author of *Plant Like Jesus: The Church Planter's Devotional* (Upper Room Books, 2021).

In today's reading, Asaph, a temple musician in Jerusalem, observes the Assyrian invasion of the northern kingdom of Israel. Ten tribes are being swept away, leaving the southern kingdom of Judah exposed to the foreign threat. It is a great tragedy that shakes their faith foundations.

Under such dire circumstances, grief overtakes the writer. He begins by recounting Israel's favored history of Exodus and the United Kingdom of David and Solomon. They believed they were God's vine—that God had transplanted them from Egypt and cultivated their growth and fruitfulness over the years. With that collective memory, the people react to God with shock, denial, and anger: "Why did you let this happen to us? Why have you permitted foreign vermin to ravage your vineyard?" The demand for answers then pivots to a bargain never to fail again: "We are the vine you planted that now is being torched. Return your favor to us and we will never turn away again" (AP).

We can relate to these words of desperation. It could be any number of circumstances—a lost job, a failed relationship, or compromised health. Suddenly the landscape changes, and we desperately rehearse the past and wonder how things changed so dramatically for us. Then come the alternating jabs and pleas to God: "Awaken!" "Why?" "We promise!" We turn the words over and over. They become our lament.

The thread of hope that runs through the psalm—the hope that the people hold on to—is our hope as well. Like the Israelites, we believe we are God's vine and therefore that God is invested in us. The vine may require pruning (see John 15:6); but in troubled times we find, and maintain, hope in the One to whom we belong.

Today, Lord, I claim my identity as part of your vineyard, and I accept seasons of growth and pruning that you permit. Help me to deeply and fruitfully claim that identity. Amen.

The book of Isaiah is so full of hopeful references to "good news for the poor" (61:1), the "Prince of Peace" (9:6), the "wolf dwelling with the lamb" (11:6), and "Immanuel" (7:14) that it has been named by some as the fifth Gospel. Indeed, the writer often sounds more like a hopeful evangelist than a dour prophet. But the surrounding circumstances cannot be denied. The northern kingdom of Israel has been assailed by Assyrian invaders. That national calamity sets the stage for a parable delivered through a love song.

Like the parables of Jesus in the Gospels, this love song uses vivid images to draw us into its story of hopeful promise and then tragic disappointment. Picture a carefully prepared plot of ground, the best vine rootstock for planting, a fence and a look-out to guard the produce, and even a winepress in anticipation of fine vintage. Imagine the keeper's expression when he first tastes the bitter yield. There is nothing to do but abandon the field. Now we are ready for the surprise ending: The people of God are a foul harvest. They have produced injustice and misery instead of righteousness. All appears to be lost.

It is tempting to correlate a point of reference for every element of the story, but we are wise to remember that the concluding summary is the point. God delights in justice and cultivates that principle in his people so that they will carry it into the world. The prophets' lessons lift up kingdom values that are both a blessing and a responsibility for those who receive them.

Like Israel, we have to decide how we respond to God's righteous nurturing, tending, and cultivation. Those choices come in large and small ways throughout our lives.

Today, Lord, I am aware again of the responsibility I have to live as a recipient of your grace and truth. Help me to be alert for the ways I can demonstrate your kingdom in the world. Amen.

In Luke 12, Jesus is focused on our choices. He first warns a rich man not to be a fool with his money. Later he warns his disciples to remain watchful. Now Luke records the sober words in today's text. The choice we make regarding Jesus and his kingdom will affect others around us. Calling for our decision is not easy. We can hear in our Lord's voice a deep longing that this reckoning with choices be over and done with: "How distressed I am . . ." We would say he wants to "get past this." That said, Jesus will not hide the cost of discipleship.

Jesus will not mislead us about the kingdom separation that is coming. He wants us to see it for what it is. Two times in this text he says he has come to bring "fire" and "division." Then he bears down on the hard news. Three times "division" is branded onto his narrative. He then proceeds to itemize the potential schisms in painful detail.

It is striking how intimate these divisions are. Family members are separated. Generations are divided. Indeed, this sounds very much like one of those manufacturer disclaimers that lawyers draft to protect sellers from legal claims: Buyer beware. The decision Jesus is calling you to will break your closest relationships.

Change brings discomfort. The kingdom-defining moments in our lives affect us and those we love. The relational friction shows up in differing values and priorities. We can try to avoid this discomfort and circumvent the change that God is working, but Jesus invites us into his kingdom with full disclosure. God is doing a new thing.

Holy God, we struggle to hear the words of the scripture today. We would prefer to have Jesus delay a call to decision and division. Help us accept the choices that are before us and act faithfully, trusting you with the outcome. Amen.

Earlier in Luke 12, Jesus was speaking to his disciples, but here he is talking to a crowd. These are people who depend on their crops for survival. They study the skies and winds for any indication of what weather is coming. They know by experience that westward clouds passing over a body of water bring rain, and southern winds bring warmer temperatures. They can see these indicators right before their eyes.

But there are other indicators before them that they cannot comprehend. The religious leaders are arrogant and prideful. Herod and the Romans are bearing down with their unjust agenda of occupation. By contrast, Jesus has been walking among them, performing miracles and teaching the pure religion of the kingdom of God. Why can they not see the signs and accept what is before their eyes?

Jesus has a single-word diagnosis: *hypocrisy*. They know the truth, but they live in denial of it. Their problem is not their capacity to understand; it is their unwillingness to accept the truth. They don't like what it could mean for them if Jesus is indeed who he says he is. There is a proverb that captures this tragedy: "A person convinced against their will is of the same persuasion still." Jesus understands this powerful reality, and he calls it out.

Like the crowds who followed Jesus, we too must recognize the hypocritical dilemmas we face. We know the right action, but something overtakes us and we fail to do what we know to be right. That "something" is the very thing Jesus illuminates.

We are not always ready to accept and believe what being a disciple of Jesus means for us. It is not easy to hear these words, but we can trust that Jesus wants us to know abundant life.

Holy God, I am not yet as I hope one day to be. Grant me your grace, and lead me into abundant life in Jesus' name. Amen.

Transitions can be tricky. Are we under the old or new rules? Do we honor the past or announce the future? For the writer of the book of Hebrews the question was: Is religion about the outer practices or about the inner life?

To answer, the writer took a step-by-step comparative path through the practices of the older and newer covenants. One step represents Moses, the sacrificial rituals, and the priestly class. The other step represents Christ, the maker of a new covenant. The point of the first half of Hebrews is to contrast a religion of externalities with a religion of the inner spirit. And chapter 11 represents a climax in that contrast.

The point we find in today's reading, however, is that religion of the inner spirit is not new or confined to one Testament. Joshua, Rahab, Gideon, Samson, and many others are from the old system. Yet they possessed the essential core: faith. In some cases, their faith led them to take great risks for the sake of a cause; in others, their faith moved them forward in liberation. Faith led them to acts of justice and sustained them in profound suffering. Faith was what God was after all along.

Yet, Hebrews shows that for every person who wrestles with the mysteries of God, many more lean on the rituals that can be contained, measured, and checked off a list.

The New Covenant brought a renewed emphasis on matters of the heart. Chief among them is the capacity to face the future without all the answers in front of us. This pleases God. This faith leads us to take risks for the causes of God. This faith draws out acts of justice and liberation. This faith sustains us through affliction and suffering. Believing in the present what God has made clear in the past guides us through difficult transitions.

God, today I hear your invitation to believe you in both the unclear and the focused seasons of my life. Draw from me the fruits of faith in acts of mercy, justice, and truth. Amen.

The writer of Hebrews looks all the way back to Abel and then forward to the days just preceding John the Baptist. This whole time was an era of unfulfilled (or incompletely fulfilled) promise. God's covenant through Abraham was that Abraham would be a great nation and that all the peoples of the earth would be blessed through him. God's promise through Moses was that God would show God's glory through Israel to the nations. God's covenant with David was to establish David's throne perfectly and forever. Finally, the new covenant spoken by the prophet Jeremiah was to overcome national exile and forever press a holy identity onto the people's hearts. These promises were made yet unfulfilled for multiple generations.

While the writer commends the faith of these generations, we know from the record that they did not always wait perfectly. Abraham jumped the gun with Hagar, and Moses lost his cool on Mount Sinai. Jeremiah wished he had never been born, and Jonah ran from his mission. These important ancestors in our faith often stumbled toward the promise.

Despite all the imperfections of faith, God planned something better—a better promise, hope, covenant, and sacrifice. Christ is the fulfillment of all this! He has secured the completion (perfection) of hope for all those who wait in faith. This is God's better plan. We have the benefit of seeing in retrospect this great legacy of faith and God's faithful keeping of the covenants with Abraham, Moses, David, and the prophets. Now we join them, waiting in hope for the ultimate consummation.

Christ has died, Christ is risen, Christ will come again!

Holy God, I humbly join those who await your final consummation in Jesus Christ. I too am impatient with your plan at times. Help me trust you and live today with hope. Amen.

We are surrounded by witnesses. The idea here is not of a great Olympic moment with grandstands and spectators but rather a host of individuals who can bear witness to the practice of a life of faith.

Imagine them standing one by one to tell their stories—Gideon, Rahab, Samuel, David, and Jesus. Each story is an authentic witness to the risks and rewards of believing God. Jesus himself is the pioneer witness who entered our human experience in a way never done before. He is the perfect witness who always trusted the mission he was sent to perform with an eye on the joyful outcome.

Hebrews 11 ends with these witnesses awaiting the promised "something better." Chapter 12 begins with Jesus' anticipating a "joy before him." The life of faith is in anticipation of a much better day to come.

Between the hopeful future and the present challenge is our race. Our challenge is to throw off the things that hinder and entangle us. In human terms these are things that divert our attention—challenging setbacks or the temptation to quit. Anything that draws our attention away from Jesus and the path he has made before us must be jettisoned in favor of finishing the race.

Our race is just that—ours. No one can throw off these things for us. We must do that work ourselves. No one can provide persistence for us. We must do that work too. Jesus has cut the path for us in his life, death, and resurrection. It's our turn now.

Today, Lord Jesus, I see you with fresh eyes. What a persistent race you ran for the sake of the kingdom! Help me to follow you more closely and to release lesser things. Amen.

Journeying with God

AUGUST 15–21, 2022 • CORY DRIVER

SCRIPTURE OVERVIEW: The readings in Jeremiah and Psalm 71 are repeated in a pair from earlier in the year (January 24–30). They describe the authors' confidence that God has had plans for their lives since even before they were born. God similarly knows each one of us and has a calling on our lives. The reading in Hebrews gives us confidence in the permanence of the kingdom of God, to which we have access through the sacrifice of Jesus Christ. We are not to take this lightly; we should worship God with due respect. In a synagogue on the sabbath, Jesus teaches a lesson about mercy. When he encounters a woman in need, he places her need above religious regulations. If religious traditions trump mercy, then our priorities are out of alignment.

QUESTIONS AND SUGGESTIONS FOR REFLECTION

- Read Jeremiah 1:4-10. How can you trust God to empower you to follow God's call? How can you encourage others to live into their calling?
- Read Psalm 71:1-6. How can you continually praise God as your refuge?
- Read Hebrews 12:18-29. How do you discern what is required of you in praising God in the new covenant?
- Read Luke 13:10-17. How do you observe the sabbath now? What sabbath practice might you start that puts God's reign into action?

Director of the Transformational Leadership Academy of the Indiana-Kentucky Synod of the Evangelical Lutheran Church in America (ELCA); adjunct professor at Pacific Lutheran Theological Seminary.

The book of Jeremiah begins with Jeremiah's reasons why he was unsuited for prophetic ministry. He was just a young man. He felt unwise in the ways of the world and also unable to speak eloquently to the kings, priests, and rulers to whom God would send him. How many of us have felt this way in the first weeks of a new job, when we do not yet know all our co-workers or how things are done in this new setting?

But God will have none of Jeremiah's protestations. Pointedly, God does not say that Jeremiah is qualified, skilled, or mature. Instead, God simply informs Jeremiah not to dwell on his lack of experience, but to acknowledge that Jeremiah will go everywhere and say everything that God intends.

Friends, not many of us are called to prophetic ministries like Jeremiah. And yet, God does have words for us to say, places for us to go, and deeds of loving-kindness for us to fulfill. To focus on our own shortcomings and uneasiness is to miss the invitation to a journey with the One who knew us before we were born and prepared righteousness for us to fulfill—if we will but begin the journey.

The writer of the letter to the Ephesians was no doubt familiar with Jeremiah and other prophets like him who were not sure of God's call and what answering that call meant for their lives. In Ephesians 2:10, he writes, "We are what [God] has made us, created in Christ Jesus for good works, which God prepared beforehand to be our way of life."

As we begin, or restart, our journeys with you, remind us, O God, that your grace is sufficient for us. Amen.

God's words to Jeremiah remind us that we are called to witness to the love of God wherever we go. But what are we to make of this list of acts that God has called Jeremiah to do?

At first, the list sounds rather grim: pluck up, break down, destroy, overthrow, build, and plant. At least we get a bit of relief in the last two. In fact, I think seeing those last two verbs in context is key to understanding the rest.

One of the strange places that my journey with God has taken me is the Arava Desert in southeast Israel. I worked on a cooperative farm, growing tomatoes, mangos, and herbs in the desert sand. We used ultra-efficient drip agriculture and about twenty cubic centimeters of organic fertilizer to grow each tomato plant each season under massive tents that contained moisture and blocked out the worst effects of sandstorms and blazing desert sun.

During those desert adventure years, I learned that all the tasks of Jeremiah's ministry are those of a farmer looking to produce a harvest. We built a growing tent and planted the seedlings. But we also plucked up the plants after harvesting their fruits. We destroyed the tomato plants by grinding them up to use as fertilizer for the next crop. Some of the most fun of the whole growing season was tearing down and "overthrowing" the tents, so that we could set up someplace else and let the desert return to its natural state.

I believe the tasks for which God called Jeremiah and for which God calls us as well are the work of a master gardener who is deeply in love with creation and expects humans to produce good fruit (see Matthew 7:17-20). Planting, overthrowing, and destroying all work together for good.

God, as we journey with you, show us how to build, plant, tear down, and overthrow so that your kingdom will grow. Amen.

We know that as we journey with God, there will be ups and downs, successes and failures. I love this reading because it recognizes the cyclical nature of our relationship with God. The psalmist knows God as a reliable refuge. I love the detail in the third verse that says that God is a rock of refuge that I can always go to (NIV).

When my older son was a little boy, he would run just a little bit farther ahead of me than I was comfortable with when we were out walking. But when he would see anything that would scare him, especially seagulls, he would come running back to me because he knew that I would keep him safe. He would cling to my legs, and I would wave my arms like a madman to drive away the seagulls that were after his snacks. His fear turned to joyous laughter as I dramatically flailed about long after the seagull threat had passed. I think that is the image that the psalmist is trying to portray here: God is a refuge and fortress who not only provides safety and deliverance from enemies but is also a comforting, loving presence who turns fear into joy.

No matter how many times my son took his french fries and walked ahead of me instead of holding my hand, he knew that he could run to me, and that he (and his french fries) would be saved from hungry seagulls. Just so, we as children of God are always welcome to run to God in times of trouble on our journey. The psalmist confesses our faith for us: From the beginning of our journey together, God has been our refuge and fortress, ready for us to continually come home to the rock of life.

God, when the journey is difficult, remind us that we are always welcome to find safety in you. Amen.

The writer of Hebrews describes two different journeys that God's people have undertaken. One journey was from the house of slavery in Egypt to Mount Sinai. The Israelites were overwhelmed by the fiery mountain, storms, darkness, and most of all the awe-inspiring voice of God. This is an overwhelming journey, indeed!

The other journey of God's people leads first to Mount Zion and the city of the living God, and ultimately to the heavenly Jerusalem, the collections of angels, the saints in heaven, God the divine judge, and Jesus. This is an even more overwhelming destination on a journey with God.

The writer of Hebrews preferred the latter journey. But the truth is that God has been bringing people on journeys to God's self in different ways throughout scripture and throughout time. Only a chapter earlier in Hebrews, we heard about those heroes whose faith led them to travel and wander, conquer and retreat, flourish and suffer.

If the wisdom, love, and grace of God bring some to mountains of storm, fire, and divine voice, we say, "Amen, praise God!" And if the wisdom, love, and grace of God bring others to mountains of communion with angels, the church triumphant in heaven, with Jesus and God, we say, "Amen, praise God!" Either way, it is to the same God that we journey. And it is the one true God that sent the beloved Son to rescue us all from the powers of sin and death, freeing us for whatever journey God calls us to undertake.

God, as we follow you on the journeys that you call us to, remind us that we seek the same goal: to encounter you through the life, death, and resurrection of your Son, Jesus. Amen.

The verses that conclude this chapter come as a warning: God has shaken the earth and will again shake the earth and the heavens. The writer of Hebrews urges the readers and hearers to cling to the kingdom that cannot be shaken.

This passage makes me think back to where I was when I experienced my first earthquake. As luck would have it, I was on Mount Scopus, just north of Mount Zion and the Mount of Olives. I had come to the Holy Land and felt the shaking of the earth in a subterranean computer lab at the Hebrew University. No one else seemed particularly worried (it was only a small earthquake), but I was, forgive the pun, rather shaken up. I kept feeling phantom vibrations under my sandals in class and under my bed at night. I could not get rid of the feeling that the earth was unstable under my feet.

I think that is the goal of this passage—to remind us what is stable and unshakable (God and God's kingdom) and what is shakable and combustible (everything else). This realization of what is and is not stable then leads to worship. The letter to the Hebrews urges us to show God gratitude, reverence, and awe "since we are receiving a kingdom that cannot be shaken" (NRSV). On our journey of faith, we travel with an unshakable God who leads us to an unshakable kingdom—both here and in heaven.

God, help us to put our trust in you alone. You and your kingdom are the only refuge to escape the shaking of creation and the consuming fire. Thank you for your love and grace that call us to safety. Amen.

I just cannot get over Jesus' calling this woman forward. Luke notes that Jesus was teaching in the synagogue. There was a woman there who had been sick for eighteen years because of an evil spirit, and she was bent over double. But the woman apparently did not come straight to Jesus. She did not speak for herself. Jesus was teaching, and then he stopped to call her over to him.

I wonder about that woman. Was she content to listen to the words of the great teacher? Was she, perhaps, waiting until Jesus was finished with his lesson to catch up with him and ask him for healing? Or was the woman outside an open-air synagogue, not even listening to Jesus when he saw her and called her over? All we know is that Jesus called this woman to a very short journey that, in her bent-over state, was probably difficult and possibly embarrassing. Was this rabbi going to use her as an example to illustrate some sort of point about people getting what they deserve? Just how had she gotten that evil spirit eighteen years ago anyway? No! The rabbi from Nazareth traveled with healing in his wings (see Malachi 4:2). And so, at the end of her short journey to the center of the synagogue, she began another journey of glorifying God with a healed body.

The Gospels are full of stories of Jesus' going to people: the Syro-Canaanite woman (see Matthew 15:21-28; Mark 7:24-30), the Samaritan woman at the well (see John 4:1-42), and Jairus's daughter (see Luke 8:40-56). And yet, Jesus called this woman, possessed for almost two decades, to come to the center of the crowd so that Jesus could straighten her out. I wonder if Jesus is calling any of us on short journeys of faith so that we can experience the healing we need.

Lord, we know that you come to us always. When you call us to you, help us respond with faith. Amen.

As we finish this week's journey with God and ready ourselves to begin another week, we end with a cautionary note. When the leader of the synagogue saw Jesus call the crippled woman over and heal her on the sabbath, he became indignant. He believed that healing was a kind of work that was prohibited by sabbath regulations. Notably, the official was not opposed to the healing itself: He told people in the congregation who might be interested in healing to come back any day other than the sabbath.

Jesus, of course, did not stand for this. Untying knots was explicitly prohibited on the sabbath, but an exception was allowed to release tethered farm animals so they could eat or drink. How much more then should healing a human body, which does not involve any actions forbidden on the sabbath, be a cause for rejoicing?

Friends, we dare not try to limit the progress of those on their journey toward God. We might find ourselves working against God's loving outreach toward our neighbors or ourselves. Just as responsible farmers or pet owners make sure their animals receive water every day, God makes sure that humans are unbound and led to the water of life every day of our lives.

God is taking us all on a journey. Let us never stand in the way of God's freeing, healing, and loving actions. Let us be awake and alert to ways that God is bringing freedom, healing, and love into the world!

Lord God, we love you. Thank you for loving us first and best. Strengthen us for the journey that you have set out for us. Help us to love and encourage our neighbors. Prevent us, God, from inhibiting your kingdom. Instead, help us to follow you faithfully on the journey. Amen.

You Are Cordially Invited

AUGUST 22–28, 2022 • KATHRYN HAUEISEN

SCRIPTURE OVERVIEW: Jeremiah had the unenviable task of speaking truth to power. While others were proclaiming how good things were, he was called and compelled to insist things were not all that great. The people kept ignoring Yahweh's persistent invitations to abandon their pseudo-gods and focus on Yahweh. The theme of God's hospitality continues in our texts from Hebrews as the author reminds readers that when we extend a genuine welcome to strangers, we may actually be hosting the Lord God. Luke picks up the hospitality thread by proposing a radical new way of deciding whom to include. He extends God's compassion for all humanity by suggesting that we start our invitation lists with those who would not typically be included. God's central message to humans through the centuries, through the scriptures, and most certainly through Christ, is consistent: You, personally, are invited to be God's precious guest on the journey through life.

QUESTIONS AND SUGGESTIONS FOR REFLECTION

- Read Jeremiah 2:4-9. When have you needed to tell authority figures that something was wrong? Where did you find your courage to deliver the message?
- Read Psalm 81. What treasured traditions do you have in your family or with your friends?
- Read Hebrews 13:15-16. Where do you observe people going out of their way to show compassion to others? Where have you received unsolicited kindness?
- Read Luke 14:12-14. When have you extended hospitality to someone who couldn't pay you back?

Retired ELCA pastor living in Houston, TX, with her UMC husband; consults with congregations to conduct capital campaigns and enjoys blogging about good people doing great things at *HowWiseThen.com*.

Jeremiah wrote sometime around 600 BCE, when Josiah was king of Judah. A little more than a decade after Josiah assumed power, it was beginning to look like independence from domination by Assyria was possible.

Jeremiah did not share the confidence of his fellow countrymen but rather continued to warn that Judah was in danger of an invasion from the north. He chastised the people, claiming they had strayed far from God's expectations. During Jeremiah's time, workers found the Book of the Law scrolls that had been abandoned in the Temple (see 1 Kings 22–23). Many of Jeremiah's contemporaries considered this discovery a significant turning point in Judah's spiritual renewal, but Jeremiah remained cautious.

We often ignore people who deliver facts we don't want to hear. Many simply dismissed Jeremiah as a doom-and-gloom malcontent. But Jeremiah kept calling out what God directed him to say and what his own convictions compelled him to proclaim. He accused the people of abandoning Yahweh, making the case they had mistreated the Lord.

Like a skilled prosecutor, Jeremiah demanded to know if the people had completely forgotten everything the Lord had done for them. Did they not remember that astonishing escape from slavery in Egypt to freedom in a land of plenty?

Human nature hasn't changed through the centuries. We're eager to call upon the Lord for help but are quick to forget how God has rescued us. We neglect to listen to God's word until we're in trouble; then we call on God to bail us out—again.

Gracious God, forgive us when we fail to listen to you. Thank you for faithfully inviting us to return when we stray. Amen.

Jeremiah's efforts to reach the rebellious people of his generation remind me of the challenges faced by medical and public health officials during the COVID-19 pandemic. Jeremiah tried again and again to call the people back to a position of health and well-being. But the people didn't believe and insisted on their right to be out and about, without any protective measures, regardless of how their actions affected others.

The people in Jeremiah's time preferred little gods they could hold and manipulate. They wanted the gods of other communities—such as those of the people in Cyprus to the west or those of the Kedar desert tribes to the northeast.

Jeremiah kept proclaiming that Yahweh is the one who would give them what they most longed for; but they had forsaken Yahweh. They turned down living water for cracked, empty cisterns.

During the 2020 pandemic, some people refused to follow the recommended safety precautions from infectious disease specialists. They quite literally adopted the "give me liberty or give me death" philosophy. Their desire for the freedom to do whatever they wanted pulled them away from practices that would protect them and contribute to public safety.

In Jeremiah's day people chose the impotent gods of their neighbors over worshiping the omnipotent Yahweh of their ancestors. Empty promises lured them away from life-enhancing choices and toward life-diminishing consequences.

Yet God would not give up on them. Again and again God sent Jeremiah to invite the people to return to Yahweh.

God of infinite patience, thank you for continuing to call us back to a life-giving relationship with you. Amen.

People like rituals. We like predictable, daily rhythms as we progress from early morning to bedtime. We mark time by the changing seasons and the calendar of special occasions.

It was no different when the psalms were being composed, often to commemorate special events through the year. The beginning of Psalm 81 is a travel psalm people might have sung on their way to the Temple for a festival to mark the transition from one year to the next.

The rest of the psalm, however, shows that the people had forgotten the original reason for the celebration: the Lord's freeing them from bondage in Egypt. The Lord who brought them up out of slavery is ready to fill their open mouths again, but the people will not listen. They will not submit to Yahweh, so the Lord gives them over to their stubborn ways.

Can you sense God's disappointment and frustration? It reminds me of someone who has tried in vain to help a family member overcome an addiction. Again and again the long-suffering relative or friend provides empathy, money, lodging, and trips to professionals, only to have the one suffering with the addiction get into trouble again. Sometimes these cycles are too much for humans, and the only healthy thing to do is trust in God. But God always comes to people, in ancient Israel and in modern situations, inviting us away from death and destruction toward health and wholeness.

We are slow to remember God's saving grace but quick to turn God's interventions into reasons to celebrate. God has to intervene continually with each new generation. Thanks be to God that God is more than willing to do just that.

God of our past, our present, and our hope for the future, thank you for coming to us when we neglect to come to you. Amen.

Hospitality is a major theme throughout the Bible. The unidentified author of this letter emphasizes the central role hospitality played in the early Christian community, noting that welcoming strangers may mean hosting angels without knowing it.

In the early church, hospitality meant more than just being welcoming or friendly. For example, visiting prisoners was an extension of hospitality, taken to those who could not come out to receive it. In Roman-occupied communities, people often ended up in prison for such offenses as not showing adequate respect for Roman gods or being poor. People were persecuted and tortured for expressing their faith. The support of the Christian community was an act of solidarity and a form of hospitality to those suffering for their faith.

Modern economic systems still imprison people for the "crime" of being poor. Those who have resources often buy their way out of jail, if they don't use the legal system to avoid it in the first place. But those lacking financial resources stay behind bars, cut off not only from their family but also from any means of making the money to pay their bail. Members of the Christian community are often the advocates coming to protest the inequity of this system.

People are also still persecuted for their religious beliefs in many parts of the world. In my diverse city of Houston, Christian congregations frequently go to great lengths to show solidarity with Muslim and Jewish neighbors as a way of demonstrating hospitality across interfaith lines.

Lord who invites us to fellowship, strengthen our resolve to extend your hospitality to others. Amen.

The author of Hebrews ends on what some scholars speculate may have been an afterthought. If so, perhaps the author wanted to leave readers with one final encouragement: Praise God and remember to do good, including sharing what you have.

My favorite local evening news program closes each broadcast with an inspirational story about people showing kindness to neighbors. Through hurricanes, floods, and pandemics, they always manage to find someone doing something great for other people. It is a real morale booster after a half hour of disturbing and distressing reports of crime, greed, and corruption.

Many people do acts of kindness. What sets the Christian community apart is our conviction that we show mercy and kindness to others because of what Christ first did for us on the cross.

Perhaps equally important, as we try to figure out how to live together in our global village, are the many ways Jesus demonstrated how to treat others. He showed grace to those that society tends to reject—people with contagious diseases, poor people, foreigners, and immigrants. But Jesus also showed kindness and grace to those who seemed to have more than they needed. He was a frequent guest in the homes of those others looked upon with suspicion and contempt.

In one way, the Christian life is easy. In Christ, God has already done everything to bring us into relationship with God's self. But it is also an extremely challenging path because we are called to set aside our prejudices and to reach out to those we would prefer to ignore.

Lord and lover of all people, forgive us when we fail to follow where you lead. Thank you for your endless supply of grace and forgiveness. Amen.

You Are Cordially Invited   285

In our scene for today, Jesus is at the house of a leader of the Pharisees to share in a meal. As he watches the other guests arrive, he takes notice of how they choose to sit in the places of honor. Jesus then tells a parable on the meaninglessness of social status: "Take the lowest status seat available and wait to be asked to take a better seat. That way you won't be humiliated when the host asks you to move to make room for someone more important" (AP).

I was on the return flight from an international trip, comfortable in my aisle seat near the front of the plane. A flight attendant asked me to switch seats so a man in the back could sit with his family, who were sitting in the seats adjacent or across the aisle from me. I tried to maintain a positive attitude as the attendant led me to a middle seat near the back of the plane. I wasn't feeling particularly hospitable at the moment but decided to make the best of it so the family could stay together.

I tried to get comfortable sandwiched between two other passengers. Then the attendant approached me again. The person in the emergency aisle seat did not speak English, which was a requirement to sit in that row. Would I mind moving again? I flew home with an entire row to myself, with extra leg room.

Hospitality comes in many forms. Sometimes extending it includes doing things that weren't in our original plans so others can have a better seat. Sometimes we're invited to take the better seat.

Lord of community, increase our awareness of ways we can extend hospitality to others. Amen.

Aguest would not normally presume to tell the host who should be on the invitation list, but Jesus is not your typical guest. He uses his status as a guest to advocate for those who would never be invited to such a fine banquet. The poor would be excluded because they could not reciprocate with an invitation to a banquet they would host. In Jesus' day, people who were lame or blind were excluded from events in the Temple and generally left out of social events. But the Son of God came to include those typically ignored and left out by the community, turning social conventions upside down.

One of my daughter's elementary school teachers had a firm rule: If a child in the class wanted to pass out birthday party invitations, there had to be an invitation for every child in the class. The same rule applied for the annual February tradition of passing out Valentines. I suppose the teacher had seen her share of devastated children, crying when no invitations or Valentine cards were deposited on their desks. Being left out hurts to the core. Being included heals.

One summer I witnessed the healing power of inclusion at the summer camp I helped run. For the weekly Thursday night dance, one of the summer-staff counselors learned enough sign language to invite a camper who was deaf to dance with him. The girl was stunned but readily agreed. She couldn't hear the music, but she could feel the vibrations of the excited campers and staff and happily joined in the dancing. Her mother later told us that dance was the highlight of the girl's summer.

Exclusion wounds. Inclusion mends.

God of inclusion, teach us how to issue your invitations to everyone to be part of your community. Amen.

God's Loving Hands and Heart

AUGUST 29–SEPTEMBER 4, 2022 • JERRY OWYANG

SCRIPTURE OVERVIEW: Jeremiah brings another warning of impending judgment. If the people will not turn to the Lord, God will break the nation and reshape it, just as a potter breaks down and reshapes clay on a wheel. The psalmist praises God for God's intimate knowledge of each one of us. Even from the moment of conception, God knows us and has a plan for our lives. Philemon is often overlooked, but it packs a punch. A text that some used in the past to justify slavery teaches a very different message. Paul warns Philemon not to enslave Onesimus again but to receive him back as a brother. Secular power structures have no place in God's kingdom. In Luke, Jesus uses striking examples to teach us that the life of faith cannot be lived well with half-hearted commitment.

QUESTIONS AND SUGGESTIONS FOR REFLECTION

- Read Jeremiah 18:1-11. As clay, how can you better respond to the Potter's guiding hand?
- Read Psalm 139:1-6, 13-18. God knows you better than you know yourself, yet God has given you the ability to make your own decisions. How do you respond to God?
- Read Philemon 1-21. How do you honor the full humanity of those who serve you through their work?
- Read Luke 14:25-33. What does it mean for you to take up the cross in your life?

Ordained deacon and retired pastor of several multicultural churches in the California-Pacific Annual Conference of The United Methodist Church; active with Kairos Prison Ministry and grandparenting.

When I was in college, I often went to the campus ceramics center to relax from my studies by crafting earthenware dishes, vases, and other vessels. I would take a lump of clay and throw it down several times on a hard surface to remove any air bubbles that could explode when the pottery was fired in the kiln. Throwing the clay also softened it and made it easier to shape on the wheel. If I discovered a hard lump or a hidden air pocket while manipulating the clay, I would smash the project down and begin again.

After hand-molding the spinning wet clay into its intended form, I would relax my grip and set my work aside to be dried, decorated, and finally baked in the fiery furnace, where a transformation takes place. The clay, once nothing more than wet mud, experiences an internal structural change that gives it a hardened crystalline permanence that can never be reversed.

With a fresh vision, Jeremiah watched the potter fashion an ordinary, everyday vessel. As the potter shaped the clay, Jeremiah realized that he was looking at himself, humanity, and Israel. The turning wheel was essential for the potter to squeeze and nudge the clay into the desired product—much like how circumstances will give a particular fit or form to life. But when an imperfection was revealed, the potter remolded the clay into a new vessel. Once just slimy mud, the clay in the potter's hand became the beginning of something elegant and permanent. And then Jeremiah saw that God is the Great Potter, with the power and skill to make the clay whatever he wants it to be, glazed with grace and beauty.

How willing are you to allow God to shape your life to fit into God's perfect design?

Everyone was affected in some way by the great uncertainty of 2020. The COVID-19 pandemic was global, and social unrest reached nearly every part of the United States. We all discovered new ways that we are interconnected, both for good and for bad. Similarly, Jeremiah had a growing awareness—and apprehension—of the disaster and ruin that were coming for the nation of Israel.

As Jeremiah watched the potter, he saw that there was a flaw that caused the potter to stop and reform the clay. The potter could throw away the clay and begin with a new piece or crush the clay and start over. Jeremiah understood that the clay represented any individual or nation, and that God was the Great Potter with the skill, vision, and power to form the clay.

God was looking for the same thing in Israel that God is looking for in us today: a repentant heart. Sooner or later we are going to find ourselves on the potter's wheel confronting circumstances, and we may not understand what God is doing in our lives. But perhaps in these times of stress and confusion, God will be able to do some of God's best work. When we are in the Potter's hands, feeling the pressure, feeling the molding of God's fingers, we can relax and trust that we are being fashioned into a vessel of honor that is fit for God's use.

To visualize your life as clay for the Divine Potter is to know that God's hands are on your heart. God has a purpose in mind and the skill and ability to fulfill it.

Your heart is like clay being formed by the loving hands of God.

I used to play hide-and-seek with my children. They would hide, and I would search for them. The fun of seeking was knowing that someone was hiding, and the fun of hiding was knowing that someone was seeking. Our favorite pastime always ended in a happy reunion with smiles and laughter.

But as a pastor I am concerned for people who feel that no one is looking for them or fear that someone might really see them. My heart breaks for people who ask themselves, *Does anyone care that I was even here? Who notices me? How can I be in the middle of a crowd and feel like no one sees me? Do I matter? Would anyone love me if they really knew what goes on inside me?*

This beloved psalm responds to these worries. God knows what we are like—our heart, fears, thoughts, motives, dreams, and disappointments. God knows our past, present, and future. God understands and notices what's going on around us, to us, and inside us. There is no need or reason to pretend that we are perfect because Jesus loves us wholeheartedly, without question, including all of the not-so-perfect parts inside us.

When I read this personal psalm, I hear God's voice saying, "I've got my eye on you." It is not a warning; it is the promise of a loving, protective parent who knows, sees, and cares for us. God's complete knowledge of us is a blessing rather than a burden because of God's everlasting love.

God has given us everything we need to be loving, caring persons where "nobodies" are nonexistent.

Have you looked in a mirror and wished you were different—not just your outward appearance but the deeper, inner features? We see imperfections that no one else would notice and question whether our intelligence, social skills, and faith are good enough. For many of us, we are not happy with the way we were made. No matter how hard we try to change ourselves to win signs of love and acceptance from other people, external affirmation will never be enough.

I volunteer with Kairos Prison Ministry, whose purpose is to share the transforming love and forgiveness of Jesus Christ to impact the hearts and lives of persons who are incarcerated. While the exterior scars and tattoos cannot be changed, participants are invited to discover and embrace the genuine acceptance and authentic affection that may have been absent in their lives but are freely offered by the God who exquisitely made them and who already loves them just as they are.

When an inmate in my group realized the relentless love of this inescapable God, a tear trickled from behind the reflective sunglasses that concealed his eyes. It wasn't long before an internal reconstruction began; his heart's desire was to change his imprinted gang affiliation that was emblazoned on his chest to declare, "Jesus Christ is my life!" There is no better feeling of comfort and security in the world—or in prison—than to know that you are completely known and absolutely loved.

God loves us and made us for a purpose.

Don't be afraid of what you see in the mirror, because you are fearfully and wonderfully made!

While a prisoner in Rome, Paul wrote a carefully crafted personal letter to Philemon, a fellow Christian and owner of an enslaved person named Onesimus, who had stolen from Philemon and run away. In Rome, Onesimus came under Paul's ministry and accepted Christ, and he was now willing to return to Philemon. That's why Paul wrote this appeal for Philemon to welcome Onesimus as a Christian brother.

Paul presents in these twenty-one verses a powerful, counter-cultural message of forgiveness and reconciliation. It was vital for his friend Philemon and is essential for us as well. Paul took a position radically revolutionary for his time by asking his brother-in-the-Lord to receive Onesimus not as a slave but as a fellow believer. Paul saw how unity in the body of Christ cuts across worldly position, occupation, social or economic status, and nationality.

We have been called to this same unity as siblings in Christ. The evil of slavery still exists in many parts of the world because we do not see one another as siblings in Christ. Divisions and prejudices are everywhere—even within our churches and families. Too often we separate ourselves from others simply because of political platforms, racial identity, religious and educational background, or social hierarchies. And each instance of division saddens the Lord a little bit more.

Paul implored Philemon to see Onesimus as a brother in Christ; we too need to see one another as siblings in Christ and children of God. Jesus' death and resurrection reconciled us to God and made it possible for us to be united as one body.

Forgiveness, reconciliation, and social transformation are at the heart of the Christian message.

Over the years, I've had the opportunity to travel to different cultures and experience a kind of shopping where prices are not on display. I ask in the local language, "How much does this cost?" The shopkeeper states a price, and then the haggling begins. I say the price is too high and walk away; the seller then comes after me with a lower price, and we barter back and forth until we finally agree on a price. "A bargain!" we each believe.

When it comes to the cost of being a disciple of Jesus, however, there is no bargaining over the price. Jesus wants us to consider whether we are willing to put him first in all aspects of our lives. In this passage from Luke, the word *hate* is hyperbole. Jesus doesn't mean that we are to dislike or be hostile to the people in our families. Rather, he is emphasizing that our love and devotion to him must take priority over our love and devotion to those closest to us. Otherwise, when choosing between God's will and our own, we will say no to Jesus and yes to ourselves.

Jesus is strong and plainspoken about what it means to follow him. He doesn't hide anything from his potential followers. One who takes up a cross knows that the cost of discipleship could well be crucifixion. To follow Jesus, then, means to die to self. But dying ultimately brings new life in the giving up of self-serving, competing loyalties.

How do I loosen my grasp on those possessions and comforts that challenge my relationship with Jesus?

After graduating from law school, I worked with the Environmental Review Division of a major city to identify any potentially adverse effects of proposed construction projects, assess their significance, and recommend measures to eliminate or minimize harm. This process provided some of the information officials and the public needed to decide whether to proceed with a project.

The projects I reviewed included high-rise office buildings, transportation systems, historic preservation overlays, housing developments, and even an expansion of a fortune cookie factory. It was important to consider the immediate, long-range, and cumulative effects of a project on its physical environment and neighboring community. In other words, it was important to consider the consequences and costs of saying yes or no.

It's no different when counting the cost to follow Jesus. He tells his followers two compelling, connected parables about a building and a battle. The point of the stories was not the successful completion of the tower or the outcome of the war but the willingness and deliberation to count the cost. We know the Holy Spirit will enable us to choose correctly, but it still won't be easy. Truehearted Christian discipleship is costly.

But the cost of not following Jesus is even higher. Such a forfeiture would lead to the loss of the abundant life Jesus offers us. The gospel is much more than an ethical message about a way of life. It is about Jesus, the kingdom he came to proclaim, and loving God before all else. It's our choice. The cost, whatever it may be, is worth paying.

What keeps you from fully following Jesus?

From Death to Life, Lost to Found

SEPTEMBER 5–11, 2022 • BETH LUDLUM

SCRIPTURE OVERVIEW: Jeremiah's warning of coming judgment continues. The children of Israel have become foolish, have ignored God, and have become good mainly at doing evil. God is going to respond to this situation. The psalmist describes the state of all who are foolish: They deny God and follow their own corrupt desires, including oppressing the poor. The author of First Timothy, traditionally Paul, says that this was also his former way of life. He has been foolish and ignorant, a persecutor of the followers of Christ. In fact, he had been the worst of all sinners; yet Christ has shown him mercy, not judgment. Jesus tells two parables to reveal God's heart. Rather than neglecting the ignorant, the foolish, and the lost, God searches to find each one of us.

QUESTIONS AND SUGGESTIONS FOR REFLECTION

- Read Jeremiah 4:11-12, 22-28. How do your actions show others that you know God?
- Read Psalm 14. When have you, like the psalmist, felt that no one knows God? How did you have faith that God would restore God's people?
- Read 1 Timothy 1:12-17. Recall a time when you felt unworthy of Christ's full acceptance. How has that experience made you more grateful for Christ's mercy?
- Read Luke 15:1-10. In a world full of death and violence, how do you rejoice when God finds one lost person?

Ordained elder in The United Methodist Church; Vice President for Strategic Initiatives and Enrollment at Wesley Theological Seminary; lives with her partner, Mark, their two sons, and their puppy in Washington, DC; loves to hike, bike, and bake (and eat) cookies.

It's tempting to read this psalm with an "us and them" attitude. The psalmist complains about "fools" who denounce God and do terrible things, and it's easy to think, like the Pharisee's prayer in Luke 18, *Thank God I'm not like those people!* But the psalmist quickly strips us of that defense. For the psalm is established on the principle, repeated twice, that "there is no one who does good." No one. Not even me.

The key is that these "fools" don't verbally denounce God; rather, their actions and lifestyles fail to reflect God's priorities. When put that way, it is easy to see how the psalmist's insight applies to us here and now.

Most modern societies are built upon concepts of self-reliance, autonomy, and personal responsibility. But when we strive for those qualities, they lead us to live as if there were no God. When we focus on achieving independence, we're unlikely to rely on—or truly believe we need—God or others. When we're looking out for ourselves first, we're less likely to see, dismantle, or refuse to participate in economic and social systems that benefit us but hurt others. While we might say that we are Christians, our actions don't exemplify the orientation of God's kingdom.

Today, the psalmist, like Paul, reminds us that all of us have sinned and fallen short (see Romans 3:23). We all have perpetuated systems that divide and oppress. We all have lived as if we don't need God. We all have loved our own comfort more than God's justice and mercy for the world. So we must start here: examine not only our words but also our lifestyles, repent, and turn toward God's ways.

God, help me see how I place my autonomy over your priorities, my well-being over that of others, and perpetuate injustice in our world. Help me turn toward you so that my life professes your goodness. Amen.

My toddler is a master of destruction. Every once in a while, I can convince him to build a block tower or a sandcastle, but he much prefers that I build things, the taller the better, so he can knock them down.

That kind of systematic destruction comes to mind when I read today's scripture. But Jeremiah is not describing child's play. Rather, he prophesies a reversal of the Creation account in Genesis. Where once God brought forth something from nothing, the prophet now uses the exact same language to describe the earth's return to "waste and void." The light disappears, farms and cities are destroyed, even people and animals are gone. And where once God observed each stage of Creation and declared it good, the prophet now observes and laments each loss.

The reason for this destruction? God's people are foolish (see Psalm 14) and are doing evil.

It is tempting to skip over this passage or use it to describe a wrathful God. But perhaps the prophet is describing the natural end to wrongdoing—the fact that, at some point, it all catches up with us. Perhaps the prophet is challenging us to see what we don't want to see—like the ways our selfish consumption and wastefulness are destroying mountains, rivers, farmland, animals, and people.

As long as we refuse to see the consequences of our actions, as long as we ignore the ways we have contributed to devastation and loss, as long as we don't stop to hear the earth weep and the people and animals cry out, we will not turn and seek the kingdom of God.

God, help me to see how my actions and lifestyle lead to the destruction of earth, water, air, animals, and vulnerable communities around the world. Wake me up so that I can learn to do good instead of cause harm. Amen.

When I was growing up, my father often called me "my Bethie." No one else was allowed to use a diminutive form of my name, much less with a possessive pronoun, but I loved it when he did. I felt secure in his claim, a loving promise that I would always be his. And I wanted to live into that claim by making him proud of me.

When I read Jeremiah's account, I'm struck by the way God refers to Israel. God had distanced God's self from them before; after the golden calf incident, God called them "your [Moses'] people" (see Exodus 32:7). But here, in spite of the people's sin, God invokes the covenant relationship, calling Israel "my people." Although destruction is coming, the covenant still stands, and God promises not to "make a full end."

The psalmist leans on God's claim too. The lament ends with a prayer of hope, looking toward a day when God will redeem and restore God's people, and they will rejoice.

The prophet and the psalmist remind us that even when we wander far from God, God's promises still stand. Yes, God is the refuge of the poor, the oppressed, the victims of injustice, and those left behind. But even when we are privileged, powerful, and strong, God promises to hear when we call. It may mean laying down some of our independence, our wealth, or our power—or using our resources for the benefit of others rather than ourselves. But God continues to offer a better way: a path of covenant, a path of rebuilding cities and restoring nature, a path of dismantling and replacing unjust systems. And that way, God's way, is the way of life.

God, I marvel at your claim on my life. Give me the courage to confess my sin and turn toward your love. Give me the courage to live into a covenant life with you. Amen.

Imagine you've spent an entire day running errands around town. When you get home, you realize something is missing. Would you go back and retrace every step if you were missing a penny? What about a favorite book? Your wedding ring or favorite piece of jewelry? If you're like me, you would run an internal cost/benefit analysis to determine an item's worth before deciding to go back to find it. Penny? No way. Ring? No question.

So Jesus' opening question leaves me scratching my head. Would a shepherd leave ninety-nine vulnerable sheep in the wilderness to go find one, no matter how long the search takes, no matter that the one is likely beyond saving? Probably not. It doesn't make economic sense to risk ninety-nine to save one. So maybe Jesus' question wasn't rhetorical but ironic, showing the difference between the world's economy and God's.

In the world's economy, we are constantly weighing the value of each activity, possession, and, yes, human life, whether consciously or unconsciously. In the world's economy, we hold on to the ninety-nine who have stayed rather than risking everything for the one who has wandered. In the world's economy, we maintain systems that keep us comfortable even when others are left out.

But in God's economy, no one is lost or forgotten. In God's economy, no matter how many are safe, God doesn't rest until ALL are found and restored. This is the good news: When we are lost, before we even realize that we are lost, God is searching, sweeping, traversing the wilderness, ready to carry us home. And once we are found, God calls us to join the eternal search for every last person who is vulnerable, alone, or lost.

God, we keep drifting, wandering, losing our way. Find us and carry us home. Then help us to be finders like you, seeking the ones in our families, communities, and world who are lost, left behind, or overlooked. Amen.

I t's not about you."

It was just an exasperated retort by my then-boyfriend, but it turned out to be one of the more liberating and clarifying statements of my life.

It's interesting how Paul retells his story in today's scripture. We often think about his Damascus road experience as a religious conversion—but he didn't change religions. The big change? Suddenly, in light of Jesus' call, Paul's life was not about him—or even his religion or its institutions. It was all about God's glory and following the Way of Jesus by serving others. Paul got a transformed heart and a calling to serve.

I've worked around seminary admissions for more than a decade. If there's one place where you consistently hear call stories, it's a seminary admissions office. Day in and day out, people call, email, or walk into the office with a story on their tongues and a fire in their hearts. Sometimes they've sensed a call for years but have just recently gained the courage or aligned life circumstances to follow it; sometimes the call is brand new, and they still struggle to articulate it. While every person's story is different, a few things are almost universally true: God's call is not about them. It's not even about maintaining the church or Christianity. It's about following Jesus and serving his people. Following God's call requires sacrifice.

Paul gave up a powerful religious career to become an itinerant preacher who would be beaten and imprisoned. Yet in his retelling, Paul overflows with joy in his calling. Yes, God's call brings struggle, but it also brings freedom, meaning, and joy.

Think of moments when you realized that life isn't all about you. How is God's grace propelling you to serve God and others? How can you share the freedom, mercy, and love you've found in Jesus Christ?

Water is remarkable. While sometimes soft and soothing, its fearsome power is on display in ocean waves or during floods. But water's most remarkable transformations come over time. If you visit a canyon, look carefully at a stream bed, or enter a cave, you will see how water has cut through sand and silt, dirt and roots, and even the deepest levels of bedrock. Sometimes quickly, sometimes almost imperceptibly, water shapes, forms, and changes its environment.

It is no wonder, then, that water imagery is so common in Judaism and Christianity. Through the prophecy of Amos, God gave this command: "Let justice roll down like waters, and righteousness like an ever-flowing stream" (5:24). Ezekiel saw a river flowing from the temple that brought life to everything it touched (see Ezekiel 47). Through baptism, Christians enact our dying to self and rising in Christ with water.

Paul's description of his "before and after," caused by God's overflowing grace, evokes images of God's movement as water. When Jesus entered his life, Paul didn't become someone different; rather, like a riverbed, his gifts were redirected as he was caught up in the flow of God's love. He was still zealous; but rather than protecting traditional Judaism from supposed heretics, he poured himself into sharing the good news of abundant life for all. His eloquence and erudition were refocused. God's love had flooded Paul's life and redirected his skills, creating new channels to deliver grace and mercy to the world.

Salvation is a beautiful mystery, at once a flood of God's grace and a lifetime journey in God's channel of mercy.

God, thank you for the ways I experience your mercy and grace—at times like a flood, sweeping me up; at times like a soft, life-giving rain, nourishing my soul. Amen.

Several months after I moved to China, a friend invited me to her cousin's wedding in a remote village. When we arrived at the bride's home, the family surrounded me and began a debate I couldn't understand. Eventually my smiling friend turned to me and said, "As a foreigner, you are the most honored guest. You must be the maid of honor." With that, the next several hours became a blur, as I was thrown into a celebration of food, music, dancing, and, yes, toasts. ("Say anything in English," my friend instructed. "I will make you sound good when I translate.")

But perhaps my favorite part of the day was when we traveled from the bride's home to the ceremony site. Cars and buses and people on foot paraded across the village, honking and calling to neighbors. The whole community was welcomed—even compelled—to come join the celebration, from the poorest neighbor to this confused, awkward foreigner.

Jesus tells of a God who doesn't just seek, sweep, track, and venture out to find the lost one; when the lost one is found and retrieved, God celebrates extravagantly. God throws parties, the kind where everyone is invited.

The question is this: Will we will accept the invitation? For some of us, we must let go of the pride that keeps us from dancing in the street. Others of us, like the Pharisees, must overcome our sense that we (and others) must earn the right to be celebrated. We may have to let go of our biases that keep us from associating with the sinner/wanderer/lost one who has been found. But God is there, in the middle of the party, dancing with the sinners and the wanderers, inviting us to join the celebration, and compelling us to extend the party to our homes, our neighborhoods, our workplaces, our nation, our world.

Friends, we have serious work to do. Let's get to it. Let's party.

God's Community

SEPTEMBER 12–18, 2022 • LAYTON E. WILLIAMS

SCRIPTURE OVERVIEW: Jeremiah, "the weeping prophet," grieves for the plight of his people. They have provoked God's judgment by following foreign gods, and now there is no comfort to be found. The psalmist cries out to God from a similar situation of despair. Foreign nations have overrun the land, destroyed Jerusalem, and killed many of its people. The psalmist cries out to God for compassion and restoration. The author of First Timothy gives his readers two commands. They should pray for and honor their leaders, and they should be faithful to the one true God, with whom they have a relationship through Christ Jesus. Jesus in Luke tells a strange parable about a dishonest manager who is commended for his shrewd business sense, but Jesus turns his story into a teaching about good stewardship.

QUESTIONS AND SUGGESTIONS FOR REFLECTION

- Read Jeremiah 8:18–9:1. When have you called out to God in distress?
- Read Psalm 79:1-9. As you search for solutions to life's problems, how do you demonstrate God's call to love and to justice?
- Read 1 Timothy 2:1-7. How do you pray for your local, state or province, and national leaders with whom you agree? with whom you disagree?
- Read Luke 16:1-13. How do you negotiate the complexities of Jesus' call to be a good steward of your resources as you work to serve God rather than money?

Minister in the Presbyterian Church (U.S.A.); director of New Dawn Ministries at Sunrise Church, Sullivan's Island, SC; communications specialist for NEXT Church; author of *Holy Disunity: How What Separates Us Can Save Us.*

We live in a broken world. All over the globe people suffer from conflict, disease, natural disasters, exploitation, bigotry, and injustice. We witness these struggles up close, in our communities, in the lives of our loved ones, and even in our own experiences. In the face of such difficulty, we seek comfort and security wherever we can find it.

One place where we might find comfort and security is in the stories of those who came before us. Our faith and our holy scriptures are full of generations of God's people who have suffered and struggled through agonizing ordeals, exile and enslavement, famine and war, and who have wavered in their faithfulness to God, as we ourselves might do in our most difficult moments. It can be hard to believe in God's goodness and mercy when our world and our own lives seem to be devoid of those gifts of a loving Creator.

In this passage, Jeremiah is reflecting on his people's suffering. He is crying out to God, weeping tears for the slain. It is clear that Jeremiah is striving to maintain faith in God in the midst of a broken world. He questions when—or even if—his people will be healed and delivered. But the fact that he brings those questions to God shows that he still believes that God is listening.

We know that God was always faithful to God's people. And knowing these stories, knowing this history, we can trust that God is also always faithful to us. We can learn from Jeremiah and hold on to our knowledge that God is good, merciful, present, and listening, even in the midst of struggle.

God, thank you for your steadfast presence in our lives and world. Help me to remember the signs of your faithfulness in my own life and experience. Amen.

Jeremiah reaches out for refuge in God as his people suffer. Jeremiah trusts, even as he is filled with questions, that God is listening and that God cares. The prophet offers us an example of faithfulness in the midst of struggle and brokenness. Yet Jeremiah's people offer a different example. Jeremiah writes:

Hark, the cry of my poor people
>from far and wide in the land:
"Is the LORD not in Zion?
>Is her King not in her?"
("Why have they provoked me to anger with their images, with their foreign idols?")

Because of their suffering, the people are questioning whether God is present with them at all. They have turned to foreign idols. They have placed their trust and reliance on something other than God.

We have been taught that idolatry is wrong, that we are meant to trust in God alone. We know we are supposed to condemn Jeremiah's people as wayward and faithless. But we make a mistake if we identify only with the prophet and not with the people in this passage. After all, how often do we root our sense of security in something other than God? We rely on money, our worldly leaders, and our routines. These earthly realities are not inherently bad, but when we look to them for our ultimate sense of certainty and comfort, we wander from a faithful focus and relationship with God.

This passage invites us to return our focus to God and to uphold our trust in God over and above our reliance on any earthly comforts or leaders. We need not question whether God is present; we know and believe that God is always with us.

Holy God, I know you are always faithful. Help me to lean on you in times of trouble. Amen.

The world seems more divided than ever. Pundits argue on news networks, politicians pit themselves against one another, people attack one another on social media. Even families find themselves at odds. When division is so present, it is easy to see people we disagree with as our enemies. And it is easy, once we have designated them as enemies, to reject their humanity and wish them ill.

There's a striking juxtaposition in Psalm 79 that touches on this impulse. The psalmist writes about the devastating destruction of the Temple in Jerusalem and the hateful violence of the Israelites' enemies. The psalmist begs God to unleash vengeance on them and pour out anger on the nations who do not know or worship God. Then, in the next breath, the psalmist acknowledges the failures and inequities of Israel's own ancestors and asks God to ignore those and have compassion for the Israelites.

It's interesting how easy it can be to expect compassion for ourselves and those we love without extending it or wanting God to extend it to others. We want to believe that God shares our ire, our hatred, our rejection. Too often we confuse retribution with justice. We're happy to have a God of grace to forgive us, but we want a God of vengeance to punish those who harm us. The truth, though, is that God loves and offers compassion and mercy and grace to all people. As recipients of that grace and mercy, we are called to offer them in turn to others, even to those we deem our enemies.

God, thank you for the love and compassion and mercy you show me. Help me to remember that you love all people and that I am called to do the same. Amen.

The author of First Timothy first urges that prayers, supplications, thanksgivings, and intercessions be made for everyone, but then he singles out one particular group: kings and all who are in high positions. The implication is that praying for one's leaders isn't a natural impulse. Is this true for us?

I imagine it depends on how we feel about particular leaders. If we're sympathetic to their perspective and strategies or are connected to them personally, it likely feels more natural to concern ourselves with them in our prayer lives. If it's a leader we despise or vehemently disagree with, I suspect most of us rarely spare a thought for her or him that isn't an angry one.

This passage suggests, however, that concerning ourselves spiritually with those in power is crucial to "quiet and peaceable life in all godliness and dignity." It says that God wants everyone to follow God's will, including—perhaps especially—those with power. We are to pray that our leaders behave and lead in ways that promote God's love and justice. Whether we support and defend or decry and reject a given leader, it is our responsibility to seek a world in which those in power live in ways that reflect God's love and care for all people.

I've often heard it said that sometimes we pray with our words and sometimes we pray with our feet. It seems that seeking faithful and righteous behavior from our leaders requires more than silent prayer. It requires that we engage our leaders in ways that call upon their better angels and our own. And we must do so from a place of love and faith.

God, guide our leaders in your wisdom. Give them hearts of courage to enact your love and justice. Amen.

Though this passage begins with an exhortation about the importance of praying for our worldly leaders, the author quickly shifts away from earthly authority to true divine authority. The author asserts that, regardless of mortal leadership, there is only one God and only one mediator between God and humanity—Jesus Christ.

We generally understand this theological belief as the doctrine of divine sovereignty, the belief that God is omniscient (all-knowing), omni-benevolent (all-good), and omnipotent (all-powerful). Essentially this means that even if kings and principalities hold sway over people on earth, God is still the only one with true authority and power. It matters, moreover, how God, in Christ Jesus, uses this power and authority as described by the author of First Timothy. The author writes, "Christ Jesus, himself human, . . . gave himself a ransom for all." Jesus Christ, who has access through God to absolute power, chooses to express that power through mercy and grace and self-sacrifice for the sake of humanity.

We know that all humans are flawed and that power often corrupts those who have it. When we look at worldly leaders now and throughout history, it's easy to grow discouraged by their shortcomings. Even those with true hearts for justice and care are often deeply flawed, and this reality can leave us unmoored and unsure of where to place our trust. This passage reminds us that ultimately we must place our trust in Jesus.

God, thank you for sending your Son to connect us to you. Thank you for using your power in the service of love and grace. Help me to place my trust in you. Amen.

This strange parable seems on its surface to be about the morality of money, but deeper examination points to Jesus' countercultural vision for human relationship and community.

The framing of this story introduces a familiar worldly hierarchy: The rich man has the most power and oversees the manager, who in turn has power over those in debt to the rich man. However, when the manager finds himself suddenly at risk of losing his job, the very people who can help him are those with the least amount of worldly power. And the manager's selfish actions to help himself—collecting a reduced amount of debt from each debtor—end up helping everyone.

In a vacuum, this story may demonstrate a moral framework of *quid pro quo:* If you help me, then I'll help you. But within the larger context of Jesus' teachings and ministry, it becomes an invitation to connection and interdependence.

How do we survive through times of struggle? How do we endure and respond to the brokenness of the world? We could shore up our defenses, cling tightly to what we have, and worry only about ourselves. But our faith proclaims a different truth and calls for a different response. Jesus teaches us that faithfulness in the face of difficulty and brokenness is about leaning toward relationships, community, and one another, even when it goes against the "way things are done." Contrary, perhaps, to our instincts, our survival depends on one another. Only together can we move through brokenness into the whole and healed kingdom of God.

God, thank you for all people and for the ways you have connected us to each other. Help us to be in community together and to help one another live faithfully within your reign on earth. Amen.

These philosophical observations from Jesus come as a summary to his unusual and confusing parable about the Rich Man and the Dishonest Manager. The first few verses are as confusing as the story they reference. However, the final—and perhaps most famous—verse offers some helpful grounding for Jesus' ultimate point. He says, "No slave can serve two masters; for a slave will either hate the one and love the other, or be devoted to the one and despise the other. You cannot serve God and wealth."

Essentially, Jesus is saying that no matter what situation you're in, your behavior and its impact will be determined by what you prioritize and allow to guide you. But Jesus gets more pointed than that. He specifically juxtaposes wealth and God. Does this mean that money is inherently bad? Does it mean that someone with a lot of money is inherently bad? What exactly constitutes a lot? It's easy to be vexed by these questions, but Jesus' statement is really about what we value.

Regardless of how much money we have, if acquiring wealth is our goal above all else, we will be tempted to behave in ways that separate us from other people and from God. God's ways call us to work for the good of all people and to be generous and open with what we have.

It is common in our world today—as it was in Jesus' time— to base our sense of security on our possessions. But true security comes only when we grasp on to God's love and trust above all else in how God calls us to live.

God, help me not to hold on so tightly to the pursuit of wealth on earth that I fail to take hold of the abundance of love, grace, and hope I can have in you. Amen.

God's Story of Abundant Life

SEPTEMBER 19–25, 2022 • AMY ODEN

SCRIPTURE OVERVIEW: While Jeremiah is in prison, God tells him to buy a field. This transaction shows that in the future, life will return to normal. It is an "enactment prophecy," where a prophecy is given through actions instead of just words. The psalmist rejoices in the protection that God provides to the faithful. God is a fortress, a covering, and a shield. Paul admonishes his readers not to fall into materialism. The love of money, not money itself, is the root of all kinds of evil, and those obsessed with it build their hopes on shifting sands. Jesus tells a parable about a rich man who has fallen into that very trap. Only after death, when it is too late, does he realize his mistake.

QUESTIONS AND SUGGESTIONS FOR REFLECTION

- Read Jeremiah 32:1-3a, 6-15. How do you live as if God's promises were already true?
- Read Psalm 91:1-6, 14-16. How do you turn toward God with hope in times of darkness?
- Read 1 Timothy 6:6-19. Whether you have few or many possessions, how do they get in the way of your following Jesus?
- Read Luke 16:19-31. God knows each of us by name. Do you know the names of the persons in your community who have obvious or internal unmet needs?

Seminary professor who looks forward to each day with students; born and raised on the prairies of Oklahoma; her spiritual home is under the wide-open sky.

The world as the Israelites knew it is ending. With an enemy army moving in on Jerusalem, it is clear that Judah is lost to this foreign, conquering power. Their families, livelihoods, and way of life will all be destroyed as Babylon takes them captive far away from Jerusalem.

We might feel some of this same sense of things falling apart as the world has been reshaped in recent years by pandemic, racial injustice, and economic loss. Entire social structures of work, church, school, and commerce have been wiped away in a matter of weeks. We know something of Jeremiah's time.

Into this disintegration and disorientation, the Lord speaks a word of hope. In fact, the Lord tells Jeremiah to do something that seems crazy: Go buy property. Go buy this land that is soon to belong to a foreign power, this land the Israelites are soon to be exiled from, this land on which they will no longer live! It seems ridiculous to invest in land they are leaving behind; yet the Lord says, go buy a field on this land.

The fall of Jerusalem is not the end of the story; it is only one chapter. God insists here that Jeremiah stake a claim for the future. Jeremiah's purchase of this field commits him to the future, an expectation that they will return to this promised land, trusting that captivity in Babylon is not the final word. God promises that "houses, fields and vineyards will again be bought in this land."

What in your life right now feels like the end of the story but perhaps is not? What concrete step is God inviting you to take toward the future? How might your expectations stay open for God to do a new thing?

O God, remind us that this is not the end of the story, that you are calling us into your abundant life. Amen.

The story of Lazarus and the rich man is a warning about getting so caught up in our own ideas of success that we miss out on the real story of our lives. The rich man enjoyed fine food and clothing yet did not know mercy or the depths of God's love in his own life. His wealth numbed him to the pain of others. His riches robbed him of the true story God called him to live.

The rich man thought he knew the end of his story. He thought he had arrived, had achieved success because he had wealth and ease, feasting to his heart's content. It's easy to imagine that he was regarded with esteem and respect—even admiration—because of his riches. The world around him would have told him he had made it to the top! But the rich man was lost. He was lost in his status, in his version of success, in others' esteem. He was unable to see that real, abundant life eluded him. Only torment would make that plain.

I think about the many versions of success that can drive our lives: professional accomplishment and esteem from colleagues, financial comfort with a padded retirement fund and small luxuries, and approval from others for conforming to their values. Yet all these can prevent us from living the abundant story God invites us to live. These seductive versions of success make us think we have arrived. Yet they draw our gaze away from the Author of our lives, whose story is the only true one.

To be sure, riches are not inherently bad. But they are more likely to confuse than to clarify. Jesus warns us that it will be devastating to mistake riches for abundant life.

I wonder what versions of success distract me from abundant life? How do I confuse the two?

Reflect on any false versions of success that hold your gaze. Invite God to shed light on them.

God asks Jeremiah to do this seemingly crazy thing—buy property in a land that is being conquered by a foreign enemy. Just as his people are taken captive into Babylon, Jeremiah obediently buys the land they all have to leave behind. Crazy, right?

What's more, Jeremiah is very public about it. He carries out the transaction in front of "witnesses . . . and all the Jews." The community bears witness to this outrageous commitment he makes to the future, to a promised abundant life ahead. Did they think he was crazy? Wasting his money?

This was a bold witness, a wake-up call that challenged any assumptions about "the end of life of as we know it." God was telling a different story: a story of abundant life ahead with a signed deed as a promise on the future.

Today it's easy for us to doomscroll through newsfeeds and wring our hands in worry. Neuroscientists tell us that this repetitive behavior creates neural pathways in our brains, physical circuitry that wires our brains to seek out ever more bad news. We are held captive to paralyzing anxiety, unfree for the story God is telling about the future.

In order to be free to be part of God's dream for the world, I want to listen to the narratives God is telling. How is God calling us to stake our claim on the future? What commitment for the future makes a crazy, bold witness for God's abundant life? Maybe God is inviting us to invest in the failing elementary school down the block. Or maybe God calls us to the work of racial justice when it can seem to be a lost cause. Or maybe God dreams for us to plant our lives in our hopes for the future instead of planting in disappointment and regret.

O God, free us from our captivity to stories of doom, and open our ears to your story of abundant life. Amen.

Jesus offers a rare and shocking picture of God's keeping score with Lazarus and the rich man. Jesus usually presents God as generous and forgiving. Just one chapter earlier (see Luke 15), Jesus makes clear that God is not the Divine Accountant with a giant ledger in the sky but rather is the tenderhearted Father who extravagantly welcomes home his wayward son.

This parable, then, is not so much about keeping score as about paying attention. Jesus' story makes plain the consequences of refusing to listen and not having "ears to hear."

The last sentence is the key line. Father Abraham says to the rich man, "You did not listen." The rich man was too smug and self-satisfied, too comfortable in his success to listen, and so he refused to let God transform his life. Jesus says to us, "Have ears to hear! Pay attention! Don't miss out on what God is up to!"

When we attune our ears to God's narrative, we hear the strains of abundant life and are called to repentance and transformation. We know this. In those fleeting moments when we have ears to hear God's dream-song for our lives and for all creation, our hearts break open with possibility. We step into God's story, turning (repenting) from self-satisfaction to true life, abundant life, eternal life.

Yet our hearing is numbed by overstimulation, multitasking, and preoccupations. We have a cacophony of voices around us and inside our heads: the "to-do" list and the "others' expectations" list, the inner critic and the inner gossip. It gets crowded!

When our ears are full of the world's messages about success, we need daily practices to help us pause, breathe, and listen for the voice of Jesus.

Pick three times today to use a breath prayer to become more aware of Jesus' presence and his offer of real, abundant life. As you inhale, say "abundant." As you exhale, say "life." Repeat in five slow breaths.

In Psalm 91, the psalmist runs to God for refuge from danger and destruction.

I don't hear the word *refuge* much these days. It's not really American to want to take refuge. We are encouraged to stand and fight, to strive harder, to never back down or walk away. Refuge sounds like a cop-out, like giving up. Only losers run to safety. Seeking refuge can sound like weakness or even failure.

Maybe that's the problem. If we never seek refuge, then we never wake up to tell the truth about what we can and cannot do. In the most disturbing places of our lives, we are, in fact, often powerless. When we face a life-threatening diagnosis, the loss of a loved one, or an unpredictable financial hardship, we quickly realize we are not in control and cannot achieve our desired outcome on our own. We live in the illusion that we can fix anything if we just try hard enough. This deception distorts our understanding of ourselves and of who God is for us.

When we tell the truth about our lives, we take refuge "in the shelter of the Most High" where there is freedom and peace. This is neither weakness nor failure. It is truth-telling at its most vulnerable and real when we too "say to the LORD, 'My refuge and my fortress; my God, in whom I trust.'"

To be clear, we very often do have the capacity to effect change, take initiative, and make things happen. God has given us gifts to be disciples of Jesus in the world, and we follow God's call to use those gifts. But we also must learn to recognize our limits and seek God's refuge and peace.

When you tell the truth about your life, where do you long to seek refuge? Share that with God now.

Lately for me, abundant life has meant taking refuge under God's wings. Here I can completely lay down any illusion that I can fix whatever is wrong. Over the last eight years, I've been journeying with my husband through early onset dementia, a painful reality that I can't fix. To be sure, there are plenty of things I can do, such as be mindful of the present moment and the sheer miracle of our lives together or learn to adapt and flow with his latest version of reality. Still, at the heart of it, I am powerless to stop his decline. I am unable to prevent this long, slow goodbye.

In the early days of our dementia journey, as I became more and more frustrated and unhappy, I had to reckon with my illusion of control. It took me the first couple of years to come to accept that I couldn't just manage our way out of this. As I began to relax into the refuge of God's arms, I came to accept my own inability to fix it and also to accept my husband more fully. I was able to see that he was not a problem to fix but a gift to receive.

For most of us, letting go of control feels like moral failure. We do not easily admit the limits of our own power to create the outcomes we want. It takes practice. I've found that the more I entrust my life to God's keeping, the more grounded and grateful I am. The truth-telling of "I don't know" and "This is hard" frees me to ask for help. In fact, seeking refuge in God has become a path of resilience.

Where in your life today are you finding the limits of your power? What invitation is God offering you in this?

Imagine taking refuge under God's wings or in God's arms. Notice what you experience as you settle into this posture.

Many of us connect eternal life with life after death, something that happens after we die. Paul offers a powerful vision of eternal life *now*: a life rooted in gentleness, love, endurance, and faith. It is a life seeking to love as God loves and to walk in God's ways, following Jesus into the world. He describes this as the life "to which you were called and for which you were made." This, he says, is eternal life.

Eternal life is not only some other plane of existence after we die. It means living the depth dimension of the now. Eternal life means expanding our field of vision to see the bigger picture of God's life moving in us and others, a life that is bigger and more permanent than our immediate circumstance. Paul says this is abundant life, eternal life, living squarely in the presence of God right here, right now.

To make his point, Paul contrasts eternal life with a picture of a painful life. He describes a life never satisfied, chasing more and more, inevitably empty and broken. We can easily be "trapped by many senseless and harmful desires that plunge people into ruin and destruction." Echoing Jesus' parable in Luke, Paul warns against mistaking affluence for abundant life.

Abundant life is not built on the stuff we buy, our bank accounts, our appearance, or our status. These are the world's marks of a successful life. Jesus offers much, much more: eternal life that we start living now, rooted in love, full of energy and vitality that cannot be destroyed by changing circumstance. This abundant life—walking with God, loving as God loves with gentleness, faith, and endurance—is your truest and eternal life. The life "for which you were made."

O God, open my eyes to the eternal life before me right now, your abundant life in me. Amen.

Where Do I Find You?

SEPTEMBER 26–OCTOBER 2, 2022 • WESSEL BENTLEY

SCRIPTURE OVERVIEW: Lamentations opens with a description of the plight of the people of Judah, the southern kingdom. The people have been taken into exile as part of God's judgment for their idolatry. The psalmist struggles to sing the songs of the Lord. In fact, those who overthrew Jerusalem have forced them to sing for their amusement, so the joy is gone. The psalmist prays that one day God will repay the invaders. In Second Timothy, Paul praises God for Timothy's faith and for the legacy of faith that comes through his family. He charges him to preach boldly and without hesitation the gospel of Christ. In the Gospel reading, Jesus challenges the disciples to show greater faith and to understand that we are all servants in God's kingdom.

QUESTIONS AND SUGGESTIONS FOR REFLECTION

- Read Lamentations 1:1-6. How do you allow your imperfections and failings to transform you?
- Read Psalm 137. How do you remember your spiritual traditions and sacred places? How do you look for God's work in change?
- Read 2 Timothy 1:1-14. What spiritual practices help you to "guard the good treasure entrusted to you"?
- Read Luke 17:5-10. How might a posture of cyclical servanthood to and with all creation transform or increase your faith?

Professor at the University of South Africa; specializes in the field of science and religion; ordained minister in The Methodist Church of Southern Africa; resides with his family in Pretoria, South Africa.

Our readings from Lamentations and the Psalms reflect on the same historical events from two different perspectives. The Babylonian Empire conquered Judah, leaving the capital city of Jerusalem desolate and in ruins. Many of its citizens were taken into captivity.

Lamentations was written as if the narrator stood outside the city, looking at what was once a thriving hub. The psalm was written from the perspective of a person who was taken into exile, about to cross into the heartland of the captors. To both these storytellers, the feelings of shock and loss are surreal: *Could this all be true? Is it possible that Jerusalem, especially the Temple—the dwelling place of God—could be left in such a state? Is it at all possible that God may have been defeated?*

These questions set the scene for our journey this week. At the time of writing these meditations, the world is in the midst of the COVID-19 pandemic. South Africa implemented a swift and thorough lockdown. The world changed overnight—no traffic on the highways, no airplanes in the sky, malls and parking lots empty, schools and universities suspended, church buildings empty on Sundays. No one would have thought this scene to be possible, much less how suddenly it all unfolded!

At times life springs unpleasant surprises on us, leaving us dazed, not knowing how to make sense of it all or how to move forward. We become speechless.

We can learn from the authors of these scriptures. The first step for them was to put down words, naming their emotions, vocalizing their fears and giving voice to their sense of chaos. Try to do this today with words, images, or music.

Almighty God, when I don't have words, you assure me that you know my innermost thoughts. Help me to put my feelings into sounds and symbols so that I can start making sense of life's surprises. Amen.

My therapist starts each session by asking the same question: "Where do I find you?" The first time I went to see her, the question annoyed me. If everything had been normal, I would have said: "Right here, in your room, sitting on a couch." Not this time. The question cut deep. I couldn't be flippant; words failed me. She unlocked my words by posing a series of further probes: "Tell me what you are feeling." "Tell me what you are thinking about." "Tell me what you see."

Read the text for today again. This time imagine the writer sitting speechless on a couch in God's counseling room. God asks, "Where do I find you?" and the writer starts by unpacking what he sees, his feelings, his fears, and his doubts. The author apportions blame, tries to find the answers for himself, and makes every effort to make sense of this chaotic situation. God does not interrupt. God does not argue with his assumptions, his accusations, or his logic. God listens patiently and empathically, allowing the writer to let go of the words that had been locked up deep inside.

Healing does not come immediately, and it definitely does not come with concrete answers or by satisfying the difficult questions that we ask. It does not manifest in our eloquence or lack thereof. Healing starts when we know that we are received with empathy and compassion, when we are heard even when our words do not make sense (either to others or to ourselves).

Yesterday's challenge of putting words on paper or paint on canvas or playing a musical instrument may have felt overwhelming. *Where do I start?* Start with one word, or one stroke of the brush, or one note. This is where the writer of our scripture started, by humbly stating what he saw in front of him: a lonely city on top of a hill. And then the rest followed.

Lord, you ask me, "Where do I find you?" I know you ask as one who knows the answer already. I pray for courage to utter at least one word, paint one stroke, play one note. Amen.

The psalmist is bitter and angry. When the words start to flow, giving expression to his inner hurt, they come out filled with wrath. Perhaps you have found the words you wrote in your journal, or the paint you put on the canvas, or the musical notes played to be anything but "Christian." Let me remind you again of who receives these words, strokes, or notes—it is God, listening lovingly and patiently.

I grew up in a culture where any prayer, any God-talk, had to be filled with pious and reverent words. There was no room for expressing anger, disappointment, or hurt toward God. Prayers were supposed to be filled with flowery words of admiration, devotion, and praise, as if anything else would turn God into a lightning-wielding punisher of disrespect. That was until I started reading the psalms.

More often than not, psalmists start by giving God their worst, while eventually finding healing as they let off steam. Psalm 22 is a great example of this. But Psalm 137 is purely a psalm of venting with no healing yet. But, in letting go of those inner feelings of pain, the psalmist unknowingly starts down a road toward healing.

God is big enough to receive these bitter words from a psalmist who is disillusioned with life. God is big enough for when we lash out. I think God appreciates our honesty when we use words, images, and notes that answer God's question, "Where do I find you?" While we spit venom, God hears, "Lord, this is a mess, I am in a mess, and I need you to hear my cries for help." God is big enough, God is patient enough, and God understands.

Lord, thank you for receiving me lovingly and compassionately. You are my rock, my redeemer, and the one who leads me to peace. Amen.

The disciples asked Jesus to increase their faith in the same way we might ask a doctor for a vitamin B boost when our bodies feel run down. Did they think that more faith would make them feel stronger, more resilient, more trusting, and more able to navigate life's challenges? Or did they expect that an extra dose of faith would allow them to have more control over what they were facing?

Their request seems reasonable enough. More faith would mean more power and ability to do their work. But Jesus' response shows that they have missed his point. Although their faith is outwardly small and insignificant, it is all that they need to accomplish what God calls them to do.

When we encounter life's frustrations, it is tempting to think that more faith would make the troubled waters smoother. This logic leads to teachings like this: "If you have enough faith, you will be healed" or "If you had more faith, your finances would be sorted out." But Jesus teaches that we don't need to be given more faith; we need to act on the faith we have. To Jesus, faith is reflected in things like love, hope, compassion, responsibility, self-care, empathy, honesty, and humility. These acts of faith are what pull us through, not the over-the-counter doses of faith that the apostles requested.

We need to trust God when God asks us to move forward by taking what may appear to be small and insignificant steps. That is what Jesus' kind of faith is about.

Almighty God, I hear you asking me to do small things, such as asking for advice or seeking assistance from others. Help me understand, Lord, that being open to the small things is a significant act of faith. Amen.

How is it going with your journaling, painting, or music? Where is God finding you today? Let's go back to my therapist. On my way to her office, I often find myself planning what I would like to share. My thoughts run ahead, and I start to think about her possible responses. In turn, I formulate responses to her responses, until the whole session is mapped out in detail in my mind, leaving me questioning why I need to see a therapist in the first place! (I recognize this is silly.)

Then I arrive, and she asks the predictable, "Where do I find you?" I don't know why, but from that point on, the sessions rarely follow the route I had mapped out. Expectations are not always reality, especially when we open ourselves to the possibility of being guided.

Jesus highlights this point by posing a thought-problem that shows that the disciples' expectations are somewhat "off the path." They expected Jesus to respond to their request for more faith by saying, "Sure, here you go—another helping of faith! Who wants more?" The reality was more challenging, and I paraphrase: "Faith is not something you acquire; it asks that you trust and obey."

In my therapist's office, when I have talked about what I think my road should look like, I need to spend some time listening, being challenged, and receiving suggestions. I need to leave the session with a certain measure of trust, knowing that my therapist has my best interests at heart, even if what I received is different from what I expected.

Find some time today to listen to God and those who have your best interests at heart. Is it possible that your road to healing may take some detours, veering off the path you had in mind?

Almighty God, sometimes I come to you telling you how my life should unfold. I pray for the humility to listen, trust, and obey, especially when your way is not mine. Amen.

Where Do I Find You?

Having faith does not make life's problems magically disappear. Who better to testify to this than the apostle Paul? Writing to Timothy, Paul finds himself in prison, reflecting on a life filled with trials. Yet Paul is quick to remember God's faithfulness in all situations. He does not downplay the trouble he has known but owns the fact that despite his suffering, outbursts, venting, anger, and hurt, God was always faithful.

Paul writes this letter to encourage and strengthen young Timothy, his apprentice in the faith, with a realistic picture of what it is like to follow Jesus in the context of the persecuting Roman Empire. Paul reminds Timothy that the faithful are not exempt from life's trials; but when we travel in God's presence and calling, we carry hope that gives us the strength and motivation to take just one more step, to breathe one more breath, to try just once more.

Hope is a gift from God that does not depend on our own strength or abilities. Instead, it is a gift that journeys alongside us when we do our best, reminding us that we are not alone. Read this passage again, but this time read it as if Paul were writing to you. In verse 5, replace the names of the people who were pillars of strength to Timothy with the people who give you strength. Receive this letter of encouragement, knowing that God's strength is enough to meet us where we are.

Lord, give me reminders of your presence with me so that I can take one more step, breathe one more breath. Amen.

Today is Sunday. Perhaps we will have the opportunity to join our siblings in the faith in a time of worship. Sometimes, when I go to church carrying a burden, it feels as if I am the only one who does so. I mean, look at the smiling faces, the ease with which some people are able to raise their hands and their voices! It is at these times that I remind myself that each person present has their own story to tell.

A faith community is not made up of people who have it all together. We are surrounded by fellow sojourners who are on their own paths of struggle, healing, and redemption. All who are here, like me, have had their own Lamentations 1 or Psalm 137 moments. We join people, who, like us and like the disciples, have asked God for more faith. This is also a community of people who, like Paul and Timothy, can listen, empathize, and encourage one another. And we find new meaning too when we join our Christian family at the Communion rail. Jesus invites us all the same, and we share around the same Table, each bringing our own stories to the Lord.

At the end of Communion in my church, the minister says, "You have come to this Table in faith; go in peace and may the God of peace go with you." It is at this moment that I know that the Spirit of the Lord is present. Verse 14 of today's reading then comes to mind. While God is faithful and promises God's presence in all situations, I am asked to treasure this gift that has been entrusted to me, holding on to the promise of the Spirit that we will never be left on our own. So at the end of this week's journey, I leave you with theses words: "The God of peace go with you."

Almighty God, I know that I am not alone. You are here. My siblings in Christ are here. As we join in fellowship and worship, may we draw strength through our togetherness. Amen.

Where Do I Find You?

By Heart

OCTOBER 3–9, 2022 • JONATHAN WALLACE

SCRIPTURE OVERVIEW: Through Jeremiah, God sends a message to the people in exile: They are to seek good for the city of Babylon, their new home. God will bless the city and in doing so will bless God's people. The psalmist encourages the people to praise God with songs recounting past challenges through which God's powerful deeds have brought them. This can be encouragement for those currently experiencing difficulties. In Second Timothy, Paul encourages his protégé to endure suffering if necessary. In fact, Timothy should expect to experience resistance. Although the apostle Paul is in chains, the word of God is powerful and can never be chained. The story in Luke reminds us of a basic truth: We should remember to show gratitude to God for answered prayers.

QUESTIONS AND SUGGESTIONS FOR REFLECTION

- Read Jeremiah 29:1, 4-7. When have you experienced physical or metaphorical exile? How has God helped you to thrive in your Babylon?
- Read Psalm 66:1-12. Recall a time of division in your family or community of faith. How did God bring you individually and collectively to a spacious place?
- Read 2 Timothy 2:8-15. How do you remember Christ in your actions toward others?
- Read Luke 17:11-19. What boundaries keep you from full wellness that can be found in Jesus Christ?

Pastor of First Presbyterian Church (PCUSA), Foley, AL.

In Luke's world it was a given that having leprosy meant your life was over. You were a kind of walking dead, isolated from your community and a threat to public health. Only the town priest could restore you to the community. Without dramatic improvement in your condition, that was not going to happen.

In a situation like that, one either dies or decides there's nothing to lose. So when Jesus comes through, ten such afflicted souls cry out to him for mercy. Jesus, being in the mercy business, tells them to go to the priest. On the way, they are cured! If you had been standing between them and the synagogue, you would have soon had footprints on your back!

There is one person in this group who is different. Specifically, he is a Samaritan. (There goes Luke again, always surprising us with our own prejudices—as in the Parable of the Good Samaritan in Luke 10!) Yet there is something more fundamental here. This man discovers that with God there are no givens, only gifts. There had been no guarantee of healing; yet, he is healed anyway. Then, since gratitude seemed his only way of responding, he thanks Jesus for healing him. By that act of gratitude, everything changed; it brought not only healing but salvation.

Gratitude allows us to see everything with strange, new sight. Gratitude is not interested in givens or guarantees, only gifts. Oh, you can accept gifts without gratitude. But then you cannot see that the only given, the only constant, is God's love. In a world with more than enough heartbreak, forgetting God's love is a tragedy that, thankfully, we can avoid, no matter who we are!

Dear Lord, in the times when I feel hopeless and helpless, you are there. Your gift of unconditional love is always surprising. Thank you for healing my body, heart, and soul. Amen.

In the movie *Groundhog Day*, egotistical weatherman Phil Connors heaps snobbish scorn on the people of Punxsutawney, Pennsylvania, as they celebrate their special day. The next morning, he discovers that he is living the same day over again. This happens so often that he sinks into despair, even trying to kill himself—only to wake and live February 2 once again! Finally, Phil tries a new approach. He takes an interest in the people around him, learns their stories, and does good deeds all over town. He lives the same day until he gets it right.

Luke's text is also a story about getting it right. Ten people are afflicted by leprosy. They are isolated from their families and feared by their community. They approach Jesus as he enters their village. Jesus tells them to go to the village priest. During their journey, the disease disappears. They are free. They can go home. Nothing can stop them from breaking down the synagogue doors!

No response was sufficient to repay that debt, but one man knew that something had to be done before he saw the priest. He went and thanked Jesus for giving him his life again. All ten of the men with leprosy had their bodies made clean. But only one was made whole again. He was the one who got it right!

There is a difference between being cured and being healed. The cure went to all. The healing came to the one who recognized the Healer. This one man understood his own vulnerability. He learned that every day is a gift, an opportunity to live fully, not only for himself but for others.

Every day is a chance for us to get it right, to thank the One who gives us life and to reach beyond ourselves and care for others. Every day is not Groundhog Day. But, thank God, every day is Thanksgiving Day!

Lord, thank you for forgiving my mistakes and for the time to "get it right." Your love and forgiveness are never-ending gifts for which a simple thank-you can never be enough. Amen.

The news has become predictable. Whatever your news source, chances are you will find expected interpretations of the day's events. We usually hear what we want to hear from our leaders. Surprises are truly newsworthy.

In this text, Jeremiah makes news. Judah had been overthrown by the Babylonians. The people were exiled from their homes, their sacred places, and their country. Back in Jerusalem there were predictions of a short-term captivity. That's the kind of news the exiles wanted to hear. Jeremiah's letter, however, was not what anyone expected.

Jeremiah tells them freedom is a long way away. There is no light at the end of the tunnel right now. They are to settle in for the long haul. They are to get married, have children, plant fields, and start businesses. Most of all, they are to pray, which will be challenging, since they are away from their Temple. Even more surprising were for whom and for what they were to pray. They were to pray for themselves AND their new land. The people discover that God is with them not just in the Temple, but wherever they are. They can pray to God just as easily in Babylon as they did in Jerusalem, and God will hear them. Most startling of all, God is not just their God but a universal God who rules over all people, even their enemies.

This is startling news, the kind of news one would never expect. It is an entirely new way of viewing God and the world around us. God is playing the long game here. In the meantime, we need to get to work being the people of God wherever we are, in all kinds of circumstances. That may not be what we expect. It may not be what we want to hear. But with this God, expect the unexpected!

O God, you hear my cries in the dark and in the light. Help me to remember that I am your child, as are all my neighbors, wherever they may be in your world. Thank you for your guidance and love, no matter where I am. Amen.

It has been said that the only constant in the world is change. The evidence is all around us. We hardly recognize the world anymore. We feel disconnected, even exiled from what we used to be. It is tempting to spend our time bemoaning the passing of "the good old days." The siren calls of those who deny reality and claim we can return to our former lives with ease are difficult to resist.

All of this makes the word we get from the prophet Jeremiah even more startling. Instead of rallying his people to believe deliverance is just around the corner, Jeremiah gives some blunt news that is a version of the popular saying "It is what it is." He offers a provocative and deeply practical message: Get used to your situation. Put down roots. Enlarge your community. Invest in your new home. Pray for your captors. Make the best of the situation, knowing that God is still with you, even in this strange, new land.

Of course, there are situations that demand a much different response. Jeremiah is not calling for passive acceptance of injustice. He is saying that God's vision is much larger than the present circumstances. Pining for the past is a waste of energy. Instead we are being challenged to believe that God is with us still, and we can find faithful ways of living even in the most challenging of circumstances. We can do that because the only thing more constant than change is the promise of God.

Living in a world of truth and knowing the work we have to do to get where God wants us to be is more important than always living life looking through rose-colored lenses and then being surprised when reality shows up. Being as prepared as we can be for what is to come is our challenge from God.

Lord, help me remember that I am a member of your community no matter where I am. Help me to live in ways that give others hope regardless of their circumstances. Amen.

Feelings of defeat, loss, and suffering have been turned into songs for millennia. From the poems of early civilizations to every contemporary genre, there is something irresistible about songs reflecting human pain. This view is summed up by the old joke about what happens when you play a country music song backwards: "You get your truck back, you get your dog back, you sober up, you get your wife back, and you get out of jail."

It is not surprising that the great hymnbook of the Bible is full of laments, complaints, and the primal screams of a people at the end of their rope. The Psalms are often a mirror of a community's long struggle with disappointment and broken dreams.

Psalm 66 is a good example of those kinds of lyrics. In its verses there is acknowledgment that times have not always been easy. There have been moments when the people went through "fire and water," and times when those around them were hostile. But instead of continuing on with that list of woes, the singer notes a surprising but inescapable fact: They were not destroyed. They survived. Their defeats were temporary. They came through their ordeal stronger than when they entered it. They survived because God was with them through it all.

While I tend to resist the idea that God intentionally induces suffering and trial, there is no doubt that life is full of both. What the psalmist claims is that God is with us in the midst of those trials and has a plan not only for our survival but our thriving. God even has a habit of saving us from ourselves. Defeat is temporary. Hope in God springs eternal. Suffering is inevitable, but grace is eternal. News like that is enough to make one break into song . . . not a sad song, but a joyful noise!

Lord, in the midst of suffering, I find your strength. In adversity, I find resilience. Your presence through hardship and jubilation is my comfort. Thank you for your eternal faithfulness. Amen.

One of my favorite patriotic songs is "America the Beautiful." I often find my voice catching a little as I sing it. Being a city guy, however, I never fully appreciated the power of those words until I visited Arches National Park in Utah. Staring over the vast desert dotted with some of the most unique geological formations on earth, my spirit soared like it never had before. I started softly singing, "O beautiful for spacious skies . . ."

The words of Psalm 66 soar as well. The song reminds the faithful of God's mighty deeds and amazing grace. Though they have experienced defeat, trials, and setbacks, God has been faithful to them through it all. Now God has led them to a "spacious place," where they remember that the future is in God's hands and is wide open.

"Spacious places" are often hard to come by; that surely held true for the exiled Israelites. Yet they were led to that space not by viewing breathtaking vistas but through their worship of God. They sang songs like Psalm 66 that reminded them of all that God had done for them. It's not hard to imagine them dancing and singing as they remembered God's dramatic rescues in the past. Those joyful noises restored their hope for the future.

Worship should be healing. It is a time to remember the moments when despite what was happening around us, we knew we would survive. It involves memories of beloved people, words of promise, and joyful singing and praise. Over the years, we have argued so much about form in worship that we have often forgotten its function: joyful praise of a faithful and loving God, thanksgiving to God for healing both past and present struggles, and hearing God's promise of hope for the future through Jesus Christ. Whatever form it takes, may worship lead all of us to "a spacious place" of God's unlimited horizon.

Lord, help me to worship you in peaceful solitude as well as in joyful communion with my siblings in Christ. Amen.

On the first day of my seminary Old Testament survey class, my professor listed about a dozen scripture verses for us to memorize. Even in the mid 1980s, this kind of teaching was considered antiquated. The days of Presbyterian kids having to memorize Bible verses and the Westminster Shorter Catechism for confirmation were long gone. We chafed at parroting words rather than engaging in deeper exegetical exploration. My professor was unmoved. He said, "Every Christian should have certain verses burned into memory. They will remind you of what is truly important. They should be a central part of who you are. There are certain things you should know by heart."

The author of Second Timothy is writing his young protégé from prison. Ironically, he, the prisoner, is the one trying to encourage and comfort. The times are confusing and uncertain. His friend is sinking into immobility. The writer had no books or better management strategies to offer his young friend. Yet he had something of even greater value. He knew it from memory. The author tells him to recall what is central to their very identity: "Remember Jesus Christ, raised from the dead, a descendant of David." That is what all this fuss and effort is really about. If he can remember that, then the rest will take care of itself.

Few things are more destructive than spiritual amnesia— getting so caught up in what we are doing that we forget why we do it in the first place. As Christians, we are responsible for many things. Above all, however, we are to remember. *Remember* is a word that traverses the entirety of scripture. Perhaps my professor was right. Our most important spiritual discipline is to remember what matters most: Jesus Christ, crucified and raised. There just are some things we should know by heart.

Dear Jesus Christ, in days that are hectic and filled with the attitude of "just get it done," help me remember why I am here and the plan you have for me. Amen.

"Give Thanks!" For What Exactly?

OCTOBER 10–16, 2022 • W. SCOTT HALDEMAN

SCRIPTURE OVERVIEW: At last Jeremiah is able to bring a message of restoration and hope. God promises a new covenant with the people, and they will internalize the law in their hearts so that they will keep it. The psalmist rejoices in such a reality. He meditates on God's law all day and has been granted profound understanding. This allows him to walk faithfully in God's paths. The reading from Second Timothy confirms the ongoing power of God's law in scripture, which is given by God for our good. Timothy is charged always to be ready to preach it faithfully. Luke hits on a different theme: the importance of persistent prayer. In the parable a heartless judge finally yields to a persistent widow, so we should be similarly tenacious with our prayers to God.

QUESTIONS AND SUGGESTIONS FOR REFLECTION

- Read Jeremiah 31:27-34. How have you broken your covenant with God? How has God responded?
- Read Psalm 119:97-104. The Jewish laws of the Hebrew scriptures are part of our Christian heritage. How can you delight in the law?
- Read 2 Timothy 3:14–4:5. How can you learn or teach from scriptures you do not normally read?
- Read Luke 18:1-8. Through the familiar call to pray always, the author reminds us that we are called to pray for what God wants. What is at stake when you pray for justice and mercy?

Associate Professor of worship at Chicago Theological Seminary in Chicago, IL; he is a member of the Presbyterian Church (U.S.A.).

Thanksgiving Day, Canada

It was not until 1957 that the Canadian Parliament declared the second Sunday of October as "a day of General Thanksgiving to Almighty God for the bountiful harvest with which Canada has been blessed." The day's roots reach back, however, to rituals for a plentiful harvest among the First Nations; to a meal of gratitude for surviving the transatlantic voyage by Sir Martin Frobisher and crew in 1578; and to the "Feasts of Good Cheer" established by Samuel de Champlain at Port Royal after enduring scurvy in 1604.

In a nation committed to the separation of church and state and acutely aware of the shadow side of settler colonialism in conquest and genocide (both physical and cultural), for what exactly should Canadians be giving thanks? And what might those of us in the United States learn from such reflections?

The ambiguities of Deuteronomy 26 suggest that we should cultivate gratitude for what sustains us—the firstfruits of bountiful creation where we are—but always with caution. The land has been made available for us but was neither uninhabited nor barren before we arrived. This may be land promised to our ancestors, but its bounty is both for us and for the "aliens" who dwell among us. The *Shema*, the statement of identity of all Israel, challenges our comfort in occupation: Our ancestors were wanderers!

We are called to modes of thanksgiving that remember those who died by violence and disease; that support the displaced, refugees, and immigrants who dwell among us still; and that lead to reconciliation as we wander gratefully toward a just future.

God of wanderers, we give you thanks not for what we have taken but for what we receive. Amen.

Our psalmist's words exude self-satisfaction. Somebody is having a very good day!

For people like the writer—who ruminates constantly on the divine commandments—there is never a misstep. They are immersed in God's ordinances, enjoying the sweetness of these venerable scrolls of wisdom. Surpassing the elders and the educated in insight, wiser than their teachers and any enemies who might set a trap for them, they embody faithfulness and shun evil. The precepts provide understanding so they can avoid paths that would lead them astray.

From the text we have no reason to doubt this self-portrait. From the larger story, we might be a tad skeptical.

It is easy to lean less on divine wisdom and more on our own. We claim, with perhaps a bit too much self-assurance, that we know what the Bible says about this or that. On this teaching or that moral issue or this social justice struggle, we declare emphatically that our interpretation is correct, and all others are wrong.

Giving thanks for our own gifts and talents is a worthy exercise. Confusing them with uncontainable divine wisdom is a huge mistake. Like the land we occupy, the Word of God is less our possession than a gift we continually receive, one that we are called to grasp lightly so that we may deploy it in love and service among neighbors, strangers, and enemies. We seek understanding but not for our own sake. God's precepts are both guardrails that keep us secure and vehicles through which we can speak good news of assurance, hope, and peace. In this way the honeycomb of sweet truth with which God entices us will be both a delight and nourishment to all with whom we share it.

Lawgiver, we give you thanks for the sweet honey of your Word and pledge our humble obedience to serve those in peril. Amen.

The epistle continues the commendation of scripture to us as a firm foundation for a life of faith and ministry, this time in a Christian key. In this first half of our reading, Paul counsels his mentee to recall the lessons he has learned from a lifetime of immersion in scripture. Earlier, in the opening of the letter, Paul invokes not only his own teaching and mentoring of Timothy but also the formation Timothy received from his mother and grandmother. Within this family, within this young man, the gospel message and the stories upon which it is based are deeply rooted indeed.

But anxiety abounds also. Wicked impostors are attempting to deceive weak minds and lead the flock astray. Scripture can function as a guide, as a source of right teaching, as a reproof and rebuke of those who would misinform and misshape the naïve. It can also be misused to corrupt and mislead. Scripture, then, requires prayerful and faithful reading. Its open-endedness and ambiguities require a critical reception—what interpretation is faithful and what teaching deceives? The two possible translations of verse 16 illustrate this. Is it, as the text of the NRSV says, "All scripture is inspired by God and is useful . . . for training in righteousness"? Or is it, as the critical note of the NRSV says it could be, "Every scripture inspired by God is also useful"?

Our gratitude for the received canon and the faithful witness of the church, therefore, is not simplistic but involves a lifetime of formation and discernment. Our seeking, again, is not for knowledge alone but for knowledge that clarifies and sustains our service to God, within the church, and for the increase of justice and mercy locally, nationally, and globally.

Our Way, Truth, and Life, we give you thanks for those who formed us—mothers, grandmothers, teachers—and for teachings that bring about justice. Amen.

The time is coming when people will not put up with sound doctrine, but having itching ears, they will accumulate for themselves teachers to suit their own desires." The time is coming? Really? Is it not always such a time?

Is not, for most of us, the challenge also slightly different? It is not so much that our congregations will stop listening to us and turn to authorities more conducive to their lifestyle preferences and privileges. That may happen, but it is probably not under our control—especially with so many false prophets who comfort the comfortable and afflict the downtrodden surrounding us. No, the more common challenge is that we get worn down. We learn to hold our tongues. We let important hard truths soften as we seek to maintain membership numbers, the flow of donations, and a positive atmosphere for everyone. Our fundamental calling is, of course, to love the people among whom we minister. But to love them involves communicating that they are acceptable to and accepted by the Source of wisdom and compassion while also leading them to someplace new. And sometimes they lead us more than we lead them in acts of service, justice, and witness.

To my ears this passage is for preachers. I actually question if these verses should be read as a part of public worship at all. The portrayal of the assembly is harsh, but the advice to preachers is sound, if complicated. Be patient, even as you endure suffering, but convince and rebuke. Encourage, but proclaim "the message." Be always sober and persistent . . . and loving and courageous and clear and prophetic and . . . Easy enough, right?

Dear God, we give thanks for preachers and for the challenge to preach a word that sustains the weary. Amen.

I popped a grape in my mouth the other day, expecting it to be sweet. Whew! It set my teeth on edge, the oddly satisfying pain shooting down my jawline. My daughter, however, knew nothing of this sensation.

Isn't this an odd metaphor for Jeremiah to employ to illustrate the unjust consequences that follow from a broken covenant? How does eating a grape reflect infidelity to God? The sourness is a surprise, not a choice. Yet, the echo of the promise resounds that we shall rest under our grapevine and fig tree no longer to be afraid (see Micah 4:4).

God has had enough of plucking up and breaking down. Let the one who snacks on a sour grape suffer the bite alone. Let the children be free of the punishment for their ancestors' failings. Let us also leave behind the metaphor of marriage for this relationship. The divine husband of the earlier covenant that was made in the wilderness wanderings after the Exodus was a cuckold. But that is not who God really is. The future covenant ties the divine directly to each individual—from the least to the greatest—and to the people as a whole. All will know without searching the God who forgives, reconciles, restores, and nourishes without mediation, without barrier. Humans and their livestock will know fruitfulness and will be filled with the seed of divine providence and pleasure. This covenant is neither abstract nor exterior; it is a permanent mark deep inside, written on each heart.

Our heart's desire, we give thanks for your covenant, your claiming of us in love. Soften and inscribe our hearts to you once more. Amen.

Jesus' parables rarely state the lesson that we are supposed to take from them, but the introduction to this one gives it away: the "need to pray always and not to lose heart." Where is the world turned upside down here? Perhaps Luke decided a rather obvious illustration was a welcome respite amid the whirlwind of sayings, healings, odd doings (like happily welcoming and touching the babies of strangers), and prophecies that surround this brief section.

It is no radical doctrinal claim, but I suppose it never hurts to be reminded that our God is more compassionate than a judge who has no fear of the divine or respect for any person. I certainly hope so. It's a pretty low bar.

We know judges who seem to lack any sense of mercy. Those who, for instance, believe the so-called literal meaning of the words found in a 235-year-old document is more significant than the spirit of those words, a spirit that fuels the yearnings of the vulnerable who struggle for dignity today.

But our judge in the parable seems less interested in making and enforcing this or that social policy than in merely avoiding doing his job. He has nothing to say on the merits of the widow's claim. He simply sends her away over and over again. When he grows tired of her pleadings, he abruptly decides the case in her favor. As I said, it's a low bar.

Jesus assures us that God will hear and grant our petitions. God stands ready if our faith endures until the Son of Man returns. A parable after all!

Dear God who brings justice beyond law and welcome without condition, judge us in your mercy without delay so that love reigns. Amen.

Now that we've looked at our lazy, stubborn judge, let's consider the widow. All we know is that she is relentless. Convinced of the merits of her case (again, a case about which we actually know nothing), she returns again and again to this judge on whom she is forced to depend. Maybe this time . . . maybe next.

We know this woman too, do we not? Our mothers and grandmothers who kept food on the table and a roof over our heads even when they seemed to have no resources. Those like Harriet Tubman who refused to remain safely free while others toiled in bondage. Those like the suffragettes who claimed women's full citizenship and equality, including the right to vote. Those like Rosa Parks who have challenged unjust laws. Those like Stacey Abrams who continue the struggle still against voter suppression so that our democracy works for all citizens. The mothers of the disappeared and the incarcerated, and those killed by state-sanctioned police brutality too. And so many more—most of them nameless. They refuse simple comfort; they want to be heard; they want the particular injustice to be acknowledged and rectified: "Say Her Name!" Just so, "in Ramah, wailing and loud lamentation, Rachel weeping for her children; she refused to be consoled, because they are no more" (Matt. 2:18).

We "need to pray always and not lose heart." So that's what we try to do. The question is this: For what and for whom do we summon the tenacity and resilience to cry continuously, to act strategically, to petition effectively both divine and earthly powers?

O Lord who comforts the disconsolate, we give thanks that you hear and respond to our cries. Send down justice, send down mercy, and repair our broken hearts. Amen.

It's time to order

The Upper Room Disciplines 2023

Regular edition: 978-0-8358-1985-5

Enlarged-print edition: 978-0-8358-1986-2

EPUB: 978-0-8358-1988-6

Order through UpperRoom.org/store

or by calling 800.972.0433

Disciplines App Now Available
Read *The Upper Room Disciplines*
on the go with your mobile device.
Download the app through your
smartphone app store.

Did you know that you can enjoy
The Upper Room Disciplines
in multiple formats—digital or print?

The Upper Room Disciplines is available in both regular and enlarged print, but are you aware that it is also available in digital formats? Read *Disciplines* on your phone, computer, or e-reader. Whatever your preference, we have it for you today.

The Upper Room Disciplines is available in a variety of formats:
- Print (regular-print and enlarged-print versions)
- E-book (EPUB)
- Digital subscriptions (website and app)

For more information, visit UpperRoom.org/store or call 800.972.0433.

What is a standing order option?

A standing order allows you to automatically receive your copy of *Disciplines* each year as soon as it is available. Take the worry out of remembering to place your order.

Need to make changes to your account?

Call Customer Service at 800.972.0433 or email us at customerassistance@upperroom.org. Customer service representatives are available to help you with any updates.

Rescue and Restoration

OCTOBER 17–23, 2022 • DOUGLAS W. RUFFLE

SCRIPTURE OVERVIEW: The theme in the readings from the Hebrew scriptures is "abundance." Joel speaks of the time of plenty in the land of Israel. This abundance is not only physical, for it includes a generous outpouring of the Spirit of God. The psalmist sings of abundant rain that allows the land to flourish. The hills, meadows, and valleys all sing praise to God. Second Timothy 4 contains the scriptural passage that brings us closest to the death of Paul. The apostle has been abandoned by many, but the Lord stands by him as he faces his likely imminent death. In the Gospel, Jesus warns us about the dangers of pride. The Pharisee in the parable thinks his personal goodness brings favor with God, but God desires a humble heart.

QUESTIONS AND SUGGESTIONS FOR REFLECTION

- Read Joel 2:23-32. How has rain been a sign of God's impending provision in your life?
- Read Psalm 65. How has God's forgiveness freed you to participate in creation's joy?
- Read 2 Timothy 4:6-8, 16-18. When has God strengthened you in the face of evil?
- Read Luke 18:9-14. What aspect of your life do you need to approach with renewed humility?

Mission interpreter for Encounter with Christ in Latin America and the Caribbean; author of *A Missionary Mindset: What Church Leaders Need to Know to Reach Their Community—Lessons from E. Stanley Jones*, published by Discipleship Resources.

Sometimes we make such a mess of life that the only recourse is a cry for help—for someone to rescue us from the depths of despair or from our own worst actions. This week's readings carry the theme of rescue and restore. The prophet Joel proclaims God's message to the people of Israel that God, despite the people's disobedience, wants to restore the covenant. In Psalm 65 we read how God rescues the people from drought and famine, restoring barren fields into green pasture. In Second Timothy, Paul recounts that his friends deserted him in his time of trial, but he was "rescued from the lion's mouth" by the God who gave him strength. The Gospel of Luke tells a parable of Jesus concerning repentance. Our sin often leads to trouble. Confession of sin redirects us to restoration.

I know I have needed God and my fellow Christians when, through poor decisions and foolish behavior, I have found myself alone and despondent. I have learned that an important first step is to take an honest look at myself, confess my faults to God, and apologize to those I have hurt through word and deed.

The prophet Joel tells people that the "day of the LORD" is near—"a day of darkness and no light" (Joel 2:2a, CEB). People will shake with fear. Yet Joel announces God's invitation to change our hearts so that we can be rescued from the depths of fear and restored to life and to a right relationship with God.

Through Joel, God invites us to tear our hearts and not our clothing and to return to the Lord (see Joel 2:13). He announces to the people, "Rejoice and be glad in the LORD your God."

God of love and grace, rescue us from despair, and bring us into a new and full relationship with you and our neighbors. Amen.

Joel promises that God will rescue and restore God's people. Hardships will be reversed. Instead of sending swarming locusts to eat the crops, God will bring abundant rainfall in the spring and autumn. There will be fields full of grain. God's wrath had sent an army of locusts against a people who had wandered from a relationship with God, but now these same people will "eat abundantly and be satisfied." God will restore a right relationship with his people "and my people will never again be put to shame."

We do not talk much about the wrath of God these days. Maybe we should. Maybe we should inculcate a healthy respect for what God does not want to see in human behavior. The "wrath of God" is a biblical concept indicating God's anger and threat to annihilate anyone or any group who goes against God's will and purpose or who goes against God's holiness and love. In the book of Joel, God's wrath is evident when the people fall out of relationship with God. Here the prophet invites people to obey the first commandment, to know that no other God exists.

Our God has no patience when people pledge allegiance to false gods. Thus, a healthy respect for the wrath of God can lead to repentance for our complicity with the chaos and darkness in our world.

The good news is that our God is a God of grace who wants to restore a relationship with people and rescue us from the trouble we bring upon ourselves. God wants nothing less than full communion with God's people: the people of Joel's day, the people of Jesus' day, and the people of our day.

Dear God, bring us into a full relationship with you so that we know and experience the abundant life you want for us. Amen.

Our friend, whom we will call Diane, stopped communicating with my wife and me. She used to text us several times a day, but now a week would go by without word. Our messages brought no reply. Diane had changed jobs for the third time in eighteen months, and she said that each new job was less fulfilling than the one before. She had entered a dark period of depression. It pained her to communicate. Our attempts to reach out seemed to go nowhere, but we kept trying. We prayed. We waited.

The book of Psalms provides comfort and grace in times of trouble. In Psalm 65 we find solace when we need rescue and restoration. When life overwhelms us and we find ourselves out of sorts, we find the God who listens and wants to bring us into close contact. When we carry guilt for wrongdoings or beat ourselves up for poor decisions, we find the God who forgives. God is worthy of our praise because our God brings restoration to wearied lives. Our God brings us out of our funk. Our God cares and loves us far more than we can imagine.

Diane came around. She began communicating with us again. She responded to our invitation to share lunch together. In our conversation that day while breaking bread, she opened up about her struggles to cope with work and relationships. We listened. We thanked her for being our friend. We thanked her for trusting us with her struggles.

We all seek the solace that God offers when we need rescue from despair and when we need to be restored to wholeness. With patience and prayer, we can find that solace.

Dear God, thank you for your gift of love that showers us with goodness. Amen.

We have focused on rescue and restoration in the scripture lessons for this week. There is another word that begins with "R" that is appropriate for today's reading: *release*.

Paul writes to Timothy while in prison in Rome. The first two paragraphs of today's reading are personal. Paul anticipates his own death. It is time for Paul to pass the baton of ministry to Timothy, so Paul gives instructions. He urges Timothy to proclaim the gospel, to hold fast to sound doctrine, and to be wary of times when followers of Jesus will prefer messages that distract them from the truth. So Paul charges Timothy: "As for you, always be sober, endure suffering, do the work of an evangelist, carry out your ministry fully" (2 Tim. 4:5).

Paul then writes the most personal paragraph of all his writings. In his charge to Timothy, he writes, "As for you." Then he turns to "As for me." It is time for Paul to depart from the earthly confines of the body and for his soul to be released to "the Lord, the righteous judge." Paul is unafraid of death. He has dedicated his life fully to his calling. He has "fought the good fight," and he has "finished the race and kept the faith." He is ready for the crown of righteousness, which is reserved not only for him but for all who long for Jesus.

Paul is saying to Timothy, "It is your turn." Take this charge. Paul's work continues in Timothy. The same is true in every generation. We run the race of faith, teaching others to carry on the ministry when we find release from the body and fulfillment in Jesus.

Loving God, we give thanks that you hear us. Draw us closer to you as your children. May we learn to put our complete trust in you. Amen.

Phil Rizzuto, an eighty-nine-year-old Hall of Fame ballplayer for the New York Yankees, was in declining health and living in a nursing home in New Jersey in 2006. His teammate, buddy, and fellow Hall of Famer, Yogi Berra, visited weekly. Yogi was in his early eighties. How touching and human for an older man facing his final days to be gifted with the presence of a longtime friend. As humans, we all need such friendship.

Paul sought the same kind of human warmth and friendship after charging Timothy to carry on his work of proclaiming the gospel. In verses 9-13, which lie between the two passages from 2 Timothy 4 that we are looking at this week, we find Paul asking special favors of Timothy: *Come visit me! Bring Mark with you. Luke is close, and he is one of the few who still sees me. Oh, and by the way, bring some of my books and notes.*

Paul laments that his friends had abandoned him at his first trial, which was like a hearing. It was a preliminary trial before the coming of a full trial that he still faced. Though they had deserted him, Paul felt the presence and strength of the Lord during this time. He describes it as being "rescued from the lion's mouth," referring, perhaps, to being rescued from the emperor Nero himself. This rescue was the spiritual sustenance Paul needed to face the impending full trial.

Thus, Paul summons Timothy and Mark to visit him. Perhaps the parchments Paul wants Timothy to bring would help Mark and Luke write their accounts of Jesus. What could be of more consequence than such a meeting! Paul underscores the importance of personal Christian encounters to work out the challenges facing the church. We are invited to do the same.

Dear God, guide us when we meet with other Christians to plan our ministry together. Amen.

Jesus' parables frequently end with a twist, a reversal of conventional thought. Today's reading is full of reversal. It describes two persons who go to the Temple to pray. One is a Pharisee, and the other is a tax collector.

If we were Jesus' contemporaries listening to this story, we would not be surprised at the Pharisee's belief in himself and his faithfulness to the covenant with God—his fasting, tithing, and moral practices. There is nothing wrong with these rituals. In fact, they are manifestations of his desire to be faithful to God in his everyday living. Surely there is no fault to be found with solid Christian practices of daily prayer, involvement in local or distant mission, or regular worship attendance.

Listeners to Jesus' story would also understand that the tax collector is complicit with Roman government subjugation. He collects money from his people and gives it to foreign authorities. The Pharisee is not a sinner; the tax collector is not a saint.

The twist in the story comes when listeners hear that the Pharisee was one who had no empathy for another human being. The Pharisee prays in the presence of the tax collector, who stands far off. He notices him but has no compassion for his plight. This is where the reversal of the story comes in.

Luke tells the story to a Christian audience, and thus the message here is not so much about the Pharisees of Jesus' day as it is about the disciples of Jesus then and now. Do not be judgmental. Do not think of yourself too highly compared to other human beings, whoever they are—even one who collaborates with the enemy!

Dear God, save us from judging others, and guide us in the pathway of humility. Amen.

The two men in today's reading go up to the Temple to pray. The Temple was a place of restoration. When Jesus healed a man with leprosy (see Matthew 8:1-4), he instructed him to show himself to the priest who would validate his new, clean state and restore him to society.

The tax collector in the parable from today's reading needs restoration. He stands far off in the Temple. Is he afraid of the stares of others because of his complicity with Roman rule? Does he see himself as unworthy? He beats his breast, a sign of penitence. He cries out for mercy.

Luke begins the parable by stating that Jesus told it to those "who trusted in themselves that they were righteous and regarded others with contempt." It is not insignificant that Luke is telling this parable of Jesus to a Christian audience. The message is clear: Do not be like people who do not have empathy for other human beings. Strive for a humble heart. The closing verse sums up the lesson: "For all who exalt themselves will be humbled, but all who humble themselves will be exalted."

In the end, the Pharisee with no empathy (regarding others with contempt) goes away unjustified. The humble one goes away justified. Yet, it goes against the message of the parable itself for us to say, "I'm glad I'm not like that Pharisee!"

The parable invites us to aspire to humility. Humility shows itself in our attitude, behavior, and spirit. Humble hearts hold out hope that we can be restored to wholeness and find communion with God and neighbor.

O God who hears us and delivers us from evil, to you be the glory forever and ever. Amen.

Living by Faith

OCTOBER 24–30, 2022 • LISA SCHUBERT NOWLING

SCRIPTURE OVERVIEW: Habakkuk stands aghast at the "destruction and violence" all around and wonders how justice never seems to conquer. At the end of the reading, God contrasts the proud, whose spirit "is not right in them," with the righteous who live by faith. The psalmist delights in God's righteousness and in the commandments of God; however, he admits that "I am small and despised." The psalmist's "trouble and anguish" appear in Second Thessalonians also, but here the "persecutions and the afflictions" endured by the faithful serve a particular end: They stand as signs of the imminent return of Jesus Christ. In the Gospel reading Jesus tells Zacchaeus, "Today salvation has come to this house," which reminds us that the righteous who live by faith are not necessarily the socially or religiously acceptable.

QUESTIONS AND SUGGESTIONS FOR REFLECTION

- Read Habakkuk 1:1-4; 2:1-4. How can you wait actively for God's response to your prayers and complaints? How will you enact God's response when it comes?
- Read Psalm 119:137-144. How do you follow God's commandments in the face of injustice and corruption?
- Read 2 Thessalonians 1:1-4, 11-12. The work of the church has never been easy. How does your faith community work to exude God's love in a time when many reject or feel rejected by church institutions?
- Read Luke 19:1-10. When have you run to Jesus? How can you share your experience so others pursue Jesus as well?

Lead pastor of First United Methodist Church, Bloomington, IN.

"A re we there yet?" whines the small voice from the back seat. While incessant complaining irritates parents and makes short road trips seem interminable, it's a sign that children trust us. They believe we care about their situation and have their best interests at heart.

The same is true for children of God complaining to our heavenly Parent. We only lament to God about the broken, unfair ways of the world if we believe God is in the driver's seat and cares about us. Such questions are rooted in our faith, not our doubt.

The prophet Habakkuk fires questions at God about why life in the kingdom of Judah is so unjust. His corporate lament to God becomes an indictment of God's people, who have not lived up to their calling. The year is around 600 BCE, and he bemoans violent destruction from the Babylonians. The law has become "slack" because God's people have not held up their end of the covenant. Justice does not prevail; wickedness surrounds them.

Yet even in their waywardness, God hears their laments and holds space for their questions. Their cries become a powerful witness to their faith.

In our time, we hope our laments reveal our need for God. There are many historical events and current realities that make us cry, "How long, O Lord?" This honest question expresses our faith and testifies to our trust that God hears and responds to our cries. We can create space in our homes and churches for disciples of all ages to lament brokenness, question God, and grow as we live those questions together.

Heavenly Parent, may the cries of our broken hearts and the questions of our weary souls bear witness to our deep faith in you. Amen.

Living by Faith   355

After the prophet Habakkuk files his complaint with the Most High God, he stands at his watch post, waiting for God to respond. He stays awake, tossing and turning all night, because he doesn't want to miss God's answer. Finally God responds, but not as straightforwardly as Habakkuk might have hoped. "Write a vision," God says. "Make it plain. Put it on a billboard so a runner can read it" (AP). If you read ahead to chapter three, you'll see the vision is a terrifying scene of judgment.

For now, let's linger with the notion of God's vision coming into focus. When you step out of a warm building on a cold morning and your glasses fog up, you can't see anything clearly; but you trust that in time all will become visible to you. The same is true for God's vision that will be made clear at the appointed time. It isn't a vision for days of sunshine, warmth, and prosperity. It is a reminder that in times of darkness, cold, and despair, the righteous still live by faith. They rely on God and rejoice in God's faithfulness even when they can't see the future clearly.

A young adult I know spent weeks in Greece volunteering at a refugee crisis center welcoming people fresh off the boats from Syria. In the dark of night, she joined teams who waited at the water's edge for the next boat filled with nursing mothers, scared children, and young men fleeing political violence. They were willing to risk it all for a different future, even one completely unknown to them. We who will never know the fear of fleeing for our lives must also trust God to bring about a future we cannot see.

O God our help in ages past, our hope for years to come, remind us that you hold the future even when we don't know what the future holds. Amen.

In the poetry of Psalm 119, God is the teacher, and God's people are the students. Creation is the classroom, and the lessons are the laws or teachings of God. Learning is our way of life.

This particular lesson focuses on God's righteousness and our response. The Hebrew word for "righteous" or "righteousness" appears five times. It means what is right or just, but it implies a kindness and generosity as justice is being done. The psalmist declares God's righteousness even in the presence of her enemies, troubles, and anguish. Even in difficult times, she loves God's promises and delights in God's commandments.

When life is glorious, it's easy to fall asleep in class. We become practical atheists and dismiss our need for God and God's teachings. But when the news headlines haunt us, when we hear a terrible diagnosis, when we say goodbye to a loved one, or when we struggle to love our friends and family, let alone our enemies, the psalmist issues a wake-up call that God is faithful. God's righteousness is everlasting. God's promises are time-tested and true.

In those moments where we feel small and despised, we can huddle in God's classroom together. We can sing the songs of our faith as we proclaim the poetry of the psalmist. We can keep learning at God's feet until God's teaching becomes our way of life.

Righteous God, make us lifelong learners of your teachings so that we delight in your Word and trust you on all the pathways of life. Amen.

My eight-year-old hands clung to the bright red Good News Bible as Mrs. Messersmith taught my Sunday school class how to open to the Psalms in the middle of the book. I was tasked with looking up a verse from Psalm 119, the longest psalm. I was excited to find that verse on my own and eager to read more about God's promises in scripture.

The psalmist proclaims about God, "Your righteousness is an everlasting righteousness, and your law is truth." The word here for "law" is *Torah* or *teaching*. By learning how to find and read scripture under the gentle guidance of my teacher, I grew into a deeper understanding of God's love for us and God's truth for our lives.

While scripture is God-breathed, we have to inhale it in order to learn and grow in faithfulness. The teachings of God must become part of us, gathered into the storehouses of our mind, body, and spirit. This isn't something we can accomplish on our own. We need a community of faith around us and teachers like Mrs. Messersmith who help others learn the teachings of God and delight in God's commandments.

A dozen years after being in Mrs. Messersmith's class, I visited her near the end of her life. As I held her hand across a hospital bed, I thanked her for teaching me about faith and inspiring me to love the exploration of scripture. Even now I praise God for her life and pray that I may love the promises of God enough to teach others to delight in God's Word.

Everlasting God, we give thanks for the teachers who inspire us, and we pray that we will point others to your wisdom. Amen.

As my preschool-aged daughter helped me color a sign for a protest against racial injustice, we talked about how people have been marching, resisting, and protesting for decades before us. Since we are white people in a racist society, we are granted privileges not freely given to others; but as Christians we are called to use our privilege to reform our society and ensure that everyone has the same freedom and rights. We are part of something bigger than us that started long ago to bring justice for those who suffer. Even in our time, the struggle continues.

In his second letter to the Thessalonians, the apostle Paul understands the long-suffering and endurance that are part of faith. In the midst of persecution and affliction, he encourages the early believers not to veer from the truth or the traditions they've been taught. He prays for God to fulfill in them "every good resolve and work of faith."

Such good resolve and works of faith are still necessary today for those who suffer because of poverty, racism, sexism, homophobia, and other types of oppression. Part of our calling as followers of Jesus is to lift up our neighbors who suffer. And part of our calling is to urge those of us who do not suffer the same oppression to work to transform the world together.

By highlighting gratitude, Paul reminds those of us who are suffering in this life that God's grace and peace are with us. He also urges those of us in a place of privilege to recognize all we have and to hear the call to bring justice and peace in our world.

My daughter and I finished our sign, and I carried it high during the protest. "Do justly, love mercy, walk humbly with God," it read in the spirit of Micah 6:8. May we be worthy of God's call and filled with God's power, with every good resolve and work of faith.

Holy Spirit, fill us with your power to dismantle injustice with every good resolve and work of faith. Amen.

Zacchaeus isn't a billionaire, just wealthier than the average person. While his name means "clean" or "innocent," he has come about his money in suspicious ways. As the chief tax collector, he's in cahoots with the Roman government and shunned by the crowd. When Jesus comes to town, Zacchaeus, the wee little man, decides he doesn't want to miss him, so he climbs up the famous sycamore tree. When Jesus sees Zacchaeus up high, he tells him to come back down to earth and demands to go to his home. The crowds are disgruntled. "What business does he have getting cozy with this crook?" (THE MESSAGE).

That's exactly what Jesus does because that's who Jesus is. Jesus associates with people who are marginalized and with sinners who've lost their way. Zacchaeus may be hated by the crowd, but he's loved and valued by Jesus. When Zacchaeus welcomes Jesus into his home, he has a conversion moment where his entire life, including his wallet, is redeemed.

Zacchaeus recognizes his brokenness. He has defrauded his own people to get where he is. He has demanded two servings of dessert when everyone else gets only one. Zacchaeus repents. He commits himself to changing his ways and doing justice. He turns in a new direction: "I give away half of my income to the poor. And if I'm caught cheating, I pay four times the damage."

Zacchaeus reveals the miracle that happens when Jesus visits our household. Notice that Jesus doesn't argue about the numbers, tell Zacchaeus to fill out another pledge card, or demand full access to his checking account. Jesus simply says, "Today is salvation day!" The gospel comes to Zacchaeus's house when Jesus arrives, and Zacchaeus is transformed.

Jesus, may your salvation come to our household and redeem all aspects of our lives so that we are generous to all. Amen.

An old Christian adage says that every Christian needs to experience three conversions—a conversion of the heart, the head, and finally the pocketbook. Zacchaeus has all three. He slips out of the grip of his own greed. He is a changed person, living into the justice Jesus wants for the entire world.

When Jesus says to Zacchaeus, "Today salvation has come to this house," the word he uses for "house" is *oikos*, which is the source of our word *economy*. The root of *economy* is the basic needs of the household. Sometimes economic justice is personal, meaning it touches our everyday lives and interactions with people. Maybe you have given generously to help others in their times of need. You do so because salvation has come to your household and freed you to share what you have.

Other times economic justice is systemic. This kind of justice is more difficult to come by, partly because we allow our governments and institutions to be greedy for us. Systemic economic justice reminds us that we are all children of God and that the world is one household. If the salvation of Jesus has come to our household—our entire economy on a global scale—then even our institutions can be redeemed. We can pay attention to the products we buy, asking whether people and the planet were treated fairly in creating them. We can protest unjust policies around wages, poverty, education, and health care. We can take action for more affordable housing.

All of this is easier said than done. Our wallet is often the last part of us we want Jesus to redeem. As we grow in faith, we readjust our saving, our spending, and our giving because we recognize everything we have is a gift from God, and we long to be generous to God's household throughout the world.

Generous Savior, open our hearts to your economy so that we share lavishly and create communities of abundance. Amen.

This Is the Day

OCTOBER 31–NOVEMBER 6, 2022 • DEREK C. WEBER

SCRIPTURE OVERVIEW: Following the return from exile to Babylon, the people of God have much work to do to restore the city of Jerusalem. Haggai is one of the prophets sent by God to encourage them. God promises future material blessings for the people and a time of peace. The psalmist praises God and declares that future generations will tell the stories of God's wonderful works. In Second Thessalonians, Paul addresses a group that is disturbed because they think they have missed the return of Christ. He assures them that they have not missed the time and admonishes them to persevere in their faith. In Luke, Jesus is asked about marriage in the resurrection, but he focuses on God as the God of the living.

QUESTIONS AND SUGGESTIONS FOR REFLECTION

- Read Haggai 1:15b–2:9. When have you relied on God's promises for the future? How did your faith in God's provision keep you focused on the long-term goal?
- Read Psalm 145:1-5, 17-21. How can you share God's majesty and justice with the next generations?
- Read 2 Thessalonians 2:1-5, 13-17. How do you live a disciplined life, trusting in the Lord whether or not the end is near?
- Read Luke 20:27-38. How can you be open to the unexpected ways God will answer your questions?

Ordained United Methodist elder who has served churches from small to large in Indiana, Arkansas, and the UK; Director of Preaching Ministries with Discipleship Ministries of The United Methodist Church in Nashville, TN.

It was a loud party day, a celebration of what God had done for God's people, marked by movement and music and food and joy. On that day the Lord spoke to Haggai. Haggai probably said, "What?" and held his hand behind his ear. "Was that the shofar, or was that God?"

Somehow God's voice cut right through the noise of the celebration. The message was all about God's house, how it was rebuilt or not rebuilt. It didn't have the grandeur it used to have. Plus, there was a ho-hum quality to the worship. God said, "How does it look to you now?" Was God trying to shame them? "You've given me a shack," God said. "It's a dump, an eyesore!"

Maybe God was hinting about something beyond the building. The second Temple wasn't as grand as the first. But God had said, "Don't worry about it. I'm always with you. You're going to be afraid. You're going to feel . . . shaky. Then you're going to figure out what really matters. What the treasure really is."

We can value buildings and festivals and our right to think as we please, blowing horns and making a ruckus. We can value a way of life that is about placing ourselves over others. But during the noise of this protestation God says, "How does it look to you now?"

Not so great. I vote for the glory of God.

God, fill our spaces with your presence as we care for the most vulnerable among us. Shake us up until we begin to see what we are doing to one another and to those who are different. Allow us to see the treasure that they are. Only then will your splendor return. Amen.

ALL SAINTS' DAY

For all the range of emotion that permeates the Psalms, the collection ends in a crescendo of praise. In this next to last song, there is unbridled exuberance, ranging from raucous music and dancing, to shouting from the couches, to calling for justice to the nations. We are to take joy in living to the glory of God.

God too takes pleasure in God's people, the psalmist asserts. We are in a relationship of celebration and joy, even when we do the difficult task of seeking justice.

"Tomorrow Shall Be My Dancing Day" is a traditional English carol that says that Jesus invites us all to join in the dance. In his own voice and with his life, Jesus calls all to dance with joy for this gift of life eternal.

All Saints' Day might be a stumbling block for some. While we all have those we might consider saintly, most of us would never consider ourselves to be so. *Saint* sounds like *perfect*, a word we know better than to apply to ourselves. But if Psalm 149 can be believed, then the saints of God are those who accept the invitation to dance. A saint is one who knows something of the joy of living, even in the hardest moments of life. A saint is someone who knows something of the exuberance of praise, even when tears fall like rain and sweat falls like great drops of blood.

On All Saints' Day, we remember those whose dancing with their Lord has given us all hope. And we aspire to follow them in the music and dance Jesus is leading.

Tomorrow shall be my dancing day; / I would my true love did so chance / To see the legend of my play, / To call my true love to my dance; Sing, oh! my love, this have I done for my true love.

Every day I will bless the Lord. *Every day?* Yes, *every day.* What about the days I regret, the days when everything goes wrong, when I make bad choices or fall into bad circumstances? *Every day.*

What about the days when it seems like the world is heading to hell in a handbasket? What about the days when loving my neighbors seems impossible because I can't stand some of those neighbors and the ways they choose to live? What about the days when I get disgusted reading social media because everyone's opinion seems so wrong? Those days too? *Every day.*

It seems to be asking a lot, this Psalm 145. And it certainly would be if praise were a response to circumstances. Let's be honest; there are days when praise is easy. It just kind of rolls off our tongues, just pours out of us. Praise as a response is a fun and uplifting kind of thing that we all enjoy. But Psalm 145 isn't talking about praise as a response. It is talking about praise as a way of life, an act of will. *Every day I will bless the Lord* is a decision and not a reaction. *Every day.*

You can then see the rest of the psalm after the "every day" declaration as a list of ways to maintain the pledge. Meditate on God's works, seek God's justice, feel God's nearness, listen for answers to prayer. All these ways can keep us praising, even the days we don't feel like it.

Help me praise you, loving God. Every day. Amen.

Waiting is always hard. You can smell those cookies baking. You watch the clock hands move. And it seems interminable. So you try to hurry it along. You open the oven before the cookies are done. You attempt to make the clock hands move faster by sheer force of will. But nothing works. Waiting is inevitable and difficult.

That's why Jesus never just says, "Wait!" There was always something else. "Watch and wait." Or, "Keep awake and be ready." Waiting is not empty time. It is time for doing important work. We're waiting for Jesus, for the kin-dom of God, for fulfillment. So our waiting is learning to live as though it is already here. We practice kin-dom living every day. Yet, we always know there is more. That's what Second Thessalonians is telling us: Don't assume we're done; don't assume this is the best it can get. We don't wait with eyes closed, acting as if this life doesn't matter because there will be a day when someone else sets it all right. No, we wait by working with the Spirit to build the someday that is coming.

We need a vision of what is possible. The someday we long for is fulfillment, the blessed community, the experience of love. When we get a taste of it, we can rejoice. We can comfort our hearts and take strength from that experience, that kiss of grace. We strive for more, for justice, for peace, and for mercy in this life. We can smell those cookies baking and wait with hope.

Loving God, we wait for the fulfillment promised by your Son. May we never give up hope—may we never stop leaning into someday. Walk with us so that we can see and know the kin-dom. Amen.

I remember that day more than forty-two years ago when I stood before God and everybody and made promises that were impossible to keep. Oh, I didn't think so at the time. I was sure it was within my power to love and honor and cherish as long as we both should live. I was ready to take this leap, ready to remake my life around this other life, this woman I loved. It was exciting. I was happy. I was ready. Over the past forty-two years, I've learned how little I knew.

I had to learn that this kind of love is beyond us as human beings. This kind of commitment is out of our reach. At least it is beyond us on our own. For this covenantal love to work, it takes mutuality—two wills, two hearts working in tandem. It needs a supportive community to surround the couple, and it needs the abiding presence of the Spirit, pouring out love and forgiveness in abundance.

The Sadducees weren't asking about this, of course. They were asking about eternity. Since they understood eternal life to come through offspring who carry on the name, they wanted to know how this eternity thing works if there is resurrection. Jesus sidestepped the whole question. Or rather he answered the question behind the question. He said that eternity works by different rules than you thought. It isn't your effort that makes it work; it is God's. It isn't what you can do to ensure eternity; it's what God does.

Who knows how Jesus would have answered if the question had been about intimacy, commitment, and love, and not about manipulating a place in eternity. Maybe it would have been an assurance that love is what makes us alive, and that does continue in the resurrection.

Covenant God, inspire our hearts to love like you taught us to love, like the love Jesus showed us. Every day. Amen.

We've never done it that way." It's a threat, or so it feels to many church leaders. Or it's a warning or an incantation against change of any sort. Some have said they are the last words of the institutional church. *We've never done it that way.*

Yet, it's not hard to understand the desire to cling to what has always been. There is security in sameness. There is comfort in familiarity. Indeed, there seems to be an inherent good in preservation. Paul tells the Thessalonians to "hold fast to the traditions." That seems to be a call to resist change, to keep doing the same things over and over. We like our traditions; they define us. "We've been doing them since day one," we say, "since the very beginning."

But what are the traditions Paul says to cling to? Are they indeed the practices that we have been doing since day one? Are Paul's traditions the behaviors, actions, and words that we have repeated since we learned the faith? Ritual is important even now. Repeated actions can give us a sense of belonging, connection, and understanding. We partake of the Lord's Supper again and again, and sometimes something profound shines through.

Perhaps, however, what Paul is really trying to get the Thessalonians to consider is not so much the doing but the foundation. The tradition is the love that fosters the behaviors. That's what we stand firm on. Actions change by necessity. Words develop new meanings and understandings. But love that gives birth to words and actions remains the same. Stand firm on that love. That's what has been with you since day one.

Loving God, teach us to love, even when it is hard, even when it takes effort. Strengthen us to hold fast to what makes us your church. Amen.

I'm writing this during the pandemic of 2020. There are plenty of predictions about what is going to happen, but you readers will have a much better perspective on all of this from where you are. I just want to talk about one aspect for a moment: This *work-from-home thing.* This *shelter in place.* This *being here with whoever is in the house all day long.*

In my case, it is just two of us, my wife and I. Well, there's also a three-legged dog and two cats with personality to spare. But, people-wise, for months it's just been the two of us. Our kids are gone and on their own, trying to make it in a difficult economy. It is just us, all day.

It's been great, really. We get along well and have enjoyed each other's company. We've learned even more how to anticipate each other, how to serve and care for each other, and how to love.

That's what it's about, isn't it? That's why the psalmist talks about the very nature of God so confidently. It is because God is close, all day. From that closeness comes a knowing and trusting and hoping. From that closeness comes a certainty. Of course it is still faith; we don't know for sure. Just like I don't always know what my wife will say or do, but I can guess. Out of love, I can guess really well.

Be near, loving God, all day long, that I may know and love you more. Be near, loving God, all day long. Amen.

Time for a Change

NOVEMBER 7–13, 2022 • DAN R. DICK

SCRIPTURE OVERVIEW: This week we read two passages from the prophet Isaiah. In the first, God promises a total restoration, a new heaven and a new earth— a theme repeated in Revelation 21. The new Jerusalem will be filled with joy and prosperity. Isaiah 12 offers thanksgiving to God for the gift of salvation. The praise of God will be proclaimed among many nations. In the epistle, Paul chastises a lazy faction among the Thessalonians. This passage has been misapplied as teaching against providing assistance to the poor, but Paul's target is not the poor; it is those who can provide for themselves but fail to do so because they say they are too focused on waiting for Jesus. In Luke, Jesus foretells future turmoil for Jerusalem at the hands of the Romans.

QUESTIONS AND SUGGESTIONS FOR REFLECTION

• Read Isaiah 65:17-25. How can you play a part in Isaiah's vision for God's people? When do you have to accept that only God can usher in this vision? How do you know the difference between these two situations?

• Read Isaiah 12. How can your words be life-changing for others?

• Read 2 Thessalonians 3:6-13. Who has mentored you in the faith? How has their guidance helped you grow?

• Read Luke 21:5-19. How do you speak the truth of Jesus to those who say the end is near?

Ordained elder in The United Methodist Church; serving as lead pastor at People's United Methodist Church in Oregon, WI; served as assistant to the bishop and director of connectional ministries in the Wisconsin Annual Conference for twelve years, following fifteen years at the General Board of Discipleship in Nashville, TN.

The reality of a personal form of bondage came to me a few years ago when aggressive arthritis destroyed both my hips, leaving me on crutches for more than a year and leading to replacement surgeries. Many people face surgery with dread and anxiety, but for me it produced hope and release.

I came to understand Isaiah's words in a new, deep, and transformative way. I moved from a very limited and painful reality into a new world—fresh, renewed, and pain free. It was as if I had been transported from one world to a completely different one. I received a second chance and a new beginning. And throughout the ordeal I developed a new way of looking at pain and disability and cultivated a deep empathy for people whose afflictions are not so easily remedied.

We encounter people every day who suffer from physical, emotional, mental, cultural, and spiritual bondages we cannot even see. But, by God's grace and the promise of the prophet Isaiah, we can be witnesses to the transformative power of God. We are believers in new beginnings and the possibility of new realities. We have been touched by the healing power of the Holy Spirit, and we know that while not all afflictions will be cured and not all captivities will be ended, we always have hope.

I walk now without pain, and there are times when "the former things [pains] shall not be remembered or come to mind." I never fail to give thanks for my new beginning, rejoicing in my freedom, yet mindful of the many people yet to experience such release.

Our loving God of healing and hope, meet us where we are. Grant us your peace, comfort, and strength. We ask in Jesus' name. Amen.

Time for a Change　　　371

My third-grade Sunday school teacher was a dedicated but scary woman named Miss Hack. She spent most of her time putting the fear of God—instead of the love of God—into her students. For most of my childhood and adolescence, I suspected that God was carefully watching me, just waiting for me to do something wrong so that I would deserve punishment.

Poor Miss Hack had tried to instill respect and awe in her pupils, but too often it resulted in fear and dread. God was not a comfort to me for many years, but a warden. I tiptoed through life imagining a "Beware of God" sign hanging by whatever gate I passed.

After my first real girlfriend was killed in a car accident, I tortured myself for months wondering if her death was my punishment, the anger of God paying me back for all the ways I had sinned. I look back on those days with definite relief—relief that I escaped from a punitive theology that portrayed God as an angry thunderer who was eager to cast disobedient children into the fiery oven of eternal torment and damnation. Through the glorious transformation of the Holy Spirit, I came to know the God whose very name and nature is love. No longer did I live in mortal dread of condemnation and punishment. I was lifted into the reality of God's cleansing grace. Faith displaced my fear. Hope eradicated my dread. Love filled my heart and changed my entire life. I came fully into the loving, comforting, caring, and healing arms of God.

I have made—and will continue to make—many mistakes, and I will sometimes do harm. But I am a child of forgiveness not condemnation; I am a member of the incarnate body of Christ. I am not defined by my failings but by the God whose name is love.

God of loving grace, thank you for new life and the light that fills our lives. Amen.

I once overheard the following from a woman in a restaurant. "I would like the Eggs Benedict, but I don't really like ham, so if you wouldn't mind, I think I would like sausage instead; and could you fry the eggs instead of poach them? I don't like runny yolks. Oh, and please don't put any of the yellow sauce on top. I really don't care for that." The waitress helpfully suggested, "If you just want to order the sausage and eggs with an English muffin, it is almost two dollars cheaper." Indignantly, the woman informed the waitress, "If I wanted sausage and eggs, I would order sausage and eggs. I want Eggs Benedict!"

I sometimes think we approach our faith the same way. We know that we are called to be obedient to God and to imitate Jesus Christ, but we want to do it on our own terms. Certainly, we know it is important to worship and pray—when we have the time and it is convenient. We know giving is part of our commitment—but we aren't sure we want to commit to a set amount. And as for Christian service and witness—well, we are glad our church takes care of that for us.

Not everyone feels or acts this way, but many people who call themselves Christian have a faith practice that is passive or even idle. Paul warns of a complacent and convenient Christian faith. This is a Christianity of substitutions, taking what Jesus taught and modifying it to fit our desires and comfort level. But obedience to God is active. Christian discipleship demands engagement and effort. Perhaps the greatest challenge in our "have it my way" culture is to learn to want it God's way.

Teach us, Lord, to pray (and mean) as Jesus taught: "Your will be done, on earth as in heaven" (Matt. 6:9). Amen.

How often do we feel hopeful after checking the news? Natural and human-made disasters, disease and pandemics, wars and the threats of violence, climate change and ecological crises, crime in the streets, racial injustice, political and corporate corruption—the list is long and disheartening. It is hard to stay hopeful in such a world.

But this is nothing new. Jesus warned his followers that such reports and realities were natural, all signs of a broken world and a broken relationship with God. Jesus talked about the signs of the times, portents of doom, discouraging and destructive messages. His focus on the terrors of "normal" life simply highlighted the need for salvation and transformation. The world we have is not the world God intended, and it is probably going to get worse before it gets better.

So, where is the good news in all this? For Jesus, the answer is simple and straightforward: The world does not have the final word; God does. What we see with our eyes is not the ultimate reality. Our ultimate reality is the will of God, the vision of a new creation, and a future filled with hope, harmony, and grace.

Modern-day Christians who feel that their faith should be easy and their lives comfortable haven't read—or haven't understood—much of the Bible. Discipleship is hard work. Faithfulness is a full-time job. And messages of equity, justice, tolerance, and generosity are not often well received in a world of brokenness, corruption, greed, and violence. Proclaiming the good news of Jesus Christ is risky business, but God is with us, now and forever.

Almighty God, give us strength, power, and conviction to stand firm in our faith and be steadfast witnesses to your love and grace. Amen.

When I was growing up, I spent my summers on what we called my grandmother's "farm," but it was actually her orchard because she had sold off most of her land following my grandfather's death. The orchard was a slice of heaven on earth. At least this is the way I choose to remember it.

When I was young, staying at the orchard was dirty, sweaty, backbreaking, and exhausting work. On really hot summer days, there were times I felt like I was going to collapse. But at the edge of the orchard, right in the yard outside the farmhouse, stood an old cast-iron pump. I would grab a tin cup, scoop up some water sitting in the pail beneath the spout, prime the impeller, and begin pumping the handle. A faraway vacuum sound followed by a rising gurgle preceding a gush of ice-cold, clear, sparkling, refreshing water. I still remember the chill and goosebumps the cold water brought to my warm body. It was as wonderful a visceral, physical experience as I can remember from my entire childhood. When I hear the phrase from Isaiah, "With joy you will draw water from the wells of salvation," the pump at my grandmother's farm comes to mind. What an amazing image! Drawing the very water of life from the well of salvation. Immersing one's hands and face and very being in the abundant wellspring of God's love and grace. Receiving in an ever-flowing stream the freely given redemption and acceptance of God.

When we are tired, hot, and weary, God's grace restores our souls and refreshes our spirits. Too often we allow ourselves to become dehydrated in our faith. How deep is the well from which we draw? God supplies all we need to thrive, even in the most difficult times, even when we feel we cannot make it on our own.

Wellspring of faith and hope and love, we know that you will supply us with the water of your salvation. Amen.

Time for a Change

The prophet Isaiah casts a glorious vision of a new paradise, a new reality where there is peace, safety, security, health, stability, and well-being. I want to go there! I want to live there. I am tired of bad news. My heart breaks for the destructive *isms* of race, gender, and class. I am overwhelmed by the magnitude of planetary destruction, violence, famine, and disease. I am more than ready for a new heaven and a new earth.

Or am I? I can't help thinking that I might be part of the problem rather than the solution. If I were ushered into paradise, would I care for it any better than I have cared for the good creation God already gave me? Would a new beginning create in me a newer, better stewardship, or would I simply transfer my poor, destructive practices to the new reality? It is wonderful to receive the message that God is going to clean up my mess for me; but then, what is *my* responsibility?

I believe Jesus' teachings complete many of the visions of the Old Testament prophets. As Christian disciples and stewards, we are responsible for preparing our hearts, minds, bodies, and spirits to share in God's vision. We are instructed to treat others as we would treat Jesus and to love our neighbors as we love ourselves. We are taught to care for others and to do all in our power to live as kingdom people right now.

God prepares a new heaven and a new earth, but Jesus makes it clear that God will work this miracle with and through us, not in spite of us. As the body of Christ, we should live so that God's new reality emerges in and through us.

Creator God, reveal your vision for a new world through your people today. Amen.

A friend of mine was lamenting her current relationship with her fourteen-year-old daughter. "Any time I disagree with her or tell her she can't do something, she runs into her room and slams the door, screaming, 'The whole world is against me!'"

I sympathize with my friend, but I still remember that tumultuous time in my life when I also felt that the whole world was against me. It felt like nothing I said or did was good enough. I never felt confident, and I was constantly questioning whether anyone really liked/loved me. Whenever I hear someone say they wish they were young again, I shake my head. It is not easy feeling like the whole world stands in opposition to your very existence.

Jesus can relate. In Luke, Jesus tells his followers what they will face in the times to come, foreshadowing what will happen to him very shortly. The world has very little patience with people who call for radical change, social upheaval, the redistribution of power and property, and abandoning conventional wisdom. To be a faithful witness to Jesus Christ and the vision of God for a just, loving, and free world is to invite the whole world to be against you.

But this is our invitation and our purpose. We proclaim God's wisdom by speaking truth to power and calling for the transformation of the world. Thank God for the blessed and powerful gifts of Christian community and the Holy Spirit. We never stand alone. We are one with Christ, one with each other, and one in ministry and witness to the world.

Make us one, O God, so that as your people united by your love we will live to honor and glorify you. Amen.

Time for a Change   377

The Reign of Christ

NOVEMBER 14–20, 2022 • M. THOMAS THANGARAJ

SCRIPTURE OVERVIEW: Our readings for the week highlight the Reign of Christ. Jeremiah prophesies about a future King from the line of David who will bring justice, righteousness, and security for the people of God. Luke 1 records the song of Zechariah, the father of John the Baptist. Zechariah praises God for raising up salvation from the house of David as God had promised through the prophets. This child will bring mercy, forgiveness, and light. Luke 23 recounts part of the story of the death of Jesus. Here Jesus, the Light of the world, dies as an act of mercy for our forgiveness. In Colossians, Christ holds first place above everything else. Through his death we are forgiven and brought from the kingdom of darkness into the kingdom of light.

QUESTIONS AND SUGGESTIONS FOR REFLECTION

- Read Jeremiah 23:1-6. How do you trust in God's promises to bring safety and justice as you watch unjust rulers oppress and abandon their followers?
- Read Luke 1:68-79. What will you say when you break your silence?
- Read Colossians 1:11-20. Recall a time when you waited for something in great anticipation. How did your faith help you find patience?
- Read Luke 23:33-43. How do you recognize Christ as King when you experience or witness suffering?

Professor Emeritus of World Christianity, Candler School of Theology, Emory University, Atlanta, GA; now settled back home in India as a retired presbyter of the Church of South India.

One way to think about something is first to ask what it is not and then ask what it is. Today's passage guides us to follow this method in relation to the reign of the Messiah. The first four verses describe how the shepherds of Israel—a metaphor for the rulers of Judah (see Ezekiel 34)—destroy and scatter the sheep instead of caring for them and unifying them. The reign of Christ on the other hand is not a reign of destroying and scattering.

The next two verses describe the reign of the Messiah. It is the kingdom of the Davidic branch that functions with wisdom, justice, and righteousness. Peace and salvation will prevail.

We who are called to live under the reign of Christ have to ask ourselves if our lives are ordered to promote life, unity, freedom, and safety for all. When we answer this question honestly, we are humbled to confess that we have failed to live up to our calling. This admission is the start of our journey toward faithfulness. Then comes accepting that the reign of Christ is not something that we establish. We can only pray, "Let your reign come. Let your will be done, on earth as it is in heaven."

This prayer will be followed by acts of kindness, works of justice, and attempts to promote unity. In every move we make, the grace of the reign of Christ envelops and empowers us.

Gracious Lord, clear our vision, embolden our resolve, and strengthen us in our journey. Amen.

Zechariah's song celebrating the announcement of his son's birth is a wonderful hymn that highlights some of the mighty acts of God. Two things stand out in the first half of this hymn. One is that God has raised up a mighty savior for us, and the other is that we can serve God without fear.

Fear has been with us from the beginning. Adam was afraid in the garden (see Genesis 3:10), and the Bible is full of announcements that tell us not to be afraid. Most angelic appearances begin with "Fear not." Zechariah himself was afraid when an angel of the Lord appeared to him.

I have heard that the only legitimate fears are of loud noises and falling. I'm not sure about that, but I am sure most of our fear is of our own making. We need to hear the divine "Fear not!"

God raises a mighty savior to help us gain freedom from fear. How many prophets and saviors have come to us in our life! Think of all the parents, relatives, colleagues, friends, teachers, and ministers God has sent to us! We are assured that we are not walking alone; we are surrounded by "a great cloud of witnesses" (Heb. 12:1) as we run the race set before us. With this help, we can experience moments of awe and reverence rather than worry and anxiety.

God of history, help us to be mindful of your prophets among us and to experience freedom from fear and anxiety. Amen.

We are living at a time when children are offering important leadership. Malala Yousafzai from Pakistan won the Nobel Peace Prize at age seventeen for advocating for education for women and girls in her home country. Greta Thunburg of Sweden was celebrated around the world for promoting ecological responsibility and working to prevent climate change. Yet there are still several parts of our world where children are neither recognized nor respected.

Zechariah's hymn addresses John the Baptist as "child" and envisions him as a prophet, a leader who will guide us all in the way of peace. He will lead us to Christ. We know how the prophet Isaiah foretold of a time when "a little child" will lead our ecological world (see Isaiah 11:6). Such a vision of a young child should lead us to examine how children are treated in our families, neighborhoods, and Christian congregations.

Jesus said that the reign of God belongs to children and those who become like children (see Matthew 18:3). This involves recognizing and respecting children and seeing them as the messengers of God who lead us in the path of peace.

Christ's reign empowers us to work for peace. We can be thankful to God that the Christ child is the Prince of Peace and will guide and strengthen us as we do the work of peacemaking.

God, as your children we ask for your peace to be poured into our hearts so that we may be peacemakers. Amen.

Luke tells us that the first word that the dying Jesus uttered was one of forgiveness freely given to his enemies. The surprising thing is the reason Jesus gives for forgiving them. He says that the political and religious leaders who committed him to death did not know what they were doing. It is their ignorance that led Jesus to the cross.

Is this really true? Was the crucifixion not a planned, deliberate, and willful act? How is it that Jesus sees it as something his enemies did because of "not knowing"?

The mothers in my home village in India had a standard defense against the wrongs that their children did. When neighbors complained, they would say that their child did not know better, and it was the child's ignorance that led to the wrongdoing. Such a view of sin is foremost in our culture as well. Jesus' forgiving his enemies mirrors the motherly love of God because all those who are standing around are the children of God the Mother.

Those who live under the reign of Christ are invited to practice such motherly love to one another. It is not easy to live out such love; we need God's love flowing into our hearts.

God our Mother, fill our hearts with your love so that we can forgive others, even our enemies, unconditionally. Amen.

The penitent thief asks Jesus to remember him when he begins to reign. He is right away welcomed into paradise with Christ.

When we hear the word *paradise*, invariably we think of a place where joy and fulfillment abound. The garden of Eden was a paradise that was lost when Adam and Eve sinned and were driven out of the garden. Our world is far from an edenic paradise, and so we tend to think of paradise being up in the heavens, somewhere that is not here.

Do we, then, need to await death to enter paradise? We get a clue in the words of Jesus. Jesus tells the thief that he will be with him in paradise. Yes, when one is with Jesus, he or she is indeed in paradise. By taking on human flesh, the Word has come to dwell among us (see John 1:14). In the book of Revelation, John proclaims, "See, the home of God is among mortals" (Rev. 21:3).

This means that paradise is a daily possibility for us. Paradise is ours if we are willing to enter it with humility, accepting the gracious offer of God through Christ.

Every time we pray to Christ, "Remember me," we are in God's paradise. So let us begin each day with this prayer. Christ's presence with us can turn every day into a heavenly fulfilling day.

O God, thank you for being with us every day. May we awaken to that truth and experience this day as a day in paradise with you. Amen.

Paul begins his letter by addressing the readers as "saints and faithful brothers and sisters." He goes on to thank God for the life and witness of the Colossians and continues to wish them God's blessings.

The blessings Paul names may be a bit surprising. Many people today understand blessing so materialistically that only the rich are viewed as the blessed of God. Preachers who promise prosperity have adoring fans and some of the largest followings.

Strength and power are promised in this letter, but not strength and power to get anything we want. It is the strength to endure everything that comes to us as we bear our cross and follow Christ. The way of the cross is filled with pain and suffering. But God gives us the special strength and power to endure and to overcome.

In the midst of it all, we joyfully give thanks to God because we have been transferred into the reign of Christ. That reign enables us to rejoice over Christ's redemption and forgiveness of sin. To live under the reign of Christ is to accept cheerfully and thankfully moments of agony and moments of ecstasy.

A thankful heart lifts us up into the skies, so that our suffering moments look tiny. The same thankful heart takes us down to the depths of the sea to enjoy the beauty of God's grace that sustains us from underneath. What a rich blessing God has for us as we journey through our life! Thanks be to God!

Loving Lord, you have given us everything. We ask you for one thing more—a thankful heart. Amen.

THE REIGN OF CHRIST

We know that every Sunday is the Lord's Day—a celebration of Easter, the resurrection of Christ. The risen Lord ascends to the throne of God and reigns over the whole creation. But when every Sunday is a celebration day, we risk getting caught up in the festivity while forgetting the centrality and the supremacy of Christ. Today's reading invites us to focus on Christ while we adore Christ's reign.

Christ holds everything together as the creative force behind all of creation. In Christ, the whole cosmos is held together. We need not fear any scattering or splintering. The embracing love of Christ upholds the unity of the whole creation. Christ occupies the first place in the church, the community of faith in the world. The Eucharist as a celebration announces the mystery of God's wondrous transformation of us all into a single unified body. And Paul reminds us that God's plenitude resides in Christ, who has made peace through his death on the cross and his resurrection into new life.

As citizens of the reign of Christ, we inherit the love of God that invites us into the circle of God's abundant and amazing grace. We are filled with the Holy Spirit, who showers God's gifts on us so that we can share those gifts with one another and experience the oneness of God's holy family.

Now when we look at our neighbors, may we recognize the family resemblance and announce peace to them.

God of all creation, awaken in us the spirit of love, faith, and hope so that we may enjoy the reign of Christ in whatever we do today. Amen.

Life As Pilgrimage

NOVEMBER 21–27, 2022 • L. CECILE ADAMS

SCRIPTURE OVERVIEW: Advent is a season for turning our minds to the coming arrival of the Christ child. Isaiah looks forward to a future day when peace will reign in Jerusalem. All nations will come to hear the wisdom of the Lord. The psalmist rejoices in going up to Jerusalem in his own day. Jerusalem is a center of peace and a place for righteous judgment among the nations. Both readings inform Jewish expectations of a bright future with the arrival of the Messiah. Paul tells the Romans that part of receiving the reality of the Messiah is self-preparation. We should put aside immoral living and put on the Lord Jesus Christ. Matthew looks forward to the future return of the Son of God, which will happen at an unexpected time.

QUESTIONS AND SUGGESTIONS FOR REFLECTION

- Read Isaiah 2:1-5. How do you look to the Bible's stories, prayer, and the Holy Spirit to help you work toward God's reign?
- Read Psalm 122. What does it mean for you to pray for peace?
- Read Romans 13:11-14. How do you stay awake to salvation's nearness?
- Read Matthew 24:36-44. Who in your life lives as though they expect the Son of Man? What does it look like to be ready to meet Christ?

Retired diaconal minister, Christian educator, and life coach; served as a Licensed Local Pastor in The United Methodist Church (5 years in Detroit Annual Conference and 3 years in Central Texas Annual Conference); mother of two children, one who is single again and has two children and one who is married and has two stepchildren; married to Bishop Don Ott as of 2016.

This passage records what Isaiah saw and heard regarding the future of Judah and Jerusalem. If you go to Jerusalem, you will see that the Temple Mount area is not level ground but a low hill. Isaiah's vision is that at some point in the future, the Temple Mount will be the highest mountain around, so high that people will come from everywhere to access God. In fact, God will teach those who come to this mountain how to live. God will be the great teacher. No longer will there be a need for weapons of war or even learning about war. How wonderful it would be for us and the world if that time had already come!

In *The Message*, the first words in today's scripture reading are "There's a day coming . . ." It is a reminder that we are still waiting for that day, and Isaiah is quite descriptive about what that day will be. While waiting, we are both living in the present and living into the future. We are expanding our lives to benefit the world around us in the same way that God's gifts make our lives more meaningful.

Isaiah's words in verse 5 invite us to live and walk in God's light; to get on board with what God is doing among us, with us, and through us; to listen carefully; to think creatively; to be studious; to pray; to benefit from the witness of others; and to be open to God's presence with us. That is possible now, in spite of our slipping and sliding and trying to stay upright on the unlevel ground of everyday life.

Spend a few minutes reflecting on your life today, the week ahead, and God's presence with you.

God, I want to walk in your light this day, to work and serve with you, to grow in loving you and others. Guide me, I pray. Amen.

Psalm 122 is about pilgrimage—a journey to a place of religious importance. This pilgrimage is an opportunity to join others and travel together to Jerusalem to worship in the Temple.

Imagine that you, your family, and some friends decide to go to Jerusalem. What a joy to savor! Your anticipation grows as plans develop for this journey. Finally, the day comes. You are on your way! You feel a growing sense of joy as you meet others traveling to the Temple—friends, acquaintances, and strangers.

As you journey, you anticipate worshiping in the Temple with those who share faith in God. You remember from previous pilgrimages the sound of the shofar, the quietness as the rabbi prays, the rustling of papyrus as the scroll is unrolled, and the rabbi's reading the words for the day. The service of worship and the joy of being together promise to make this a memorable time.

Could it be that pilgrimage is a descriptive word for our lives? Must "pilgrimage" always be limited to a particular time and destination? Aren't we—who are prone to be creatures of habit—also people who seek and find God in many places, praise God in many situations, and serve God in many ways?

As you move through today, make note of ways that today has felt like a pilgrimage. Where did you go? Whom did you see? How did you interact? How did you worship God? Where were the "bumps in the road"? What have you learned about yourself, others, and God from this experience?

Holy One, I praise your name! I am grateful for your presence in my life and for the strength that comes through your love for us. Guide me in my daily pilgrimage so that I may be your witness and live in peace. Amen.

The Letter to the Romans was written by Paul, who had been a zealous persecutor of Christians until he quite literally "saw the light" and became a Christian himself (see Acts 9:1-6).

Paul is making an urgent appeal to the Christians at Rome. He believes that Christ's return is imminent—much closer than they may think. Paul seems to be assuming that the Christians in Rome have fallen into a false sense of security. After all, they have received Christ and the gift of salvation, so now all they have to do is wait for Christ to come and take them to their ultimate reward—eternal life! Paul knows that much more is demanded of followers of Christ.

So perhaps this is Paul's question as he writes to the Romans—and to us: "What must we give up and what must we take on in order to live fully in the light of Christ?"

First, we must wake up! We must shake off sleepiness, lethargy, fear, and anything else that tempts us to wander from our focus on Christ. We who are followers of Jesus have work to do!

Second, we must get dressed, and we are to dress ourselves in Jesus Christ. How do we do that? We step into the love, the compassion, the truthfulness, and the assurance of Christ. We wrap those qualities around ourselves before we put on our outer garments for the day. Our attitude is one of gratitude, and our commitment is to serve the risen Christ this day wherever we are, with what we have to offer, and with everyone we meet.

God, today is a gift from you! I am thankful for the gift and the Giver! I ask for one more gift. In your mercy, guide me through today so that I may focus on your children and share with them the gifts you want me to offer them. With gratitude for your love and presence, I live this day for you! Amen.

THANKSGIVING DAY, USA

One historical United States tradition is Thanksgiving Day, observed the fourth Thursday in November. There is food to prepare, there are tables to be set, a feast to be shared, family and friends to talk with, and stories to tell.

However, whether or not we actually observe an annual Thanksgiving Day, Christians everywhere are called to be thankful people. Often, our thankfulness overflows—easily seen in our actions and heard in our words. Sometimes, our thankfulness is called for in difficult times when being thankful is the last thing on our minds.

Perhaps you remember a call-and-response in worship or other group setting that has been used, especially when difficult times arise. The leader says, "God is good," and the people respond, "All the time!" Then the leader says, "All the time," and the people respond, "God is good!" How comforting it is for us to be reminded of God's nature by first hearing those words and then responding. But in those difficult times, we may well find God's healing power—God's rescue—as we remember and follow the admonition of Paul from his letter to the Thessalonians: "Pray without ceasing, give thanks in all circumstances; for this is the will of God in Christ Jesus for you" (1 Thess. 5:17-18).

What are you thankful for today? What do you want to be thankful for that is not yet on your "giving thanks" list? What could you do to make each day a "thanks-giving" day?

Consider inviting those you celebrate with today to listen to the words of Psalm 100 as words of thanksgiving to God.

God, you have made us in your image. You are our Maker! God, we are your people. Thank you for generously loving and tending us! We sing your praises as we move through this special day and every day. God is good, all the time! All the time, God is good! Amen and Amen!

Do you ever get so involved in something that you lose touch with where you are or what day it is? Most of us do that from time to time. We can be oblivious to what is going on around us. Matthew's account implies that we are not always alert, even if we think we are. We are like Noah's neighbors who had no clue the flood was coming. (One wonders why they thought Noah was building such a big boat.)

Jesus tells us: "Stay alert! The Son of Man is coming!" (AP). Trust is required here. We cannot give—nor have we received—specific information about how this event will occur. Some well-meaning Christians, however, continue to contend they know exactly when Christ will appear—regardless of what the scripture tells us. I always get a smile on my face when I read William Barclay's thoughts on this issue: "Surely it is nothing less than blasphemy for us to inquire into that of which our Lord consented to be ignorant." (See Mark 13:32.) Yet, a promise, according to our scriptures, has been made. The Son of Man will come. *When?* We do not know. *How?* We do not know. *Where?* We do not know. *In what form?* We do not know. *What will happen to us when the Son of Man comes?* We do not know that either. If you feel somewhat bewildered, you are not alone.

However, if we read again verses 43 and 44, we find direction that Matthew has given us before. The reality of the unexpected arrival of the Son of Man is still with us. Matthew records words of Jesus that encourage us again to be ready and watchful! As children of God, we have opportunities every day to love, care for, and give hope to those around us and beyond us.

Loving God, keep me alert to the promises you have made. Embolden me to live with your gifts of hope, love, and joy written large in my life. Remind me that you give me a measure of those gifts to share with those I love, those I encounter during each day, and those for whom I pray. Amen.

My spouse has told me often of his father's favorite scripture. (It is not from today's reading, but there is a link between them.) The favorite text was, "Always be prepared to give an account of the hope which is within you" (1 Pet. 3:15, AP). This verse says that life changes in ways we never expect and questions arise which cannot be answered now. Yet, our task is to be prepared for the coming of Jesus and to be ready to give an accounting of our life, our faith, and the hope that resides in us.

Noah was directed to build an ark, and he did. He did not know how deep the water would get, how long they would float, or where and when he and his passengers would land. Yet Noah and his family must have had hope. Hope must have given Noah the will and tenacity to build the ark. Surely it was hope that kept the family afloat until dry land appeared, and it was hope that enabled them to build a new life in a new location.

We dislike not knowing what is coming our way, and we certainly don't like being caught unawares by life. We want to be in control. So, Jesus encourages us to be vigilant, to stay awake, to be ready, and to be hopeful. In these words from Matthew's Gospel account, Jesus himself admonishes the disciples—both then and now: "You also must be ready, for the Son of Man is coming at an unexpected hour."

What is your hope quotient today? If it is low, how might you raise it? If it is high, how might you share it? If you were asked to tell a story about hope, what story would you tell?

God, you are my hope! I live and love in you! Help me rejoice in the gifts of this day, and keep me ever faithful in serving you. Amen.

FIRST SUNDAY OF ADVENT

Today is the beginning of Advent, the season of preparation for the coming of Christ! How fitting, then, that Psalm 122 is a song of pilgrimage to Jerusalem. The writer asks that we pray for peace, especially for Jerusalem. Perhaps it is fitting for us, in this season of expectation of the coming of the Prince of Peace, to pray for peace within the walls of all our cities and towns—for peace within the house we live in and the family and friends that make up our circle of life. We have the opportunity to start a pilgrimage, but the destination is Bethlehem instead of Jerusalem.

A religious pilgrimage is usually a journey to a designated religious site where God has done something that was life-changing and life-enriching for someone or for a group of people. Psalm 122 was one of many psalms used by worshipers on their way to the most holy of sites: the Temple in Jerusalem. Mary and Joseph could well have reflected on these words as they made pilgrimage to Bethlehem. Perhaps they prayed for peace within the walls of Jerusalem—and Bethlehem.

As we begin our Advent pilgrimage, may we show homage to the One who is coming by actively working and praying for peace. And as we do, may we not hasten through these days but rather savor our time by recalling and renewing our commitment to follow the way of Christ, whose birth we await.

Loving God, I enter this time of anticipation with gratitude for the One I await. I am grateful for the time to focus on my "armchair pilgrimage" to Bethlehem. May the gifts I want to bring to the baby Jesus be the gifts I willingly and lovingly give to the world. Amen.

Practicing Hope

NOVEMBER 28–DECEMBER 4, 2022 • BEN YOSUA-DAVIS

SCRIPTURE OVERVIEW: The readings from the Hebrew scriptures look forward to the coming of the Messiah. Isaiah describes a root from the family of Jesse, that is the family of David, that will rule fairly and usher in an age of peace. The psalmist extols the virtues of a royal son who defends the poor and the oppressed and causes righteousness and peace to abound. Christians traditionally read these psalms as prophecies about Jesus Christ. Paul in Romans quotes several prophetic passages from the Hebrew scriptures, but he begins by emphasizing that those writings were given for our instruction. Christianity without the Hebrew scriptures lacks its foundations. Just as we prepare our hearts during Advent for the arrival of the Christ child, John the Baptist prepares the way for Jesus in Matthew.

QUESTIONS AND SUGGESTIONS FOR REFLECTION

- Read Isaiah 11:1-10. What appeals to you in Isaiah's vision for the Peaceable Kingdom? What challenges you?
- Read Psalm 72:1-7, 18-19. Consider the ways you lead in your church, community, or work. How do you nurture the life God has created in these environments? How can you better lead toward God's righteousness, justice, and peace?
- Read Romans 15:4-13. How can you welcome others as Christ has welcomed you?
- Read Matthew 3:1-12. How can you prepare yourself to accept a wild or risky proclamation of God's kingdom?

Director of applied research at The BTS Center; lives on Chebeague Island, ME, with his wife, Melissa, his son, Michael, and his daughter, Genevieve; directs the local community chorus; hosts Dungeons and Dragons for island pre-teens; blogs regularly at benyd.com.

"It's going to turn out fine" was the last thing I wanted to hear as I shoved the last of our boxes into a moving van, saying goodbye to the new church my wife and I had tried so hard to plant over the last seven years.

That line, in its many forms, had hung over my head like an ax, a cheerful denunciation of my apparent failures. "Just go ahead and try! What could go wrong?" As it turned out, a lot. "Try this [insert program here]; it's sure to help!" It hadn't. "Don't give up; just trust God!" Was my broken body and spirit confirmation of my faithlessness?

We live in a culture that is addicted to the belief that a happy ending is always right around the corner. But I had learned the hard way that believing everything will magically fix itself is sometimes the very worst form of reality denial.

Isaiah writes to a community whose optimism had been proven false: Their country was conquered, people had been ripped from their homes and sent into exile, and they had lost much of what they most deeply valued, possibly forever. In this context we read, "A shoot shall come out from the stump . . . a branch from his roots."

It doesn't seem like much of a promise. But I remember holding on to it as we drove off, saying goodbye to the city we had grown to love and the dreams we had worked so hard to make real. It wasn't the promise that everything would turn out fine, but it was the promise that life would go on. In that moment I learned the difference between optimism and hope, even though our culture frequently conflates the two. Hope does not need good circumstances in order to take root; sometimes all it needs is a shoot peeking up tentatively from the stump of a now-dead tree.

Where can you discover hope, even if there are few reasons for optimism?

John the Baptist would make a lousy guest preacher. Rather than commending the piety of all the good religious people who had come to hear him, he deprecates their integrity, promises them that their religious identity won't save them, and prophesies that the one who comes after him will burn the chaff (presumably those same good religious people) with unquenchable fire.

This message would not be a winner on Sunday morning. More than a few folks would mutter on their way out the door that it was not acceptable talk in spiritual spaces: not in our churches, not on Sunday mornings, and certainly not from a guest speaker with weird clothing and odd dietary habits.

Yet John's promise of judgment also contains a seed of living hope, if we remember that every healthy forest requires an occasional forest fire. Old towering trees can grow so tall that there is no longer room for anything new; every new seed dies on the dark forest floor. When that happens, fire inevitably follows, opening up space and sunlight for the forest to remake itself.

All those seeds sleeping within us need fire so they can see the sun. When we do not make room for the new, God makes it for us. God burns down our long-held habits and ossified traditions so that something new can grow in their place.

God does not need to inflict suffering in order for this to happen; our everyday lives invariably encounter hardship, disturbance, and loss. If we listen to those moments when they present themselves, then God will take the opportunity to prune us back and help us grow in green directions again, even if it means lighting a match.

What long-cherished but now lifeless traditions or assumptions do you need to let go of?

I wonder what it felt like for John to know that he was just the warm-up act for Jesus. All his preaching and ministry were never more than prelude, setting the stage for a show in which he would only live to see the very first act.

This is not a realization that would sit well with most of us today, when being the star of our own show is considered a birthright. Our culture's logic frames everyone else as nothing more than a cast of supporting actors, useful only in how they help us when we're on stage.

It was becoming a father that changed this for me. There's nothing like the shock of instant love followed by an eternity of sleepless nights and dirty diapers to make you realize that you're not the center of your own story. As my son has grown, I have also come to realize that I don't get to possess my own hope anymore either; I find myself more concerned with protecting the world I'm leaving for my children than with exploiting the world that my parents left for me.

What if we thought of ourselves as the warm-up act for future generations? What if we considered it our task to prepare the ground for them so that their as-yet unspoken hopes and dreams will have room to flourish in a way that ours never did?

This is part of our life's most important work. We plant trees whose fruit we will never see. We water dreams that will remain under the ground for our lifetime. We offer up our own hope as the soil in which others' hopes may be planted. In doing so, we rest in the humbling hope that all of it is only a warm-up act for the glorious future that God is still persistently bringing together.

Where do you need to plant seeds that you may never see grow in your lifetime?

Every politician wants to be our next Jesus during election season. Elect them and they will fix Washington, reform healthcare, ensure economic prosperity, lower taxes, and give us hope or change or greatness in the bargain.

When we're drowning in hype and advertisements, it's easy to believe them, but these promises never come to fruition. No one person can ever fix centuries-old systems; and so, with our hope disappointed again, we crucify them or just shrug our shoulders until the next candidate comes along.

Our psalm says that we should be invested in whom we choose to be our leaders, even if the criteria it lists—seeking justice, defending the needy, tearing down the oppressor—may ring odd to our ears in a system where voting our own self-interests is considered the most legitimate form of civic expression.

As this psalm concludes, it also reminds us to limit the hope we place in our leaders: "Blessed be the Lord, the God Israel, who alone does wondrous things." It is easy to place our hope in political messiahs whom we can criticize and analyze, and whom we can vote out if they don't meet our standards. It is harder to place our hope in God, who both speaks into and transcends our partisan politics, whose priorities scrutinize and analyze our own, and who will remain God, at work for the whole world—not just our personal agendas—whether we like it or not.

When our politicians want to displace God, when we are told to look to our country as our moral guarantor, when we are told to build dreams on the backs of our leaders or catastrophize the latest election results, let us all take a deep breath and instead join in God's slow work for the redemption of all of creation—with our votes and also with our lives.

In whom or what are you currently placing your hope instead of in God?

The only way to renovate that place is with a match." That was the consensus opinion on the house we had just bought. I understood why. The weeds in the front yard stood almost taller than the building, the basement was covered with three solid inches of rabbit droppings, and a quick tour would leave you coughing for a week. But underneath all that, we saw a well-loved, well-made home with a good foundation and roof, a square frame, and a million stories that come pouring from people's lips when we tell them we bought the old Bowen place.

As I rolled up my sleeves and donned my gas mask in those first months, I learned that hope is not something we have; it's something we practice. Over time, the milestones appeared: the time the last dumpster was filled, the time the last refrigerator (there were five) was hauled away, the look of the basement after it had been cleaned and bleached multiple times, and the conversations with those same people who had told me to burn it down as they came back to tell me how wonderful the place looked after all my hard work.

Paul's talk of hope in this passage is also framed by practice. By attending to the practices of steadfastness, endurance, and hospitality, we encounter the God who renews our hope. We roll up our sleeves, get to work, and somewhere along the line discover hope standing beside us like an unexpected friend.

Hope is more habit than it is feeling. We hope in the same way that we decide to take a daily walk or clean the dishes after dinner. In doing so, we find that when we act for the future we hope for—in prayer or in protest, in public or in quiet—we become filled with hope, regardless of how the future actually turns out.

Where do you need to attend to the practice of hope?

Practicing Hope

We were chatting on the back of the ferry one day when Steve said, "So I've got to ask, Why did you decide to bring children into a world like this?"

Questions like this are not that infrequent when you live on an island and travel back and forth to the mainland with the same set of people. There is no topic that's taboo on the boat when you've lived here long enough: not theology, not politics, not existential questions like this one.

In a world where people have to wrestle with the fragility of democracy, the fragility of a warming planet, and the near certainty that the next generation will live a markedly worse life than ours has, "Why did you decide to have children?" is only the first in a long list of reasonable questions.

I took a breath and chose my words carefully. A question like this isn't really about children; it's about our future as humanity. I said, "Because if I choose to work for a better future and I teach them to work for a better future, that's enough for me: win, lose, or draw."

Hope is sometimes just a choice: a choice we make with clear eyes, one that we make even when the outcome is not assured. We may fear being hurt in a relationship, but we choose to love anyway. We may fear the death of democracy, but we choose to vote and advocate anyway. We may fear our warming planet, but we still choose to work with God for a "new heaven and a new earth."

I don't have to feel hopeful to choose hope. Rather, it's a decision I make daily in cooperation with God to live out of hope, to practice hope, and to trust that it will be enough.

Where do you need to choose hope, even if you don't feel hopeful?

SECOND SUNDAY OF ADVENT

Last week, my four-year-old son built a spaceship out of a cardboard box and invited my fourteen-month-old daughter inside. I listened to them laugh uproariously and had a vision of my toddler daughter as a fierce little preschooler and of my son's gentle face lengthening into adolescence. I had to catch my breath for a moment and blink back tears.

These visions mark my life. I saw it with my wife. We were married in our twenties, and I glimpsed the decades of love and partnership before us. I saw it when we planted a church. We gathered together for worship for the first time, and I saw a band of Jesus followers who could transform our city. I see it when I work on our future home and hear echoes of children laughing and campfires crackling on our front lawn.

Sometimes these moments surprise us, and in a flash all that possibility takes on flesh—a temporal transfiguration that lingers when the vision fades away. Isaiah offers such a moment with not only a restored Israel but a transformed creation.

When we live in hope, we encounter these glimpses, although infrequently and provisionally. They remind us that our hope for a better future is not simply dreaming into an empty void; it is cooperation with a force more powerful than time or death. They offer us the strength to entrust to God all that we cannot hold ourselves and to remember there are other places to put our faith than the exigencies of the present.

We are living in the season of waiting, expectation, and hope. The promise of a baby shows us death's final defeat and a new world awaiting. May God grant us the grace to make that hope real in this Advent season, and in all the ones to come.

Where do you see glimpses of promise for your most deeply desired future?

Twixt the Darkness and the Light

DECEMBER 5–11, 2022 • DANIEL T. BENEDICT

SCRIPTURE OVERVIEW: Isaiah anticipates a future time of total restoration. The desert will bloom, the blind will see, the lame will walk, and the people will return to Jerusalem with joy. Since ancient times, some have understood this as a description of the age of the Messiah. Luke records the song of Mary. After Elizabeth blesses her and her unborn child, Mary praises God for God's strength, mercy, and generosity. In the epistle, James encourages his audience to be patient as they await the second coming of the Lord. In the same way, we wait for the birth of the Messiah during Advent. An uncertain John the Baptist sends a message to Jesus to ask if he is the promised Messiah. Jesus responds by affirming that he fulfills the messianic expectations in the prophets.

QUESTIONS AND SUGGESTIONS FOR REFLECTION

- Read Isaiah 35:1-10. When has scripture strengthened you through personal or societal crises?
- Read Luke 1:47-55. Those with power interpret scripture differently than those who are oppressed. How can you make room for perspectives other than your own as you interpret scripture?
- Read James 5:7-10. When have you had to endure frustration with patience? How have you been strengthened by these experiences?
- Read Matthew 11:2-11. What does it mean to you to be greater than John the Baptist?

Brother in the Order of Saint Luke and retired United Methodist elder; lives in Virginia and teaches online; gardens, writes poetry, and enjoys being a husband, father, and grandfather.

Hope is in the air. Here are images of nature flourishing, bodies healing, highways leading home. You can taste it, feel it, smell it. God's covenant promise tips toward fulfillment in cosmic poetry! The whole scheme of heaven and earth is in play. Imagine it: Deportation is ending and we are going home!

The sixth-century context is specific: Babylon rules; the Jews are exiled. But the language overflows its time and place. It evokes the yearnings of all who are confined in racial discrimination, economic oppression, identity exclusion, or psychic depression. Even nature's degradation will be reversed.

For the poet-prophet the waiting is almost over. That precious ointment, hope, will be applied by the anointing Spirit. This is not just a flourishing of interior emotions. It is external, economic, political, and environmental.

What if present circumstances are not permanent? What if 400 years of racism are about to end? What if 250 years of industrial and consumer devastation of the planet are about to stop? What if centuries of retributive incarceration are about to be transformed into restorative justice for all? What if the shaming and neglect of the mentally ill is turning to compassionate care with funding and treatment to match the need? What if everlasting joy shall be on the heads of *all*, and sorrow and sighing shall flee away in jubilee?

There is a way—a way where there is no way. We are going home. Just when the darkness seems complete, someone lights a candle and the whole church is illuminated candle by candle. Christmas comes. Easter happens. The ozone layer heals. Black lives matter. God's people stand and walk home.

What would a God-given homecoming look like? Who and what would be included in such a homecoming?

In Psalm 146 the psalmist sees history—personal, societal, and cosmic—held in God's faithful care. Intervening causes and human agency shrink before God who "reigns forever." We are counseled: Do not trust "in mortals in whom there is no help." It is God who meets us in our need when we are oppressed, hungry, imprisoned, blind, bowed down in poverty, and seeking justice. So we look to God in hope for deliverance.

Do we have any role in history and the life of the planet? Humanism's emphasis of human agency is a healthy development in history. Science is essential for understanding our world. Both challenge a narrow biblical worldview that attributes all outcomes, good or bad, to God. We appreciate science and evolutionary cause and effect. We delight in discovering the 4.5 billion years of this evolving planet. We rightly celebrate when we accomplish something noteworthy.

Still, as biblical people, we sing with the psalmist: "The LORD . . . made heaven and earth . . . executes justice . . . sets the prisoner free . . . lifts up those who are bowed down . . . upholds the orphan and the widow, but . . . brings to ruin [the wicked]." The Psalms form us as we sing the Lord's song.

Gathered around font, story, and table, we acknowledge that "all our works begun, continued and ended in thee" aim to glorify God (See *Book of Common Prayer*, 1979, "Collect for Guidance," p. 832). As a eucharistic people, we join the psalmist to declare, "All honor and glory is yours, Almighty God, now and forever. Amen" ("The Great Thanksgiving," *The United Methodist Hymnal*).

Read aloud "The Great Thanksgiving" in your church's hymnal or worship book. Note how it narrates what God has done, is doing, and will do to care for and save us and all creation. Note what you feel. Then reread and rest in Psalm 146:5-10.

Mary was one of the "lowly" ones in verses 48 and 52 (Hebrew: *anawim*; Greek: *tapeinos*). In the Old Testament, the *anawim* were the poor of every sort: the vulnerable, the marginalized and socio-economically oppressed, those without earthly power who depended totally on God for their survival. Mary was one of the "bowed down" (see Psalm 146:8) who trusted for the good things of the Lord to fill their emptiness.

On the other side were the proud, powerful, and rich. They were indifferent to who got hurt and unconcerned by the suffering of the poor. In contrast to the lowly and bowed down, they were *pluteo*—the wealthy (from the Greek that gives us the term "plutocrat"). They cared nothing for who was hungry or crushed by poverty.

Class conflict seems the obvious mood here. Militant revolution seems the only tune. Is there any other way to sing it? Could Mary have sung it as a "crisis contemplation" —a spiritual centering in the midst of oppression and futility, like the moan of the slaves in the Middle Passage? Where do we go when the way is no way?

Imagine singing in solidarity with Mary our shared passage beyond our dystopian order. Moan with her, making the sounds of a new creation shaped by mercy and compassion, a new identity, a dream of restitution and balance, a day of joy, love's solidarity where we belong to each other. Imagine groaning with Mary for the day when there are neither rich nor poor, and hate and hoarding are no more. Sing the song. Moan it, groan it, march it—knowing deep down "that God still goes the road with us."

On the Internet or in your hymnal find and read (or listen to) "Cuando El Pobre" (When the Poor Ones). Meditate on the words. What happens within you? What do you feel physically?

When you are denied your share of the planet's wealth, refused your humanity, or live in unending pain or mental anguish, the counsel to "be patient" is the last thing you want to hear. If you think James is patient as a passive, pious wimp, read the verses that precede today's reading (see James 5:1-6).

James has already vented his spleen on the powerful who oppress the poor: "Your gold and silver have rusted, and their rust will . . . eat your flesh like fire" (5:3). He has condemned those who denied wages to the laborers whose outcry has reached God's ears (5:4). Justice delayed is justice denied! James is angry with we who willingly forget that we belong to each other.

The call to patient waiting is for the defamed, defrauded, poor, suffering, and excluded. James urges them not to give up; the judge who rules in their favor "is standing at the doors!" James cites the prophets and Job, and he calls for endurance that trusts God, who is "compassionate and merciful."

Waiting for God is like waiting for rain to come to the garden. The prophets proclaimed the coming of "streams in the desert" (Isa. 35:6). It is not a lie; its coming is sure and certain. The drought is not permanent, and being patient is not giving up. "If it seems to tarry, wait for it . . . it will not delay," said the prophet Habakkuk (2:3).

Waiting for the Lord is built into the creation and the seasons. But it does not mean conceding to social injustice or withholding compassion. While waiting for the Lord we are all—rich and poor—called to dream God's dream for the earth and work to make that dream a reality.

In your social and economic location, what is God saying to you in James 5:1-11? Pray a prayer in response.

Blessed is anyone who takes no offense at me," says Jesus to the delegation from John the Baptizer's inner circle. Who would be offended at Jesus? It sounds odd to us. We have been formed to think of Jesus as the fulfillment of all God's promises. Why would anyone be offended by him and what he has done and is doing? The lame, the blind, the unclean, the deaf, and the poor have been healed and helped by him. Good news! Hurts are being addressed. Hopes are soaring.

But what if you were in prison in the fortress at Machaerus across the Dead Sea? There was not one word about prisoners in Jesus' report, and John was in prison. If you are behind bars unjustly, if you are in a refugee camp, if you are chronically depressed, if you are isolated or the victim of bullying, if you are systemically excluded, reports of those whose hopes and hurts have been met and realized are of little comfort. Context is everything. John is waiting like many around us are waiting.

What about us? We are in church and praising God. Many of us have pension checks, health insurance, friends, and stability. But what if you do not have those blessings? There is little comfort for those who are on the outside looking in or on the inside looking out. When you are left out of the fulfillment of hope, you are left behind.

Since we belong to each other, saying the "prayers of the people" is an act of solidarity with those who suffer. Remembering them in our prayers will send us to them in and with the love of God.

O God, help us to bring light to those in the darkness of doubt and isolation. Give us strength to resist injustice and oppression. Amen.

What was John to think when the messengers reported through the bars of his cell? Humanly speaking, he had to have wondered, *What about me?* There was no word of hope for him.

The truth is that John had made a life choice that put him behind bars. It was not the charge against Herod (see Matthew 14:1-12), but the ultimate choice to herald the reign of God no matter what that put him in jeopardy. Baptized, we live between the darkness and the light, trusting God even in the darkness.

> Tho' the cause of evil prosper,
> Yet the truth alone is strong;
> Tho' her portion be the scaffold,
> And upon the throne be wrong:
> Yet that scaffold sways the future,
> And, behind the dim unknown,
> Standeth God within the shadow,
> Keeping watch above His own.
> (James Russell Lowell)

John's portion was the "scaffold" that swayed the future, and in the shadow of that prison God stood "keeping watch above his own." John had made one of those life choices that determine everything else for good and ill. He had thrown himself in league with the coming reign of God. If he felt disappointment and doubt in the moment, his offense was personal and human. What made him great was his willingness to become less, so that God's justice and righteousness could triumph (see John 3:30).

Abba God, by water and the Spirit you call us to resist evil, injustice, and oppression, and to profess our faith in Jesus Christ. Rekindle in us the will to live into your love and justice between the darkness and the light. Amen.

THIRD SUNDAY OF ADVENT

When we are impatient and restless, the counsel to be patient tends to evoke further impatience. Imagine James speaking these words to John through the prison cell bars (see Matthew 11:1-11). Would John have welcomed James's counsel? John was a prophet who had spoken in the name of the Lord and heralded his coming. The grain would be gathered, and the chaff would be burned (see Matthew 3:10)! Who could blame him for questioning? Was the ax at the root of the tree or not?

At the heart of James's words is a call to contemplation—to quiet the mind and enter the silence beyond words, emotions, and thoughts. Crops waiting for "the early and the late rains" is a compelling image from the creation. Nature with the planet's 4.5 billion years of emergence is full of patience. In contrast, our pace of life and the demands upon our psyche and time snarl us in anxiety and dis-ease. James calls us to the heart of prayer: a quiet centeredness, a break with the news cycle, an entry into the still point of the turning world.

Jesus said, "Whenever you pray, go into your room and shut the door and pray to your Father who is in secret" (Matt. 6:6). In contemplation—holy resting, holy seclusion—we hide ourselves from the anxious world and our own anxious selves to inhabit the presence of the One who comes near. In patience we shut the door to be the beloved with the Beloved.

In Advent, patience is waiting in the Beloved who is near. We wait between the darkness and the coming light.

Fix your attention on something in nature. Breathe deeply and rest. Let any thoughts, words, or emotions pass by like boats on the river of consciousness. Be the beloved held in the gaze of the Beloved.

Living the Tension

DECEMBER 12–18, 2022 • OSHETA MOORE

SCRIPTURE OVERVIEW: Isaiah is sent to the king of Judah to declare a prophecy of a future birth through a virgin. The boy will be called Immanuel, "God is with us." The psalmist cries out to God asking for an end to the suffering of the people. He believes that this will occur through a "son of man," an expression that Jesus later uses to describe himself. Paul's opening to Romans roots the gospel in the Hebrew scriptures. Jesus comes from the line of David and fulfills the things foretold. To understand Jesus, we must understand the Hebrew scriptures. Matthew recounts the visitation of an angel to Joseph to tell him of the coming birth of a son. Matthew interprets this birth as a fulfillment of this week's reading from Isaiah 7.

QUESTIONS AND SUGGESTIONS FOR REFLECTION

- Read Isaiah 7:10-16. How does Isaiah's prophecy continue to speak to you today? How do you hope for Christ's coming?
- Read Psalm 80:1-7, 17-19. Recall a time when you have relied on hope for God's restoration.
- Read Romans 1:1-7. What would it mean to add "servant-hood" to your list of life goals?
- Read Matthew 1:18-25. How is your life different for having listened to God's call?

Anabaptist pastor serving as Community Life Pastor at Roots Covenant Church and as Teaching/Outreach Pastor at Woodland Hills Church, both in St. Paul, MN; author of *Shalom Sistas: Living Wholeheartedly in a Brokenhearted World*.

Advent is a season when we pay closer attention to the presence and absence of light. The days are shorter—light is more scarce—as we move closer to the winter solstice, after which the days begin to lengthen again. Light is an apt metaphor for God's revealing power: God's word. God's word comes from outside of us and floods our lives like light. It is simultaneously a word of consolation and a word of judgment. God's word exposes as it illuminates and purges as it refines. How we receive it determines the depth of its transforming power in our lives. Will we stand opposed to God and receive judgment or will we open ourselves to God and receive salvation?

God's word comes to Ahaz, the king of Judah, warning him of impending destruction but also providing an opportunity for salvation. Ahaz stands opposed. What follows is both a sign of judgment and of consolation. God will show up in the sign of judgment through the force of a foreign kingdom (Assyria), and God will show up in a sign of consolation in the child born of a virgin and called Immanuel ("God with us").

When the early disciples of Jesus read the scriptures, they saw this passage with new eyes: Jesus of Nazareth is the one born of a virgin who is God with us. Most often we focus on the consolation aspect of this sign, but it was also a sign of judgment. Jesus' advent into the world is the invasion of heaven. He exposes as he illuminates and purges as he refines. How will you and I respond to God's advent in our lives? Will we be prepared to meet with openness God's word in Jesus, who is the Word, or will we double down?

Lord, this Advent we hold your light and the darkness around us in tension. Often it feels as if darkness is overwhelming. Help us to remember your light and to see how you are showing up. Help us, Lord, and bring your peace when we feel surrounded by destruction like Ahaz. Amen.

Great loss turns our world upside down and sends us to the floor; to the basics; to cold, hard truths. What's real? The loss Israel has experienced is exile—the loss of home and safety, freedom and prosperity. Israel's neighbors look on and see no special protection. They mock. Has Israel lost not only home but God too?

How can the same God who rescued Israel from Egypt with mighty power allow Israel to languish in exile? Isn't God Israel's Good Shepherd? Isn't God the King of the heavens, enthroned on high? How has this happened?

Advent gives space for our most raw emotions and guttural cries for God. Advent begins the story in the midst of the conflict. Where is God? The world is broken. God's people are conquered and need salvation and restoration. Advent reminds us that Israel longed for deliverance for generations before the Messiah was born. In our lives, too, we know longing and waiting and crying. Our stories personally and collectively mirror the story of Israel.

Covenant means being able to express grief, frustration, and anger to God. Covenant means calling on God to be who God has always been: Shepherd, King, Restorer. Israel understood this and cried out to Almighty God for mercy. Advent invites us to bring our tears and fears to God in lament.

Lord, you see our pain and you see our anger. They are not offensive to you. We will invite you in and allow you to weep alongside us. Then, we will open ourselves up to receive comfort and healing from you. Amen.

In the midst of lament, Israel finds hope in the prophetic promise of a human being who is anointed by God to be a liberating leader. Israel's national history is born from this promise. The people were once enslaved in Egypt, but God heard their cries and sent Moses to be their deliverer. This set the stage for other leaders like Joshua to follow in Moses' footsteps. Then Israel's kings took up this mantle and were anointed. Each one was seen to be in a special relationship with God—as though God had rested the divine hand on them. But David stands out. He was an anointed king to whom God promised an everlasting house. The promised "Son of Man" would be one like David—a man God raised up—but one who would reign forever. The kingdom of this Son will never end.

Advent is a season in which we await and celebrate the coming of Jesus, the Son of David whom God has raised up and upon whom the kingdom of God is conferred. Jesus of Nazareth is the answer to this psalm's cry for restoration and salvation. He is the one who has shined his face upon us—the very face of God.

What is beautiful about Jesus is that although he is God's "right-hand man," he's also right beside us. Jesus, Immanuel, came to live among us in order to reveal the love of God. This restorative and transformative love saves us not just from sin and death but from utter hopelessness.

Jesus, so many things feel broken and unjust. Hopelessness is right around the corner. You, Lord, are hope and peace. Today I will trade my heartbreak for your restoration. Amen.

What does "gospel" even mean? Some think it has to do with going to heaven when you die. Others think it has do with being forgiven even though we don't deserve to be. A lot of people know that "gospel" literally means "good news." But is any good news "gospel"? Is finding some crumpled up cash in a pants pocket "gospel"? What is the "gospel of God"?

The gospel of God stands in contrast to the "gospels" of human empires, which pretend they have a say over how history will turn out. The gospel of God begins with a promise, a word of hope and liberation. The gospel of God begins with a covenant cut with a people, a people with a history, with pain, with loss, and yet with hope.

Paul isn't talking here about some abstract doctrine or escape from this world. No, Paul is talking about a long-promised rescue of a people who are in a special relationship with God. Empires have tried to snuff them out, but God has preserved them and promised a Deliverer to once and for all establish a kingdom against which the nations will rage but which they will never overthrow. Paul makes it clear the gospel of God is the advent of Jesus the Messiah, a historical fact that was foretold by prophets and recorded in scripture. The gospel of God is about the Spirit of God who rested on Jesus and raised him up never to die again when one last empire tried to crush him. Paul also makes it clear this gospel of God calls out not only to Israel but to all the people of the world. This gospel calls us all to belong together to Jesus Christ, the Messiah—the gospel of God.

Dear Jesus, you love us, and that is good news. You are with us, and that is good news. You lived to show us a new way to be human, and that is good news. You offer forgiveness and grace when we fall short, and that is good news. Today, I respond, "Yes and Amen."

The royal announcement of the gospel creates a new way of being in community together: a holy people. This holy people group is collected together not by ethnicity, economic status, gender, or race, but because they are loved and called by God.

The gospel carves a people out of the empires of this world like an artist carves a statue from stone. Rome is stone, and the church is God's masterpiece chiseled with the power of love. This holy people will not look so different from the people around them, but they will relate to one another as family. They will love one another because they are loved by God. And the quality of their community is marked by grace and peace.

Grace means "gift," and this community has received from God the gospel that calls them and forms them. Grace makes them family; peace is their bond. Peace is the Hebraic concept of shalom, God's dream for the world as it should be—nothing broken, nothing missing, everything made whole.

As disciples of Jesus, we recognize the gift of grace we've received and try to practice shalom. Often when we integrate these two values into our relationships, we begin to see one another through the lens of God—we see those who hurt, annoy, or offend as people in need of grace and peace. This reframing becomes the foundation for how we approach people, which is one of the reasons so many letters from the apostles begin with "grace and peace." Such a greeting was a conscious decision to approach everyone with the deeply humanizing way of grace and peace.

Lord, I need your grace and peace. Lord, I receive your grace and peace. Lord, I give your grace and peace. Amen.

Living the Tension   415

At Advent time, we're reminded of Mary's role in the redemption of the world. She is the human through whom God the Son was birthed into the world. She is the vessel who carried God's sacred presence within her like the ark of the covenant. She is the also the servant who is obedient to God with her famous "yes." For nine months she was pregnant with the Christ child who came into the world to redeem us.

Pregnancy is an apt metaphor for the Advent season. Like Mary, Advent carries within it hopefulness in the midst of a threatening world. Kings and rulers may seek to prevent the promise from being birthed to protect their interests, but God will allow nothing to stand in the way of the world's restoration. The Advent season is hopeful in its waiting; the promised Messiah is almost here. The Advent season teaches us to wait for God like an expectant mother waiting for her child. These are the birth pangs of a new world.

But how do we wait? Note that Joseph decided not to wait for any word from God but rather to act on his own understanding—though it was an act of compassion to "divorce her quietly." But then the word from God came, moving him in a different direction. Where once Joseph was in a fearful state, God was now telling him not to be afraid because the Spirit of God was in the middle of the whole situation.

In our times of darkening personal and world events, how do we wait? In fear, or in trust that God is in the middle of our situation? Joseph responded in obedience to God's alternative—and from that obedience came the Savior of the world.

Yes, there is tension in our waiting; but God is with us in that tension, drawing us into a hopeful future.

With hopeful hearts and open minds, Lord, we ask you to open our hearts to your truth and strengthen us to live within it. Amen.

FOURTH SUNDAY OF ADVENT

The season of Advent takes us back to the time before Jesus was born. We imagine ourselves with Israel still waiting for the promised Messiah. There is hope but also lament. Israel has languished under the oppression of empires for generations and has cried out to God for deliverance. The prophets had foretold that God would bring the kingdom on earth as it is in heaven through a "suffering servant," one who would be God with us, to liberate them from domination. Matthew's telling of the gospel confirms that Jesus is that promised Messiah, the one the prophets foretold in the sign of a son born to a virgin.

We live in a similar tension, not between a world before the Messiah and his advent but between his first and second advents. We live in the tension between Jesus' coming into the world to redeem it and the consummation of the world's redemption. In much the same way that Israel longed and hoped for their consolation by God, the church longs and hopes for our consolation when Jesus returns to put right what has gone wrong. While we live in this tension, we have God's Spirit to guide us and comfort us. In Advent, God's Spirit reminds us that God will be faithful to finish the work God has begun through Jesus.

Lord, when I feel discouraged, I'll remember we are living in the tension and remember the times when you have shown up. When I feel overwhelmed, I'll remember that we are living in the tension and cast my cares upon you. When I'm tired of waiting for justice, I'll look for ways you are creating shalom all around me. Give me eyes for "already"—your kingdom has come near—and stamina for the "not yet" as we live in a world that does not yet fully reflect the love and peace of your kingdom. Amen.

Living the Tension

Signs of Our Time

DECEMBER 19–25, 2022 • HEATHER MURRAY ELKINS

SCRIPTURE OVERVIEW: Joy over the Christmas miracle is the theme that binds this week's passages together—unrestrained joy over what God has done and over who God is. These texts celebrate a God who reigns in strength and brings peace and light—the beginning of a new reality. As worshipers, we join in rejoicing over the coming of the messenger "who says to Zion, 'Your God reigns'" (Isa. 52:7) and the angel who brings "good news of great joy for all the people" (Luke 2:10). We celebrate with all the earth by singing a new song (Ps. 96:1). The One who was present at creation, the eternal Word, "became flesh and lived among us" (John 1:14).

QUESTIONS AND SUGGESTIONS FOR REFLECTION

- Read Isaiah 9:2-7. What or who in your life helps you to continue to walk in the world's darkness?
- Read Psalm 96. How do you join the earth in joy and worship? How does this allow you to shout for joy and sing to the Lord a new song?
- Read Luke 2:1-20. Advent reminds us of Jesus' bridging the gap between God and humanity. How does this reality change the way you experience the world?
- Read John 1:1-14. Reflect on the incarnation of God in the form of a baby. In what ways does this influence the way you see and understand God's nature?

Frederick Hannan Emerita Professor of worship, preaching and the arts, Drew Theological Seminary, Madison, NJ; elder in the West Virginia Conference of The United Methodist Church.

This meditation is being written as two branches of the government in the United States argue over the deadline for the 2020 Census. Questions about its purpose and accuracy have dogged census takers and clogged lines of communication. Census-taking, "the actual enumeration" of a nation, has been done every decade since 1790. It is an essential act of governance. According to the website for the Census, "The 2020 Census will determine congressional representation, inform hundreds of billions in federal funding each year, and provide data that will impact communities for the next decade." Everything from school lunches to highway construction will be determined based on this census and the economic health of the nation.

The empire-wide census Luke describes was seen as an essential act. Luke and Quirinius both want to give an accurate account of these matters; the census is critical for both governance and gospel. Quirinius wants an accurate head count for the purpose of taxation, statistics on migration, and places of origin. Perhaps there was an early version of the first 2020 question: "How many people are living in this house?"

This matches Luke's purpose to establish Joseph in the line of David, and Bethlehem as the center of Incarnation. "Who are your ancestors and where did your people come from?" This is not just a question of history; this is a proclamation of good news and great joy. This census will be a means of grace; Caesar may believe he rules an empire, but as the psalmist writes: "God is coming to rule the earth—to rule the world with justice and its people with truth."

You know me, Holy One. Even the hairs of my head are counted, and I matter to you who counts the stars and the grains of sand. Amen.

It's almost impossible to read these words in the King James translation and not hear Handel. His oratorio turns this text back to its original form, a song. Isaiah reassures those who are brokenhearted that God has not abandoned them. The Holy One's silence seems deafening as the nation is threatened with invasion. Have they been abandoned by their Protector because of unfaithfulness? Is the covenant broken beyond repair?

These words of promise were inscribed on a heartbroken people who face the loss of a "promised" land and loved ones. Language and memory will be threatened, and yet this song survives—a song about a child who will be the strength of God who sustains their children's children.

We do not know if Isaiah was speaking of Hezekiah or Josiah or some child ruler whose name we do not know. What the prophet wants us to hear is the righteousness of this leader. The justice and mercy of this child will be the source of shalom for the nation. What God wants us to hear is that the child whose name we do know will be the champion of peace.

Prophetic imagination proclaims future communities of faith in the same breath as naming God's faithfulness to our ancestors. The past, present, and future weave together in this witness to the child who will be a wonder, a counselor, a protector, and a champion of peace. The yoke of the oppressor will be removed. The word *yoke* was a neo-Assyrian expression for domination, yet hear how it is transformed by the Beloved: "My yoke is easy, and my burden is light" (Matt. 11:30).

Holy Jesus, be my comfort by day and my song in the night. Amen.

God's grace has appeared, offering salvation to all. It trains us to reject godless ways and worldly desires and to live temperately, justly, and devoutly in this age as we await our blessed hope—the appearing of the glory of our great God and our Savior Jesus Christ.

Wait. Hope. How?

Catherine of Siena, a medieval mystic and the first woman to be named a Doctor of the Church, speaks of how our desire for control leads to suffering. We long for and love things that will not last. We love what we will lose. We strive for security; we protect ourselves from seeing how vulnerable we are. We store up possessions and indulge our addictions. The more we desire protection, the more unbearable the pain of loss will be.

Catherine and the author of Titus offered pastoral care to their communities when political and religious structures of their world were collapsing. The writer of Titus probably experienced the First Jewish War that ended with Rome's destruction of the Temple in Jerusalem, the center of Jewish identity and worship. The Great Western Schism, an international war over rival popes that sundered the unity of the church, was underway in Catherine's day. In the midst of imperious and imperial power, religious chaos, and countless loss, how is it possible to live a temperate, just, and devout life?

God's grace appears. The Holy One enters human time in the most vulnerable form of love, and it is a love that saves us from hopeless suffering. Against this chaos of empires is the quiet assurance of God who appears in Jesus the Christ. Here is the Love that will not let us go. Here is the hope that blesses us as we wait for the One who is coming again.

O God, our help in ages past, gift us again with hope for the future through your Beloved One. Amen.

The sea is roaring the bass line; the descant of the morning stars soars above the melody line of the mountains. The trees are dancing, roots and all, as they reach the refrain. Here is a Christmas carol sung by creation in honor of the One who is coming.

People long to join in a praise chorus that includes all creatures great and small. We dream of "con-spiring," breathing together. The psalmist sings of the One who created the heavens and the earth: Yahweh, who breathes life into us, is here. The Holy One, closer than a breath, is coming to redeem all of creation. Let everything that breathes sing for joy!

Singing is a human need as deep as our DNA. We sing before we can read. We sing before we learn to write. We sang before anyone invented writing. An explosion of pent-up joy will be released when the righteous One of God arrives. This psalm of holy presence resonates deeply, particularly during the long silence due to COVID-19. When injustice takes all the oxygen out of the room, or as the air turns gray with ash and trash, the whole earth struggles to catch its breath.

Ten months into the pandemic, I have decided to clear out my "Save" Facebook files. It is a poor attempt to control the chaos. I pause at a clip of cows. I push play and a chorus springs into song. Hoot owls and hippos, blackbirds and bullfrogs sing. Their song creates a time warp. I'm now singing out loud with Peter, Paul, and Mary as they gather us all into the chorus of Bill Staines' earthy anthem, "All God's Critters Got a Place in the Choir." Con-spiring with saints and salamanders, elders and elderberries, that's how the song goes. As it was in the beginning, is now, and ever shall be, world without end. Amen.

Holy One, may every breath be a blessing for all that moves and has its being in you. Amen.

For me, Christmas day is filled with the sound of feet. Little feet, eager feet, can't-sleep-anymore feet dance down the hall searching for a tree or happy things in boxes. These are the happy-feet sounds in my memory, but this is also the undertone that can become an undertow to this scripture. It isn't Santa who announces peace, proclaims deliverance, or delivers good news.

These scriptural sounds come from a messenger who races to bring God's news to those who have been waiting in shadows. These are the feet of John, prophet of the Most High, who prepares the way for the Promised One. In Luke's Gospel, Elizabeth says she can feel her baby's feet dancing with joy when Mary, who is pregnant with Jesus, comes to visit.

There's a pair of messenger feet in Seminary Hall at Drew Theological Seminary. Broken, sandaled feet are all that remain of a sculpture of John the Baptist that was dedicated in 1965 in memory of Al Brown, a Drew senior. He had died rescuing a young girl in his youth group. The community turned to John, the preparer of the Way, in recognition of Al Brown's ministry.

The bronze sculpture was vandalized in the 80s and snapped off just above the ankles. Now the dedication plaque is lost and Al's witness is forgotten. These broken feet, however, have gradually transformed into a proclamation of Emmanuel. They bear witness to the words of Isaiah.

This is the proclamation of beautiful feet, and those who tell it on the mountain that Jesus Christ is born. These messenger feet represent all who bring the message of Christ's peace and freedom to a waiting world. "How welcome upon the mountains are the feet of one who brings good news" (AP).

Emmanuel, may my soul be jubilant and my feet be swift to answer. Amen.

CHRISTMAS EVE

What kind of sign is this? A celestial encounter between angels and shepherds leads to a baby wrapped in a simple cloth. Luke leaves all kinds of clues lying in plain sight. He carefully directs us toward Bethlehem, the city of David. David, the singer of psalms, the warrior/king, the founding father of a nation under God, is first and foremost a shepherd. "I will give you shepherds after my own heart" (Jer. 3:15). Luke weaves the words of Jeremiah and Isaiah into this birth narrative to show that the child is the Promised One, a savior raised up from the house of David.

Who are these people who receive the first glimpse of the Messiah and the coming kin-dom of God? They are hired help, the working poor, folks with such bad social credit that it's a shock to the community to hear Jesus put the words "good" and "shepherd" together. They are not "sheeple"; they recognize their world is turning upside down and they're ready to be eyewitnesses. They are not on the margins of this earth-shaking news; they are its first responders.

No wise men with their gold and costly spices clutter up this Christmas Gospel. Luke offers us these down-to-earth folks getting glory-to-God news. And how do these shepherds know they can trust this news?

It's all in the sign, just like the angel promised: A baby in the manger is carefully wrapped by Mary in a simple cloth. A simple cloth, used to bind a newborn for protection, is the evidence of Incarnation. A simple cloth, used to wash tired feet, is evidence of who Jesus is and will be. A simple cloth is used to wrap the broken body of God's Beloved; it's evidence of grief and loss. It will also be a simple cloth that provides us with the only evidence we need of the Resurrection.

Beloved, let me see your glory in the simple things. Amen.

CHRISTMAS DAY

Here is the Gospel text that illuminates this week's calendar readings. In verses four and five it concentrates our salvation story into a single sentence that burns like the tungsten filament inside an incandescent light. Creation and Incarnation and Salvation are braided together. Time itself is burning like a star; the past tense summons the present; the present foreshadows the future. What was once is now true for all time.

Mystics and spiritual teachers have recognized a truth about this Word that is lost if we reduce its depth by skimming its surface. There's a painful pattern of abuse connected to misreading this scripture, a history of rejecting or resisting anything that doesn't appear to be pure white light.

What can't we see if we're so afraid of shadows that we sleep with all the lights on? Insights about the true source of our life come from willingly encountering the dark night of the soul. "Noche oscura del alma" is the title assigned to the writings of John of the Cross, a sixteenth-century Spanish mystic and priest. Entering "noche oscura" is essential if you want to encounter the Word who is life. For John of the Cross, the only light in this dark night is that which burns in the soul. All other sources of light are artificial, distracting, blurring our vision.

Howard Thurman, twentieth-century mystic, preacher, and civil rights leader, described the struggle for justice and humanity in the language of "luminous darkness." The scriptures of this season are filled with luminous darkness. Jesus is conceived by the Holy Spirit in the darkness of Mary's womb. Angels appear in Joseph's dreams to call him to protect Mary and then Mary's son. Luminous darkness surrounds the shepherds in the fields and the place where the child who is also the Word lies sleeping. Out of this darkness will come the Risen One.

O Morning Star, enter my soul and light my way home. Amen.

The Other Side of Christmas

DECEMBER 26–31, 2022 • MARTHA C. HIGHSMITH

SCRIPTURE OVERVIEW: This week we celebrate the birth of Jesus! Isaiah reminds us that all that God does, including the sending of a Savior, flows from God's compassion and steadfast love. The psalmist declares that from the angels in heaven to the works of creation to all the kings and peoples of the earth, all should praise the exalted name of God. The "horn" is a metaphor used elsewhere in the Hebrew scriptures that is traditionally interpreted by Christians as a prophecy of the Messiah. The author of Hebrews emphasizes the humanity of Christ. Christ fully partakes of our human nature so that he would understand our weakness and fully execute his role as our high priest. Matthew interprets through prophecy the perilous early travels of the young Jesus.

QUESTIONS AND SUGGESTIONS FOR REFLECTION

- Read Isaiah 63:7-9. How has God's presence saved you?
- Read Psalm 148. How can you praise God for the glory of creation around you in your daily life?
- Read Hebrews 2:10-18. How does your relationship with God who is not only with us but like us help you understand yourself as related to all other human beings?
- Read Matthew 2:13-23. How has your church or faith community made the choice to act in the best interests of the institution rather than to follow God's way of humility?

PC(USA) pastor living close to the land on the family farm in North Carolina, keeping bees and chickens, growing food and flowers.

Christmas was just yesterday; we haven't even cleaned up the discarded wrapping paper and ribbon or started eating the leftovers. After weeks of preparation and yesterday's celebration, today seems a good time to rest and recover. But there is no rest—no easy place—here on the other side of Christmas.

The shepherds are back with their sheep, Mary and Joseph look on their child with continued amazement, while Herod is in a rage to find the "king of the Jews." He will stop at nothing until the child is destroyed. And it is a thin patchwork of faith and dreams that saves Immanuel. Joseph, like his Hebrew namesake, is so open to God that God's angels inhabit his slumber, warning and instructing him. On the basis of a memory that dissolves at daybreak, Joseph takes his family and flees to Egypt.

Jesus is safe, but all those others are killed. It is hard to imagine a small town with no toddlers. It is hard to imagine the cruelty of Herod. And yet it still happens today. Ten years ago, right before Christmas, six adults and twenty children in Connecticut were murdered by a gunman who also killed his mother and finally himself. It was, and is, terrible. Almost an entire grade in that school was wiped out, like all the toddlers of Bethlehem. And the deadly toll is not limited to one horrible tragedy. Thousands of children die from gun violence in the United States every year. The Herods of our time are everywhere. The innocents are still being slaughtered.

While the angels' words of peace and goodwill still ring in our ears, we are called to work for the holy dream of a world where all children are safe. May it be so.

Holy One, you came to us a child, innocent and vulnerable. Help us to hear your call to see you in the children of the world and to work to protect them from harm. Amen.

In her song "Blessings," Laura Story asks, "What if your healing comes through tears?"* It is a question for the Rachels in our midst.

Rachel wept for the lost children of Israel who had been taken into exile at Ramah. She would not be consoled; she did not want to be consoled. The mothers of Bethlehem also refused comfort because to dry their tears would be to forget the joy, the laughter, the love, the babies. Weeping honors the dead. Tears are a visible sign of hidden heartbreak. Mourning is an essential part of remembering.

Rachel wept, and certainly Joseph and Mary did too. Forced to flee as refugees in a strange land, they could rely only on the midnight murmurings of angels. Another question from the song is for them: "What if a thousand sleepless nights are what it takes to know You're near?"

It is a question for us too. Some feel that tears are a sign of God's presence. If that is true, then God has been close to us all. And when the tears do not cease, when sleep does not come, all we can do is hold on to that presence. Even in the midst of tears and sleepless nights, there is love. Sometimes we know the love by knowing the grief because love is embedded in every grief. Without love, there would be no sense of loss.

Birth and death, fear and faith, love and loss are intertwined in the story of Jesus. From beginning to end, from cradle to Cross, Jesus' life is in danger. And on the other side of Christmas, we are to do as Joseph did: listen for God's whispers and do what we can to keep Christ alive in the midst of the world's threats. We are called to hold on to Immanuel and know that indeed God is with us.

---

*https://www.youtube.com/watch?v=0xRNrnh__SE, accessed 8-15-2020

Loving God, inhabit our dreams, bless our tears, and fill us with your healing presence. Amen.

Why do the scriptures on the other side of Christmas call attention to suffering? This is supposed to be a season of celebration, isn't it? Christmas should be the happiest time of the year. We want everything to be peaceful and perfect. We would rather skip over the story of Herod and the Bethlehem babies. We prefer to see the Holy Family as safe and secure in the stable rather than as frightened, fleeing refugees.

But these troubling Christmastide texts have an important message for us. The one known as Immanuel is not just God with us; he is also God like us. From the very beginning, we are made in the image of God (see Genesis 1:27). When God's shining likeness in us becomes dulled by the distractions of daily life and is obscured by sin, God comes as Jesus, sharing our flesh and blood, to remind us of who we are. We are his siblings.

It is a sad fact that some people live and die knowing only suffering. It is the one constant of the human condition. Bad things happen to good people. Life is not fair. Some of us may have been spared from suffering thus far, but we will all have our share of trouble. Nothing, not even the most faithful living, will spare us.

But "because [Jesus] himself was tested by what he suffered, he is able to help those who are being tested." The One who began his life as a refugee, wept with grief at the faithlessness of his people, and died feeling abandoned, has gone before us as "the pioneer of [our] salvation." He has gone before us, and he goes with us. He is Immanuel. He is our brother. He is our Savior.

Jesus, our brother, we put our trust in you. Help us in times of testing and trouble. Go before us and with us, now and always. Amen.

At a time when God seems absent or angry, the prophet pauses for praise. This affirmation of God's goodness is embedded in a long passage that details God's grievances with the people. They have been exiled, ripped from their land, taken captive. They are suffering, and perhaps God is suffering too. With the anger that often accompanies grief, God rails against the people for their abandonment. God is grieved by the people's rebellion. God can find no helpers. It seems that this angry, anguished God wanted the people to be faithful covenant partners, but they failed.

In this desert of God's disfavor, a tiny green sprig of praise sprouts. The prophet remembers God's gracious deeds, praise-worthy acts, and mercy. In the dry place of despair, God's steadfast love overflows. These powerful memories reveal God's heart, and the prophet is assured the people are still God's children.

And if the people—then and now—are God's children, and if Jesus is our sibling, then God is our Father and our Mother too. God is the one whose care is constant and presence is unfailing. Like a mother, strong and sure, God saves us, rescuing us even from ourselves. Like a father, God lifts us up and carries us.

In the worst places, in the bleakest times, God is with us. God's presence saves us. Out of God's love and pity, we are given a second chance to be God's helpers. And we are called to respond to others as God responds to us: caring for the vulnerable, welcoming the stranger, holding the innocent ones close, and remembering that when we have done this for the least of these, we have done it for Jesus (see Matthew 25:40).

Holy One, how much you have done for us! Help us to serve you in the world by serving those in need. Help us to be your helpers. Amen.

Three years ago a small outbreak of a mysterious illness soon became a worldwide pandemic. Lives were disrupted, businesses bankrupted, schools and gyms and restaurants closed. Church buildings sat empty for a month of Sundays. Hundreds of millions of people were infected; millions died.

The pandemic exposed the evil power of death. People in poor communities died at disproportionately higher rates. Without adequate technology or the means to provide decent instruction at home, poor children fell further behind academically. Without work, struggling families in the United States had no health insurance, no rent payment, no grocery money. The rich got richer, and the poor went hungry. It is as though we let evil take control of our society.

Confronted by the overpowering reality of suffering, how can we believe that Jesus has destroyed the power of evil and death? We look to his life. He spent his ministry healing the sick, restoring the outcasts to society, feeding the hungry, mending the broken. He touched the untouchable and ate with sinners. And he challenged the powerful, calling out hypocrisy and showing the religious leaders the way back to faith.

We look also to his death and resurrection. There is a reason that so many renaissance paintings of the Nativity show a cross in the stable. All Jesus' life, the Herods were after him, but he lived without fear of death. In resurrection, he overpowered death and became a living presence with us.

The ones Jesus knew best were the ones who suffered most. If we are to be his followers, we are to renounce evil and its deathly power in the world. It is not enough just to bring gifts to the Christ child. The real work of Christmas is doing what we can to alleviate suffering.

Resurrecting God, awaken in us the will and the way to destroy the power of evil in our world. Amen.

At the very beginning of time, creation was as God intended. When everything was new, it was all good. But the shalom of Eden was soon shattered. Exiled with Adam and Eve, we have longed to return ever since. We have longed for creation restored. The praise of Psalm 148 gives voice to that deep desire.

Following the order of Genesis, the psalmist instructs all creation to "praise the LORD." From the highest heaven to the deepest depths, everything is to praise—angels and heavenly hosts, sun, moon, shining stars, plants and animals, the ground itself, and even the weather! Everything is to sing "hallelujah," which literally means "praise Yahweh."

This praise is more than a song; it is a way of being. As Walter Brueggemann explains, "'World-making' is done by God. . . . But it is done through human activity that God has authorized and in which God is known to be present. . . . Praise is not a response to a world already fixed and settled, but it is a responsive and obedient participation in a world yet to be decreed and in the process of being decreed."*

On the other side of Christmas, we are called to be co-creators with God, to let our lives be the kind of praise that remakes the world in the image of God, who is with us, is one of us, and shows us how to live. Jesus—Immanuel—was "responsive and obedient" to God; as such he participated in the work of the new creation, where the least and the last are loved and cared for, where children grow up in safety, and where evil fails. May we truly be followers of the way of Jesus. Hallelujah!

*Walter Brueggemann, *Israel's Praise* (Minneapolis: Fortress Publishing House, 1988), 11.

God of creation, remind us that we are made in your image. Through our praise, may we help to remake the world until all creation is filled with shalom. Amen.

The Revised Common Lectionary* for 2022
Year C—Advent / Christmas Year A
(Disciplines Edition)

January 1–2
Jeremiah 31:7-14
Psalm 147:12-20
Ephesians 1:3-14
John 1:1-18

> **January 1**
> NEW YEAR'S DAY
> Ecclesiastes 3:1-13
> Psalm 8
> Revelation 21:1-6a
> Matthew 25:31-46

January 3–9
BAPTISM OF THE LORD
Isaiah 43:1-7
Psalm 29
Acts 8:14-17
Luke 3:15-17, 21-22

> **January 6**
> EPIPHANY
> Isaiah 60:1-6
> Psalm 72:1-7, 10-14
> Ephesians 3:1-12
> Matthew 2:1-12

January 10–16
Isaiah 62:1-5
Psalm 36:5-10
1 Corinthians 12:1-11
John 2:1-11

January 17–23
Nehemiah 8:1-3, 5-6, 8-10
Psalm 19
1 Corinthians 12:12-31a
Luke 4:14-21

January 24–30
Jeremiah 1:4-10
Psalm 71:1-6
1 Corinthians 13
Luke 4:21-30

January 31–February 7
Isaiah 6:1-13
Psalm 138
1 Corinthians 15:1-11
Luke 5:1-11

February 7–13
Jeremiah 17:5-10
Psalm 1
1 Corinthians 15:12-20
Luke 6:17-26

February 14–20
Genesis 45:3-11, 15
Psalm 37:1-11, 39-40
1 Corinthians 15:35-38, 42-50
Luke 6:27-38

February 21–27
TRANSFIGURATION
Exodus 34:29-35
Psalm 99
2 Corinthians 3:12–4:2
Luke 9:28-43

February 28–March 6
FIRST SUNDAY IN LENT
Deuteronomy 26:1-11
Psalm 91:2, 9-16
Romans 10:8b-13
Luke 4:1-13

March 2
ASH WEDNESDAY
Joel 2:1-2, 12-17 or
  Isaiah 58:1-12
Psalm 51:1-17
2 Corinthians 5:20b–6:10
Matthew 6:1-6, 16-21

March 7–13
SECOND SUNDAY IN LENT
Genesis 15:1-12, 17-18
Psalm 27
Philippians 3:17–4:1
Luke 13:31-35

March 14–20
THIRD SUNDAY IN LENT
Isaiah 55:1-9
Psalm 63:1-8
1 Corinthians 10:1-13
Luke 13:1-9

March 21–27
FOURTH SUNDAY IN LENT
Joshua 5:9-12
Psalm 32
2 Corinthians 5:16-21
Luke 15:1-3, 11b-32

March 28–April 3
FIFTH SUNDAY IN LENT
Isaiah 43:16-21
Psalm 126
Philippians 3:4b-14
John 12:1-8

April 4–10
PALM/PASSION SUNDAY

Liturgy of the Palms
Psalm 118:1-2, 19-29
Luke 19:28-40

Liturgy of the Passion
Isaiah 50:4-9a
Psalm 31:9-16
Philippians 2:5-11
Luke 22:14–23:56

April 11–17
HOLY WEEK

Monday
Isaiah 42:1-9
Psalm 36:5-11
Hebrews 9:11-15
John 12:1-11

Tuesday
Isaiah 49:1-7
Psalm 71:1-14
1 Corinthians 1:18-31
John 12:20-36

Wednesday
Isaiah 50:4-9a
Psalm 70
Hebrews 12:1-3
John 13:21-32

Maundy Thursday
Exodus 12:1-14
Psalm 116:1-2, 12-19
1 Corinthians 11:23-26
John 13:1-17, 31b-35

Good Friday
Isaiah 52:13–53:12
Psalm 22
Hebrews 4:14-16; 5:7-9
John 18:1–19:42

Holy Saturday
Job 14:1-14
Psalm 31:1-4, 15-16
1 Peter 4:1-8
Matthew 27:57-66

Easter–April 17
Acts 10:34-43
Psalm 118:1-2, 14-24
1 Corinthians 15:19-26
John 20:1-18

April 18–24
Acts 5:27-32
Psalm 150
Revelation 1:4-8
John 20:19-31

April 25–May 1
Acts 9:1-20
Psalm 30
Revelation 5:11-14
John 21:1-19

May 2–8
Acts 9:36-43
Psalm 23
Revelation 7:9-17
John 10:22-30

May 9–15
Acts 11:1-18
Psalm 148
Revelation 21:1-6
John 13:31-35

May 16–22
Acts 16:9-15
Psalm 67
Revelation 21:10, 22–22:5
John 14:23-29

May 23–29
Acts 16:16-34
Psalm 97
Revelation 22:12-14, 16-17, 20-21
John 17:20-26

May 26
Ascension Day
Acts 1:1-11
Psalm 47
Ephesians 1:15-23
Luke 24:44-53

May 30–June 5
Pentecost
Acts 2:1-21
Psalm 104:24-34, 35b
Romans 8:14-17
John 14:8-17, 25-27

June 6–12
Trinity Sunday
Proverbs 8:1-4, 22-31
Psalm 8
Romans 5:1-5
John 16:12-15

June 13–19
1 Kings 19:1-15a
Psalm 42 and 43
Galatians 3:23-29
Luke 8:26-39

June 20–26
2 Kings 2:1-2, 6-14
Psalm 77:1-2, 11-20
Galatians 5:1, 13-25
Luke 9:51-62

June 27—July 3
2 Kings 5:1-14
Psalm 30
Galatians 6:1-16
Luke 10:1-11, 16-20

July 4–10
Amos 7:7-17
Psalm 82
Colossians 1:1-14
Luke 10:25-37

July 11–17
Amos 8:1-12
Psalm 52
Colossians 1:15-28
Luke 10:38-42

July 18–24
Hosea 1:2-10
Psalm 85
Colossians 2:6-19
Luke 11:1-13

July 25–31
Hosea 11:1-11
Psalm 107:1-9, 43
Colossians 3:1-11
Luke 12:13-21

August 1–7
Isaiah 1:1, 10-20
Psalm 50:1-8, 22-23
Hebrews 11:1-3, 8-16
Luke 12:32-40

August 8–14
Isaiah 5:1-7
Psalm 80:1-2, 8-19
Hebrews 11:29–12:2
Luke 12:49-56

August 15–21
Jeremiah 1:4-10
Psalm 71:1-6
Hebrews 12:18-29
Luke 13:10-17

August 22–28
Jeremiah 2:4-13
Psalm 81:1, 10-16
Hebrews 13:1-8, 15-16
Luke 14:1, 7-14

August 29–September 4
Jeremiah 18:1-11
Psalm 139:1-6, 13-18
Philemon 1-21
Luke 14:25-33

September 5–11
Jeremiah 4:11-12, 22-28
Psalm 14
1 Timothy 1:12-17
Luke 15:1-10

September 12–18
Jeremiah 8:18–9:1
Psalm 79:1-9
1 Timothy 2:1-7
Luke 16:1-13

September 19–25
Jeremiah 32:1-3a, 6-15
Psalm 91:1-6, 14-16
1 Timothy 6:6-19
Luke 16:19-31

September 26–October 2
Lamentations 1:1-6
Psalm 137
2 Timothy 1:1-14
Luke 17:5-10

October 3–9
Jeremiah 29:1, 4-7
Psalm 66:1-12
2 Timothy 2:8-15
Luke 17:11-19

October 10–16
Jeremiah 31:27-34
Psalm 119:97-104
2 Timothy 3:14–4:5
Luke 18:1-8

October 10
THANKSGIVING DAY, CANADA
Deuteronomy 26:1-11
Psalm 100
Philippians 4:4-9
John 6:25-35

October 17–23
Joel 2:23-32
Psalm 65
2 Timothy 4:6-8, 16-18
Luke 18:9-14

October 24–30
Habakkuk 1:1-4; 2:1-4
Psalm 119:137-144
2 Thessalonians 1:1-4, 11-12
Luke 19:1-10

October 31–November 6
Haggai 1:15b–2:9
Psalm 145:1-5, 17-21
2 Thessalonians 2:1-5, 13-17
Luke 20:27-38

November 1
ALL SAINTS DAY
Daniel 7:1-3, 15-18
Psalm 149
Ephesians 1:11-23
Luke 6:20-31

November 7–13
Isaiah 65:17-25
Isaiah 12
2 Thessalonians 3:6-13
Luke 21:5-19

November 14–20
THE REIGN OF CHRIST
Jeremiah 23:1-6
Luke 1:68-79
Colossians 1:11-20
Luke 23:33-43

November 21–27
FIRST SUNDAY OF ADVENT
Isaiah 2:1-5
Psalm 122
Romans 13:11-14
Matthew 24:36-44

November 24
THANKSGIVING DAY, USA
Deuteronomy 26:1-11
Psalm 100
Philippians 4:4-9
John 6:25-35

November 28–December 4
SECOND SUNDAY OF ADVENT
Isaiah 11:1-10
Psalm 72:1-7, 18-19
Romans 15:4-13
Matthew 3:1-12

December 5–11
THIRD SUNDAY OF ADVENT
Isaiah 35:1-10
Luke 1:47-55
James 5:7-10
Matthew 11:2-11

December 12–18
FOURTH SUNDAY OF ADVENT
Isaiah 7:10-16
Psalm 80:1-7, 17-19
Romans 1:1-7
Matthew 1:18-25

December 19–25
Isaiah 52:7-10
Psalm 98
Hebrews 1:1-12
John 1:1-14

December 24
CHRISTMAS EVE
Isaiah 9:2-7
Psalm 96
Titus 2:11-14
Luke 2:1-20

December 30–31
Isaiah 63:7-9
Psalm 148
Hebrews 2:10-18
Matthew 2:13-23

A Guide to Daily Prayer

These prayers imply worship time with a group; feel free to adapt the plural pronouns for personal use.

Morning Prayer

In the morning, Lord, you hear my voice;
> in the morning I lay my requests before you
> and wait expectantly.
> > > —Psalm 5:3

Gathering and Silence

Call to Praise and Prayer
> God said, "Let there be light," and there was light.
> God saw that the light was good.

Psalm 63:1-5

> God, my God, you I crave;
> > my soul thirsts for you,
> > my body aches for you
> > like a dry and weary land.
> Let me gaze on you in your temple:
> > a vision of strength and glory.
> Your love is better than life;
> > my speech is full of praise.
> I give you a lifetime of worship,
> > my hands raised in your name.
> I feast at a rich table,
> > my lips singing of your glory.

Prayer of Thanksgiving

We praise you with joy, loving God, for your grace is better than life itself. You have sustained us through the darkness, and you bless us with life in this new day. In the shadow of your wings we sing for joy and bless your holy name. Amen.

Scripture Reading

Silence

Prayers of the People

The Lord's Prayer (ecumenical text)

Our Father in heaven,
hallowed be your name,
your kingdom come,
your will be done,
on earth as in heaven.
Give us today our daily bread.
Forgive us our sins as we forgive
those who sin against us.
Save us from the time of trial,
and deliver us from evil.
For the kingdom, the power, and the glory
are yours, now and forever. Amen.

Blessing

May the light of your mercy shine brightly on all who walk in your presence today, O Lord.

I will extol the LORD at all times;
God's praise will always be on my lips.
—Psalm 34:1

Gathering and Silence

Call to Praise and Prayer

O LORD, my Savior, teach me your ways.
My hope is in you all day long.

Prayer of Thanksgiving

God of mercy, we acknowledge this midday pause of refreshment as one of your many generous gifts. Look kindly upon our work this day; may it be made perfect in your time. May our purpose and prayers be pleasing to you. This we ask through Christ our Lord. Amen.

Scripture Reading

Silence

Prayers of the People

The Lord's Prayer (ecumenical text)
Our Father in heaven,
hallowed be your name,
your kingdom come,
your will be done,
on earth as in heaven.

Give us today our daily bread.
Forgive us our sins as we forgive
    those who sin against us.
Save us from the time of trial,
    and deliver us from evil.
For the kingdom, the power, and the glory
    are yours, now and forever. Amen.

Blessing

Strong is the love embracing us, faithful the Lord from
morning to night.

Truly my soul finds rest in God;
    my salvation comes from God.
                  —Psalm 62:1

Gathering and Silence

Call to Praise and Prayer

From the rising of the sun to its setting,
let the name of the LORD be praised.

Psalm 134

Bless the LORD,
    all who serve in God's house,
    who stand watch
    throughout the night.

Lift up your hands
    in the holy place
    and bless the LORD.

And may God,
the maker of earth and sky,
bless you from Zion.

Prayer of Thanksgiving

Sovereign God, you have been our help during
the day, and you promise to be with us at night.
Receive this prayer as a sign of our trust in you.
Save us from all evil, keep us from all harm, and

guide us in your way. We belong to you, Lord. Protect us by the power of your name. In Jesus Christ we pray. Amen.

Scripture Reading

Silence

Prayers of the People

The Lord's Prayer (ecumenical text)

> Our Father in heaven,
> > hallowed be your name,
> > your kingdom come,
> > your will be done,
> > on earth as in heaven.
> Give us today our daily bread.
> Forgive us our sins as we forgive
> > those who sin against us.
> Save us from the time of trial,
> > and deliver us from evil.
> For the kingdom, the power, and the glory
> > are yours, now and forever. Amen.

Blessing

> May your unfailing love rest upon us, O LORD,
> even as we hope in you.

This Guide to Daily Prayer was compiled from scripture and other resources by Rueben P. Job and then adapted by the Pathways Center for Spiritual Leadership while under the direction of Marjorie J. Thompson.